THE CHOICES JUSTICES MAKE

Lee Epstein
WASHINGTON UNIVERSITY

Jack Knight
WASHINGTON UNIVERSITY

A Division of Congressional Quarterly Inc.
Washington, D.C.

Cover design: Dennis Anderson

Library of Congress Cataloging-in-Publication Data

Epstein, Lee, 1958–
       The choices justices make / Lee Epstein, Jack Knight.
          p.   cm.
       Includes index.
       ISBN 1-56802-226-3 (alk. paper)
       1. United States. Supreme Court.   2. Political questions and
    judicial power--United States.   3. Judicial process--Political
    aspects--United States.   I. Knight, Jack, 1952– .   II. Title.
    KF8742.E667   1998
    347-73'26--dc21   97-35326

To a great friend, Mark Soberman
L.E.

To my sister, Julie Knight
J.K.

Contents

Tables and Figures

Preface

Just over thirty years have elapsed since Walter F. Murphy published *Elements of Judicial Strategy* (University of Chicago Press, 1964). Relying on intuitions derived from the rational choice paradigm, Murphy sought to demonstrate that Supreme Court justices operate in a political context not wholly unlike elected officials.[a] He painted a portrait of policy-minded jurists who make choices ranging from which cases to hear to which opinions to join, while paying some attention to the preferences of other actors (such as their colleagues and members of Congress) and the actions they expect them to take. *Elements,* in other words, elucidated the strategic nature of judicial decision making.

Like their earlier counterparts, today's political scientists have mixed reactions to Murphy's work. Judicial specialists often include *Elements* on their lists of truly classic works, but they also point to its limited influence on the direction of the field: simply put, few have adopted Murphy's vision of the way the Court operates. The explanation, it seems, is that the book

---

a. Throughout this book we use the term rational choice to refer to theories that offer explanations grounded in the following assumptions: (1) social actors make choices to achieve certain goals; (2) social actors act strategically in that their choices depend on their expectations about the choices of other actors; and (3) these choices are structured by the institutional setting in which they are made.

may be a "good read," but it does not comport with the methodology that has come to dominate political science studies of judicial behavior. Murphy explored his thesis only against examples (typically landmark cases) designed to illustrate his point, while most scientific investigations of judicial decisions use much bigger samples of cases and claim more rigor in their methodology and analytics. What is more, when large-scale studies attempted to put Murphy's predictions to the test, they failed or, at least, that is the conclusion some scholars have reached.

Debates over *Elements* are not only interesting but also significant. Just as scholars were finding Murphy's intuitions inviting, they were rejecting them on the ground that more systematic evidence, especially pertaining to the votes of justices, seemed to prove them wrong. This rejection had an immeasurable impact on the direction of the field.

It is now the case, as it has been for nearly thirty years, that political scientists largely view justices as unconstrained decision makers who are free to behave in accord with their own ideological attitudes, rather than the sophisticated actors Murphy made them out to be. Therefore, the "attitudinal model"—and not theories grounded in assumptions of strategic rationality—dominates the study of judicial politics.[b] To put an even finer point on it, political scientists have published *relatively* few articles in disciplinary journals or books that invoke rational choice to explain Court

---

b. The attitudinal model holds that the U.S. Supreme Court "decides disputes in light of the facts of the case vis-à-vis the ideological attitudes and values of the justices." In other words, "Rehnquist votes the way he does because he is extremely conservative; Marshall voted the way he did because he [was] extremely liberal." See Jeffrey A. Segal and Harold J. Spaeth, *The Supreme Court and the Attitudinal Model* (New York: Cambridge University Press, 1993), 65.

To be sure, the attitudinal model dominates studies exploring judicial votes. See, for example, Jeffrey A. Segal et al., "Ideological Values and the Votes of U.S. Supreme Court Justices Revisited," 57 *Journal of Politics* (1995): 812, asserting, "A, if not *the,* predominant, view of U.S. Supreme Court decision making is the attitudinal model." But, because this model, at least according to its most important contemporary advocates (Jeffrey A. Segal and Harold J. Spaeth), *is designed to explain only voting behavior,* political scientists have developed a range of explanations to account for other choices that justices make, such as the choice of whom to assign responsibility for writing the majority opinion—explanations that typically emanate from the findings of previous empirical investigations, such as the notion that chief justices, who assign the bulk of majority opinions, strive for equity—rather than from any overarching theory.

decisions—a phenomenon in direct contradistinction to many other fields.[c]

It is also a trend that runs counter to the direction in which students of courts in other disciplines are pushing their research programs. Over the past decade or so, numerous law and business school professors have been touting what they call positive political theory (PPT), consisting of "non-normative, rational-choice theories of political institutions," as an appropriate framework for the study of judicial decision making.[1] In some sense, then, these professors are asking us modern-day political scientists and our students to take Murphy's intuitions seriously and to integrate them into our work. Should we take heed?

The answer we offer in *Choices* is yes. On our account, which we call a strategic account, justices may be primarily seekers of legal policy, but they are not unsophisticated characters who make choices based merely on their own political preferences. Instead, justices are strategic actors who realize that their ability to achieve their goals depends on a consideration of the preferences of others, of the choices they expect others to make, and of the institutional context in which they act. In other words, the choices of justices can best be explained as strategic behavior, not solely as responses to either personal ideology or apolitical jurisprudence. The implications of this claim, pursued throughout *Choices,* are many. Most important is that law, as it is generated by the Supreme Court, is the long-term product of short-term strategic decision making.

---

c. We do not mean to imply that political scientists studying the judicial process have completely rejected rational choice. Even before Murphy published *Elements,* Glendon Schubert invoked game theory, a set of tools to study social situations involving strategic behavior, to examine the voting behavior of Supreme Court justices during the New Deal period. See "The Study of Judicial Decision-Making as An Aspect of Political Behavior," 52 *American Political Science Review* (1958): 1007–25. Moreover, in the immediate aftermath of *Elements,* J. Woodford Howard explicitly attempted to provide more systematic support for one of Murphy's predictions: internal bargaining on the Court occasionally produces vote shifts. See "On the Fluidity of Judicial Choice," 62 *American Political Science Review* (1968): 43–56. And another scholar applied theories grounded in assumptions of rationality to the study of opinion coalition formation. See David W. Rohde, "Policy Goals and Opinion Coalitions in the Supreme Court," 16 *Midwest Journal of Political Science* (1972): 208–224. Finally, interest in choice approaches appears to be on the rise. A partial list of recent work produced by political scientists includes: Robert Lowry Clinton, "Game Theory, Legal History, and the Origins of Judicial Review: A Revisionist Analysis of *Marbury v. Madison,*" 38 *American Journal of Political Science* (1994): 285–302; and Forrest Maltzman

We recognize that it is one thing to make a claim and quite another to provide support for it. So, in *Choices,* we do more than simply lay out our account. We attempt to demonstrate its plausibility and to explore its explanatory power with data mined from the Court's public records and from the private papers of Justices William J. Brennan Jr., William O. Douglas, Thurgood Marshall, and Lewis F. Powell Jr. This is not to say that we assess our account against empirical evidence on the range of judicial decisions. *Given that strategic rationality seeks to explain all the choices justices make—from the initial decision to grant review to the policy enunciated in the final opinion, not just the vote to affirm or reverse*—it would be virtually impossible for us to do so in one volume. But it is to say that we hope *Choices* makes a compelling case for the importance of injecting strategic analysis into future studies of the Supreme Court.

For the primary purpose of our book is to develop a *conception* of judicial *decision making.* It is an account of how justices make decisions. We do not pretend to offer a complete *explanation* of any particular line of decisions or body of law. We offer instead a perspective of judicial decision making that will form the theoretical basis of such substantive explanations. If we succeed, our conception should provide scholars with an approach for identifying strategic behavior, understanding its various roles, and incorporating its implications into their explanations of the Supreme Court—whether those studies focus on the choices justices make or the doctrine they produce.

DATA NOTE

In recent years, it has become a matter of course for political scientists to describe in some detail how they went about collecting and analyzing their

---

and Paul J. Wahlbeck, "May It Please the Chief? Opinion Assignments in the Rehnquist Court," 40 *American Journal of Political Science* (1996): 421–443; Edward P. Schwartz, "Policy, Precedent, and Power: A Positive Theory of Supreme Court Decision Making." *Journal of Law, Economics, and Organization* 8 (1992): 219–252; and Jeffrey A. Segal, "Separation-of-Powers Games in the Positive Theory of Congress and Courts," 91 *American Political Science Review* (1997): 28–44.

But, as our emphasis on *relatively* suggests and as a systematic inventory of articles published in the leading disciplinary journals shows, rational choice work has received a far warmer welcome from scholars working in almost every other field of political science. See Lee Epstein, "The State of the Field of Judicial Politics" (remarks delivered at the 1995 annual meeting of the Southern Political Science Association, Tampa, Fla.).

data. Many scholars now make their data sets available for public inspection. We applaud these trends and attempt to follow them. For all of the original data appearing in *Choices*, we provide the rules we used to code them and we have made the data available on a Web site: *http://www.artsci.wustl.edu/~polisci/epstein/choices.* These steps, we felt, were particularly important because so many of our data come from the papers of justices, which may be difficult for readers to access.

One final comment on the data. For many of the investigations in *Choices*, we rely on two samples of cases: (1) 1983 term cases that were orally argued and that are listed in Justice Brennan's register ($N = 157$) and (2) landmark cases handed down during the Burger Court years (1969 through 1985 terms) ($N = 125$).[2] Our logic in drawing these particular samples was as follows. We thought it important to examine both important cases and an entire term, and a typical one at that, to ascertain whether strategic behavior is commonplace or whether some critics of Murphy are correct in arguing that strategic behavior (if it exists) may be limited to landmark litigation.[d] Moreover, our focus on the Burger Court era is by no means accidental. We needed to collect most of the data from the justices' papers rather than from published sources. For the Burger Court years, we could access (1) the case files of Marshall and Brennan, who served during the entire period;[e] (2) Justice Powell's records, including case files, docket books, and conference notes, dating from January 1972; and (3) Brennan's conference notes and docket books—records that scholars have deemed highly reliable and comprehensive[3] In addition, a number of important changes in the Court's internal record-keeping procedures came about during the Burger years. Before the 1969 term, for example, justices did not regularly note where they had made changes on their opinion drafts; now they almost always do. Certainly, such procedural changes were designed to facilitate the decision-making process for justices, but they also help scholars trace that process in a systematic way.

These data constitute our primary samples. Occasionally, we depart from them and use published data or information from other eras—both pre–

---

d. Even if these critics are right, it is worth noting, approaches competing with strategic variants of choice theory cannot readily explain (or do not attempt to explain) such behavior, regardless of whether it occurs in ordinary or important cases.

e. Both justices also served on the Rehnquist Court, but Brennan's post-1985 term files are not yet available to researchers. Scholars may access the entire Marshall collection, but his some of his important records, such as his docket books, are available for only a few terms.

and post–Burger Court. When we do so, we try to explain why with some degree of care.

ACKNOWLEDGMENTS

Choices has been a work-in-progress for nearly half a decade, so it will come as no surprise that we have accumulated many debts—both jointly and individually. To begin, we could not have conducted this study without access to the papers of Justices Brennan, Douglas, Marshall, and Powell. While the Douglas and Marshall collections are open to all scholars, we needed to obtain the permission of Justices Powell and Brennan to use their papers. We are grateful to both for granting our requests. Along the same lines, we express our sincere gratitude to all the archivists and staff— Fred Bauman, Ernie Emrich, Jeff Flannery, Michael Klein, Katie McDonough, David Wigdor, and Mary Wolfskill at the Library of Congress and John Jacob at Washington and Lee School of Law—who helped us work with the collections. We also thank the following Washington University graduate students who assisted with data collection and management: Scott Comparato, Lauretta Conklin, Timothy Johnson, Andrew Martin, Madhavi McCall, and Beth Wilner.

Amassing data from the justices' papers and other sources is not only time-consuming, but also costly. We are therefore grateful to the National Science Foundation (SBR-9320284, SBR-9614130) and the Center for Business, Law, and Economics at Washington University, which have supported our efforts over the years, and to two former NSF program directors, Susan White and C. Neal Tate, who provided wise counsel.

We have more than a few words of thanks to two editors at CQ Press. Brenda Carter has been with this project every step of the way, from encouraging us to recraft the first chapter (which we did) to providing many of the ideas contained in the conclusion (which we took). Her faith in *Choices* has been so completely unwavering that we truly hope the final product lives up to her expectations. It is an understatement to say that this book presented Carolyn Goldinger, our copy editor, with many challenges. Especially important to us was that the material be presented in a way that students as well as scholars would find accessible and interesting. To say that Carolyn lived up to this challenge would again be an understatement. We simply could not have had a better copy editor.

Over the years, we presented bits and pieces of *Choices* to many professional audiences, composed of faculty members and students from various departments and schools at SUNY/Stony Brook, Texas A&M, University of Arizona, University of Virginia, University of Texas, Vanderbilt, and Washington University. We gained much from their reactions and acknowledge their contribution.

We also express gratitude to those colleagues whom, we fear, we bored to near death with our preoccupation with *Choices* but who stuck with us. Epstein thanks, in particular, members of the judicial dinner group—Greg Caldeira, Micheal Giles, Jeff Segal, Harold Spaeth, and Tom Walker—and her compatriot at the Library of Congress, David J. Danelski. They will find more than traces of our conversations throughout this volume. Knight wishes to note the value of his ongoing discussions with William Eskridge, John Ferejohn, Jim Johnson, Edward Schwartz, and Barry Weingast. We both thank Chuck Cameron, Jeff Segal, and Harold Spaeth for their comments on an early version of what is now Chapter One; Caldeira, Segal, and Spaeth for their willingness to provide data within minutes of our (many) requests; and Stuart Banner, Saul Brenner, Richard Brisbin, Nancy Maveety, Gerry Rosenberg, and Cameron and Segal (again) for their insightful suggestions on the final draft of *Choices*.

We end with some personal acknowledgments. Epstein, as always, thanks her husband, Jay, and her parents, Ann and Ken Spole, and her in-laws, David and Janet Epstein, for all the encouragement they have given her over the years. She dedicates this book to Mark Soberman, without whose support *Choices* literally could not have been done. For four years now, Mark has put her up in his Washington, D.C., apartment, poured great wine, and, most of all, wanted to talk about anything other than political science—a great relief after very long days in the Library of Congress. She knows that this is one debt that she can never fully repay but hopes that the dedication will provide an indication (however small) of her gratitude. Knight also thanks his family and friends, especially his wife, Lou Brown, for her ongoing support and encouragement. He dedicates this book to his sister, Julie Knight, who has always been supportive, even when she wasn't particularly interested in what he was doing at the time.

L.E.—St. Louis

J.K—St. Louis

ENDNOTES

1. Daniel A. Farber and Philip P. Frickey, "Foreword: Positive Political Theory in the Nineties," 80 *Georgetown Law Journal* 80 (1992): 461. The PPT literature is considerable in size. For an accessible taste, see William N. Eskridge Jr., "Reneging on History? Playing the Court/Congress/President Civil Rights Game," 79 *California Law Review* (1991): 613–684; and Eskridge, "Overriding Supreme Court Statutory Interpretation Decisions," 101 *Yale Law Journal* (1991): 331–417; for an important empirical investigation, see Pablo T. Spiller and Rafael Gely, "Congressional Control of Judicial Independence: The Determinants of U.S. Supreme Court Labor-Relations Decisions, 1949–1988," 23 *RAND Journal of Economics* (1992): 463–492; and, for a good review, see Daniel B. Rodriguez, "The Positive Political Dimensions of Regulatory Reform," 72 *Washington University Law Quarterly* (1994): 1–150.

We should also note that the PPT group includes a few important political scientists. Most of these political scientists developed their reputations as students of Congress or the executive. They include Charles M. Cameron, John Ferejohn, Mathew D. McCubbins, Roger G. Noll, and Barry R. Weingast.

2. The 1983 term case list is located in the Library of Congress's guide to the papers of William J. Brennan (pages 171–179); important cases are those listed in Elder Witt, *Guide to the U.S. Supreme Court,* 2d ed. (Washington, D.C.: Congressional Quarterly, 1990), 915–927. Because of its reliability and because it includes statutory cases, Witt's list has been used by many scholars. See, for example, Saul Brenner and Harold J. Spaeth, *Stare Indecisis* (Cambridge: Cambridge University Press, 1995). See Jeffrey A. Segal and Harold J. Spaeth, "The Influence of Stare Decisis on the Votes of U.S. Supreme Court Justices," 40 *American Journal of Political Science"* (1996): 971–1003.

3. See Forrest Maltzman and Paul J. Wahlbeck, "Inside the U.S. Supreme Court: The Reliability of the Justices' Conference Records," 58 *Journal of Politics* (1996): 528–539. Pursuant to a grant from the National Science Foundation (SBR-9614130), Harold J. Spaeth and Lee Epstein are in the process of coding vote data contained in Brennan's docket books. These data will be available to all faculty, staff, and students of colleges and universities who are members of the Inter-University Consortium for Political and Social Research in Ann Arbor, Michigan.

THE CHOICES JUSTICES MAKE

CHAPTER ONE

A Strategic Account of Judicial Decisions

Driving while intoxicated (DWI) and driving under the influence (DUI) are now familiar terms to most Americans, but that was not true during the 1960s. With the Vietnam War and the civil rights movement monopolizing the media, drunk driving was just not one of the pressing issues of the day.

Even so, various researchers and government agencies began to explore the problem as early as 1968.[1] Although these initial studies differed in design and sampling, they reached the same general conclusion: teens, particularly males, had a greater tendency than the general population to be involved in alcohol-related traffic incidents. A 1972 FBI report, for example, indicated that between 1967 and 1972 national drunk driving arrests among those under eighteen increased 138 percent and that 93 percent of those arrested were males.

Despite the accumulation of statistical evidence, another decade elapsed before most states even considered raising the legal drinking age. Oklahoma was a notable exception. In 1972 it passed a law prohibiting men from purchasing beer until they reached the age of twenty-one, but allowing women to buy low alcohol-content beer at eighteen.

Regarding the Oklahoma law as a form of sex discrimination, Curtis Craig, a twenty-year-old male who wanted to buy beer, and Carolyn Whitener, a beer vendor who wanted to sell it, brought suit in a federal

TABLE 1-1

Arguments in *Craig v. Boren* over the Appropriate Test to Assess Sex-Based Classifications

Party	Test Advanced	Policy Implications
Craig/Whitener	*Strict Scrutiny:* The law must be the least restrictive means available to achieve a compelling state interest.	If adopted, the Court would almost never uphold a sex-based classification. It would (presumably) strike down the Oklahoma law.
Oklahoma	*Rational Basis:* The law must be a reasonable measure designed to achieve a legitimate government purpose.	If adopted, the Court would (presumably) uphold most sex-based classifications, including the Oklahoma law.
ACLU	Something "in between" strict scrutiny and rational basis.[a]	If adopted, the Court would sometimes strike down laws discriminating on the basis of sex and sometimes uphold them. The ACLU argued that application of this test should lead the Court to strike down the Oklahoma law.

[a] This test is now called "heightened scrutiny": the law must be substantially related to the achievement of an important government objective.

trial court. Among the arguments they made was that laws discriminating on the basis of sex should be subject, at least according to rulings by the U.S. Supreme Court, to a "strict scrutiny" test.[2] Under this standard of review, as Table 1-1 shows, a court presumes a law to be unconstitutional, and, to undermine that assumption, the government must demonstrate that its legislation is the least restrictive means available to achieve a *compelling* state interest. As one might imagine, laws reviewed under this standard almost never survived tests in court.[3] In Craig and Whitener's opinion, the Oklahoma statute was no exception: no compelling state interest was achieved by establishing different drinking ages for men and women.

In response, the state argued that the U.S. Supreme Court had never explicitly applied the strict scrutiny test to laws discriminating on the basis of sex. Rather, the justices had ruled that such laws ought to be subject to a lower level of review—a test called "rational basis" (Table 1-1). Under this test the state need demonstrate only that the law is a *reasonable* measure designed to achieve a *legitimate* (as opposed to compelling) government purpose. Surely, Oklahoma contended, its law met this standard because statistical studies indicated that men "drive more, drink more, and commit more alcohol-related offenses."

The trial court held for the state. While it acknowledged that U.S. Supreme Court precedent was murky, it felt that the weight of case law supported the state's reliance on the lower standard.[a] Moreover, the state had met its obligation of establishing a rational basis for the law: given the statistical evidence, Oklahoma's goal of reducing drunk driving seemed legitimate.

Refusing to give up the battle, Craig and Whitener appealed to the U.S. Supreme Court. While they and the state continued to press the same claims they had at trial, a third party advanced a somewhat different approach. The American Civil Liberties Union entered the case as an ami-

---

a. The problem was that a majority of the justices had not backed a particular standard of review since 1971, when a unanimous Court used the rational basis test to strike down an Idaho law that gave preference to men as estate administrators. *Reed v. Reed,* 404 U.S. 71 (1971). Two years later, however, a plurality adopted the strict scrutiny approach saying that the military could not force women officers to prove that their husbands were dependent on them while presuming that wives were financially dependent on their male officer spouses. *Frontiero v. Richardson,* 411 U.S. 677 (1973). But, in *Stanton v. Stanton,* 421 U.S. 7 (1975), the case most proximate to *Craig,* the Court seemed to give up the search for an appropriate standard. At issue in *Stanton* was a Utah law specifying that, for purposes of receiving child support payments, boys reach adulthood at age twenty-one and girls at eighteen. The Court held that the law constituted impermissible sex discrimination, but it failed to articulate a standard of review. Instead, the majority opinion concluded that "under any test—compelling state interest, rational basis, or something in between—[the Utah law] does not survive . . . attack."

It is no wonder that trial court judges were confused over the appropriate standard of review. As one district court judge wrote, "Lower courts searching for guidance in the 1970s Supreme Court sex discrimination precedents [prior to *Craig*] have 'an uncomfortable feeling'—like players at a shell game who are 'not absolutely sure there is a pea.'" Quoted in Herma H. Kay, *Sex-Based Discrimination* (St. Paul: West, 1981), 70.

cus curiae, a friend of the court, on behalf of Craig (see Table 1-1).[b] ACLU attorneys Ruth Bader Ginsburg and Melvin Wulf argued that the Oklahoma law "could not survive review whatever the appropriate test": strict scrutiny or rational basis or "something in between." This argument, which Ginsburg and Wulf had taken directly from the Court's decision in *Stanton v. Stanton,* was interesting in two regards: it suggested that (1) the Court could apply the lower rational basis standard and still hold for Craig, or (2) the Court might consider developing a standard "in between" strict scrutiny and rational basis.

What would the Supreme Court do? That question loomed large during the justices' conference, held a few days after oral arguments.[4] As it is traditional for the chief justice to speak first, Warren Burger led off the discussion. He asserted that *Craig* was an "isolated case" that the Court should dismiss on procedural grounds. The problem was that, because Curtis Craig had turned twenty-one after the Court agreed to hear the case, his claim was moot. So, to Burger, the dispositive issue was whether Whitener, "the saloon keeper," had standing to bring the suit. Burger thought that she did not.[c] But, if his colleagues disagreed and thought Whitener had standing, Burger said he was willing to find for Craig if the majority opinion was narrowly written. By this, Burger meant that he did not want to apply strict scrutiny to classifications based on sex.[d]

---

b. Despite the literal meaning of amicus curiae, most amici are not friends of the court; rather, they support one party over the other. Nearly 85 percent of all orally argued Supreme Court cases contain at least one amicus curiae brief, and the average is 4.4. See Lee Epstein, "Interest Group Litigation During the Rehnquist Court Era," 9 *Journal of Law and Politics* (1993): 639–717. In *Craig,* however, the ACLU was the only group to file an amicus curiae brief.

c. The doctrine of standing prohibits the Court from resolving a dispute if the party bringing the litigation is not the appropriate one. The Court has said that Article III of the U.S. Constitution requires that litigants demonstrate "such a personal stake in the outcome of the controversy as to assure that concrete adverseness which sharpens the presentation of issues upon which the Court so largely depends for illumination of difficult constitutional questions." *Baker v. Carr,* 369 U.S. 186 at 204 (1962). In *Craig,* Burger felt that Whitener, being over the age of twenty-one and female, did not have the requisite personal stake.

d. He made this point again in an October 18, 1976, memo to Brennan: "I may decide to join you in reversal, particularly if we do not expand the 'equal advantage' clause or 'suspect' classifications! In short, I am 'available.' " He reiterated this position in two subsequent memos dated November 11 and November 15.

TABLE 1-2

Justices' Conference Positions on the Issues in *Craig v. Boren*

Justice	Conference Position		
	Standing	Standard	Disposition
Burger	No	Rational?	Dismiss/Lean toward Craig if decided on merits
Brennan	Yes	[Strict]/ In-between★	Craig
Stewart	Yes	Rational	Craig
White	Yes	Strict/ In-between?	Craig
Marshall	Yes	Strict	Craig
Blackmun	No	Undeclared	Dismiss/Lean toward Craig if decided on merits
Powell	No	Rational?	Dismiss/Lean toward Craig if decided on merits
Rehnquist	No	Rational	Dismiss/Lean toward Oklahoma if decided on merits
Stevens	Yes	Above rational	Craig

Data Sources: Docket sheets and conference notes of Justice William J. Brennan Jr., Library of Congress; and conference notes and vote tallies of Justice Lewis F. Powell Jr., Washington and Lee University School of Law.

? = Implicit but not explicit from conference discussion. ★ "Strict" represented Brennan's most preferred position, but at conference he offered the "in-between" standard. See Chapter One, note 5.

Once Burger had spoken, the other justices presented their views in order of seniority, another of the Court's norms.[e] They were, as Table 1-2 shows, all over the map. Lewis Powell and Harry Blackmun agreed with the chief justice: both would dismiss on the standing issue, and both thought they could find for Craig. William Rehnquist also wanted to dismiss on standing, but would hold for Oklahoma should the Court resolve

---

e. The order of speaking is a norm, as is the tradition of the chief justice speaking first at conference. Norms structure social interactions (here, among the justices) and are known to the community (the justices) to serve this function. See Jack Knight, *Institutions and Social Conflict* (Cambridge: Cambridge University Press, 1992). We have more to say about norms in the pages to come.

the dispute. The remaining five justices would rule in Craig's favor, but disagreed on the appropriate standard. Thurgood Marshall favored strict scrutiny, as did William Brennan, but Brennan suggested that a standard in between rational and strict might be viable.[5] Byron White seemed to go along with Brennan. Potter Stewart intimated that the Court need only apply the rational basis test to find in Craig's favor. John Paul Stevens argued that some "level of scrutiny above mere rationality has to be applied," but he was not clear on what that standard should be.

According to the Court's procedures, if the chief justice is in the majority after the conference vote, he decides who will write the opinion of the Court. If he is not part of the majority, the most senior member of the majority—Brennan, in the *Craig* case—takes on that responsibility. According to Court records, Brennan assigned the *Craig* opinion to himself. When he took on the responsibility, Brennan knew, as do all justices, that he needed to obtain the signatures of at least four others if his opinion was to become the law of the land. If he failed to get a majority to agree to its contents, his opinion would become a judgment of the Court and would lack precedential value.

The majority requirement for precedent is another of the Court's many norms, which for Brennan, in *Craig,* must have seemed imposing. Only three others—Marshall and possibly White and Stevens—tended to agree with his *most* preferred positions in the case: (1) Whitener had standing; (2) a strict scrutiny standard should be used; and (3) the Court should rule in Craig's favor. From whom would the fourth vote come? Rehnquist seemed out of the question because his position was diametrically opposed to Brennan's on all the main points, and he would surely dissent. Blackmun, Powell, and Burger also favored dismissal but were closer to Brennan on point 3.

That left Stewart. He, as do all justices, had several feasible courses of action, as shown in Table 1-3: join the majority opinion, concur "regularly," concur "specially," or dissent. Based on his conference position—he had voted in favor of both standing and Craig, but was not keen on the strict scrutiny approach—it was possible that Stewart, as well as Blackmun, Powell, and Burger, might join Brennan's disposition of the case (that Craig should win) but disagree with the strict scrutiny standard the opinion articulated. This situation would not be good news from Brennan's perspective because such (dis)agreement—called a "special" concurrence—meant that Stewart would fail to provide the crucial fifth signature. Stewart might, however, join the majority opinion coalition and write a regular

TABLE 1-3
Major Voting and Opinion Options

Option	Meaning
1. Join the majority or plurality	The justice is a "voiceless" member of the majority or plurality; the justice writes no opinion but agrees with the opinion of the Court.[a]
2. Write or join a regular concurrence	The justice writes or joins an opinion and is also a member of the majority or plurality opinion coalition.
3. Write, join or note[b] a special concurrence	The justice agrees with the disposition made by the majority or plurality but disagrees with the reasons in the opinion. The justice is not a member of the majority or plurality opinion coalition.[c]
4. Write, join, or note a dissent	The justice disagrees with the disposition made by the majority or plurality. The justice is not a member of the majority or plurality opinion coalition.

Source: Jeffrey A. Segal and Harold J. Spaeth, *The Supreme Court and the Attitudinal Model* (New York: Cambridge University Press, 1993), 276.

Note: A justice may be assigned to write the opinion of the Court. But, with the exception of self-assignment, a justice does not make this decision for himself or herself. It is the responsibility of the chief justice, if he is in the majority, or the senior associate in the majority, if the chief justice is not, to assign the opinion of the Court.

[a] Or the judgment of the Court, which results when the opinion writer cannot get a majority of the participating justices to agree to the opinion's contents.

[b] To note is to speak, without opinion, as in "Justice Stewart concurs in the judgment of the Court."

[c] At least one justice must cast such a concurrence to produce a judgment of the Court.

concurrence. A regular concurrence, in contrast to a special concurrence, counts as an opinion "join," and Brennan would have his fifth vote.[f]

After several opinion drafts, all revised to accommodate the many suggestions of his colleagues, Brennan succeeded in marshaling a Court. The final version took up the ACLU's invitation, as well as Brennan's confer-

---

f. When justices agree to sign on to an opinion draft, they typically write a memo to the writer saying that they "join" the opinion. Many simply write "I join" or "Join me."

TABLE 1-4
Comparison of Justices' Conference and Final Positions in *Craig v. Boren*

Justice	Conference Position			Final Position		
	Standing	Standard	Disposition	Standing	Standard	Disposition
Burger	No	Rational?	Dismiss/Craig	No	Rational	Oklahoma[a]
Brennan	Yes	[Strict]/In-between★	Craig	Yes	Heightened	Craig
Stewart	Yes	Rational	Craig	Yes	Unclear	Craig[b]
White	Yes	Strict/In-between?	Craig	Yes	Heightened	Craig
Marshall	Yes	Strict	Craig	Yes	Heightened	Craig
Blackmun	No	Undeclared	Dismiss/Craig	Yes	Heightened	Craig[c]
Powell	No	Rational?	Dismiss/Craig	Yes	Heightened[d]	Craig[e]
Rehnquist	No	Rational	Dismiss/Oklahoma	No	Rational	Oklahoma[a]
Stevens	Yes	Above rational	Craig	Yes	Heightened[d]	Craig[e]

Data Sources: Docket sheets and conference notes of Justice William J. Brennan Jr., Library of Congress; and conference notes and vote tallies of Justice Lewis F. Powell Jr., Washington and Lee University School of Law.

? = Implicit but not explicit from conference discussion. ★ "Strict" represented Brennan's most preferred position, but, at conference, he offered the "in-between" standard. See Chapter One, note 5.

[a] Wrote dissenting opinion.

[b] Wrote opinion concurring in judgment (special concurrence).

[c] Wrote opinion concurring in part.

[d] With reservations or qualifications.

[e] Wrote concurring opinion (regular concurrence).

ence alternative, and articulated a new test for sex discrimination cases. Called "heightened" or midlevel scrutiny, it lies somewhere between strict scrutiny and rational basis.[g] From there, the votes and positions fell out as Table 1-4 indicates. Note that Powell, Burger, and Blackmun did not join opinions that coincided with their conference positions; that Marshall signed an opinion advocating a standard that was less than ideal from his point of view; and that Brennan's writing advanced a sex discrimination test that fell short of his most preferred standard. Even the votes changed. Powell, Blackmun, and Burger switched their positions, but in different directions.

In the end, *Craig* leaves us with many questions. Why did Powell, Blackmun, and Burger alter their votes? Why did Brennan advance the heightened scrutiny test when he clearly favored strict scrutiny? Why did Marshall join Brennan's opinion, when it adopted a standard he found less than appealing? More generally, why did *Craig* come out the way it did?

These questions become more interesting when we consider that *Craig* is not an anomaly. In more than half of all orally argued cases, the justices switch their votes, make changes in their opinions to accommodate the suggestions of colleagues, and join writings that do not necessarily reflect their sincere preferences.[6]

OVERVIEW OF THE STRATEGIC ACCOUNT

How might we answer the questions raised by *Craig* and many other Court cases? Certainly, we should begin by acknowledging the voluminous body of literature that has attempted to address them. For more than fifty years scholars have tried to develop theories to explain why justices behave in particular ways, and they have had a modicum of success or, at the very least, they have come to some agreement over the fundamentals. Among the most important of these is the primacy of policy preferences; that is, judicial specialists generally agree that justices, first and foremost, wish to

---

g. Brennan outlined the heightened scrutiny approach as follows: "classifications by gender must serve important governmental objectives and must be substantially related to the achievement of those objectives." *Craig v. Boren,* 429 U.S. 190 at 197 (1976). Using this approach, the Court sometimes strikes down sex-based classifications, such as the law in *Craig,* and sometimes upholds them. One law it upheld is the federal policy limiting the military draft to men. See *Rostker v. Goldberg,* 453 U.S. 57 (1981).

see their policy preferences etched into law. They are, in the opinion of many, "single-minded seekers of legal policy." [7]

Craig illustrates this point. During conference discussion, almost every justice expressed some preference about the way he wanted the case to come out and what he hoped the opinion would say. For example, we know that Marshall wanted the Court to hold that Whitener had standing, to apply a strict scrutiny standard to sex discrimination claims, and to rule in Craig's favor. But, as we also know, his preferences alone did not drive Marshall's behavior: he signed an opinion articulating a standard of review that fell short of his most preferred position.

So it seems that something is missing from this basic story of Court decisions. Even after we take preferences into account, important questions linger, suggesting the need for a more comprehensive approach and, in *Choices,* we offer one—a strategic account of judicial decisions. This account rests on a few simple propositions: justices may be primarily seekers of legal policy, but they are not unconstrained actors who make decisions based only on their own ideological attitudes. Rather, justices are strategic actors who realize that their ability to achieve their goals depends on a consideration of the preferences of other actors, the choices they expect others to make, and the institutional context in which they act. We call this a strategic account because the ideas it contains are derived from the rational choice paradigm,[8] on which strategic analysis is based and as it has been advanced by economists and political scientists working in other fields.[9] Accordingly, we can restate our argument this way: we can best explain the choices of justices as strategic behavior and not merely as responses to ideological values.

Is this account plausible? What leverage does it give us to understand the nature of Supreme Court decision making and the law? *Choices* attempts to answer these questions. It presents support for our conception of justices as strategic seekers of legal policy and explores how justices so motivated go about making choices. To put it another way, in this book we hope to provide valuable insights into the nature of judicial decision making by pursuing the implications of a simple argument.

MAJOR COMPONENTS OF THE STRATEGIC ACCOUNT

As we have set it out, the strategic account of judicial decision making comprises three main ideas: justices' actions are directed toward the attainment of goals; justices are strategic; and institutions structure justices' inter-actions. In this section, we explore each of these ideas in greater depth and preview the argument we make in the pages to come.

Goals

A central assumption of strategic explanations is that actors make decisions consistent with their goals and interests. We say that an actor makes a ratio-nal decision when she takes a course of action that satisfies her desires most efficiently. What this means is that when a political actor chooses between two courses of action, she will select the one she thinks is most likely to help her attain her goals. All we need to assume for the strategic account is that she acts "intentionally and optimally" toward a specific objective.[10]

This account further supposes that an actor can rank the alternative courses of action available to her in terms of her preferences according to the outcomes she expects the actions to produce. Once the actor estab-lishes the relationship between actions and outcomes, she can compare the relative benefits of the alternative actions and choose the one that produces the highest ranked outcome. To put it in terms of *Craig,* because Marshall preferred the establishment of a strict scrutiny standard more than a heightened scrutiny standard, and heightened scrutiny more than a ratio-nal basis standard, we would say he acted rationally if he made those indi-vidual choices that led to a decision by the full Court that established a standard closest to the strict scrutiny criterion.

To give meaning to this assumption—that people maximize their pref-erences—we must be sure we know what the actors' goals are. If we do not, our resulting explanations become a tautology "since we can always assert that person's goal is to do precisely what we observe him or her to be doing." [11] Typically, rational choice theorists assume that justices are "single-minded seekers of legal policy," but that not need be the case. It is up to the researcher to specify the content of actors' goals, and a few have explored objectives other than policy.[12] We adopt the more mainstream position: on our account, a major goal of all justices is to see the law reflect their preferred policy positions, and they will take actions to advance this objective.

Having said that, we recognize and appreciate the view that policy is not the only judicial motivation. Throughout *Choices,* we explore others: an especially interesting view centers on institutional legitimacy. The idea is that before the Court can make authoritative policy that other institutions, the states, and the public will view as binding on them, it must have some level of respect. *Craig* makes this point nicely. If the governor of Oklahoma regarded the Court as an illegitimate institution that lacked the authority and capacity to make policy, why would he feel obliged to follow the *Craig* ruling?

Still, we should not lose sight of the general point, which we reinforce in the next chapter: legitimacy, like most goals scholars ascribe to justices, is a means to an end, and that end is the substantive content of the law. This claim is not, as we suggested earlier, particularly controversial. Justices may have goals other than policy, but no serious scholar of the Court would claim that policy is not prime among them.[13]

Strategic Interaction

The second part of the strategic account is tied to the first: for justices to maximize their preferences, they must act strategically in making their choices. By "strategic," we mean that judicial decision making is interdependent. From *Craig*, we learn that it is not enough to say that Justice Brennan chose heightened scrutiny over rational basis or strict scrutiny because he preferred heightened scrutiny; we know he actually preferred strict scrutiny. Rather, interdependency suggests that Brennan chose heightened scrutiny because he believed that the other relevant actors—including his colleagues—would choose rational basis, and, given this choice, heightened scrutiny led to a better outcome for Brennan than the alternatives.[14]

To put it plainly, strategic decision making is about *interdependent* choice: an individual's action is, in part, a function of her expectations about the actions of others.[h] To say that a justice acts strategically is to say that she realizes that her success or failure depends on the preferences of other actors and the actions she expects them to take, not just on her own preferences and actions.[15]

Occasionally, strategic calculations lead justices to make choices that reflect their sincere preferences. Suppose, in *Craig,* that all of the justices

---

h. Some believe that such a broad (and simple) conception of strategic decision making undermines the value of the approach. See, for example, Howard Gillman, "Placing Judicial Motives in Context," 7 *Law and Courts* (1997): 10–13. We, however, see it as what underlies its importance because it acknowledges the breadth of the phenomena that might be explained.

agreed on all of the important issues: Whitener had standing; a strict scrutiny standard should be used; and the Court should rule in Craig's favor. If those conditions held, Brennan would have been free to write an opinion that reflected his true preferences, for they were the same as the Court's. In other instances, strategic calculations lead a justice to act in a sophisticated fashion; that is, he acts in a way that does not accurately reflect his true preferences so as to avoid the possibility of seeing his colleagues reject his most preferred policy in favor of his least preferred. Brennan may have followed this line of thinking in *Craig*. We know that he had to choose among three possible standards, but preferred strict scrutiny over heightened scrutiny over rational basis. Yet, he did not select his most preferred standard, opting instead for his second choice. Why? A possibility is that Brennan thought an opinion advancing strict scrutiny would be completely unacceptable to certain members of the Court, who would push for a rational basis standard, his least preferred standard. He may have chosen heightened scrutiny because, based on his knowledge of the preferences of other justices, it allowed him to avoid his least preferred position, not because it was his first choice.

Brennan chose the course of action that any justice concerned with maximizing his policy preferences would take. In other words, for Brennan to set policy as close as possible to his ideal point, strategic behavior was essential. In *Craig* he needed to act in a sophisticated fashion, given his beliefs about the preferences of the other actors and the choices he expected them to make.

But strategic considerations do not simply involve calculations over what colleagues will do. Justices must also consider the preferences of other political actors, including Congress, the president, and even the public. The logic here is as follows. As every student of American politics knows, two main concepts undergird our constitutional system. The first is the separation of powers doctrine, under which each of the branches has a distinct function: the legislature makes the laws, the executive implements those laws, and the judiciary interprets them. The second is the notion of checks and balances: each branch of government imposes limits on the primary function of the others. For example, as Figure 1-1 shows, the judiciary may interpret laws and even strike them down as being in violation of the Constitution. But congressional committees can introduce legislation to override the Court's decision. If they do, Congress must act by adopting the committees' recommendation, enacting a different version of it, or rejecting it. If Congress takes action, the president has the option of veto-

Figure 1-1   The Separation of Powers System in Action

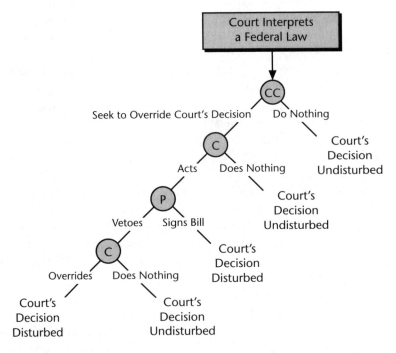

Adapted from: William N. Eskridge Jr., "Reneging on History? Playing the Court/Congress/President Civil Rights Game," *79 California Law Review* (1991): 644.

Note: CC = Congressional committees; C = Congress; P = President.

ing the law. In this depiction, the last move rests with Congress, which must decide whether to override the president's veto.[i]

It is just these kinds of checks that lead goal-oriented justices to concern themselves with the positions of Congress, the president, and the public. If their objective is to see their favored policies become the law of the

---

i. Figure 1-1 depicts a sequence in which the Court makes the first move and Congress the last. It is possible to lay out other sequences and to include other or different actors. See Christopher Zorn, "Congress and the Supreme Court: Reevaluating the 'Interest Group Perspective' " (paper presented at the 1995 annual meeting of the Midwest Political Science Association, Chicago). In another scenario the Court could move first; congressional committees and Congress again go next, but this time they propose a constitutional amendment rather than a law. The states, rather than the president, would have the last turn by deciding whether to ratify the amendment.

land, they must take into account the preferences of other actors and the actions they expect them to take. Failing to do so may have undesirable consequences: Congress could replace their most preferred position with their least, or the public may refuse to comply with a ruling, in which case their policy fails to take on the force of law.[j]

To see these points, let us consider *Newport News Shipbuilding & Dry Dock v. EEOC,* a sex discrimination case decided seven years after *Craig.*[16] While *Craig* required the Court to interpret the Constitution, *Newport News* asked the justices to interpret a 1978 amendment to Title VII of the Civil Rights Act of 1964.[k] The Civil Rights Act makes it unlawful for an employer to discriminate against an employee on account of race, color, religion, sex, or national origin. The amendment, known as the Pregnancy Discrimination Act (PDA), prohibits discrimination on the basis of pregnancy.[l] In this case, the justices addressed a number of questions flowing from the act, including whether an employer has to supply the same sort of pregnancy benefits to the spouses of its male employees that it gives to female workers.

At the time the Court was considering this case, its preferences over pregnancy discrimination legislation were to the right of Congress and the relevant committees. In fact, Congress had passed the PDA to override the 1976 Supreme Court decision in *General Electric Co. v. Gilbert.*[17] *Gilbert* held that the exclusion of pregnancy-related disabilities from an employ-

---

j. They also risk other forms of retaliation by Congress and the president: impeachment and passage of legislation removing their ability to hear certain kinds of cases, to name just two. See Walter F. Murphy, *Elements of Judicial Strategy* (Chicago: University of Chicago Press, 1964).

k. It is often convenient to talk about collectivities, such as the Court, interpreting a document, making choices, having preferences, learning, and so forth. When we do so, we must realize that it is individuals who do these things and that complete explanations of collectivities should be grounded in terms of individual choice. To understand the Court we must understand the preferences of and choices confronting its members. See Peter C. Ordeshook, *Game Theory and Political Theory* (Cambridge: Cambridge University Press, 1986), 1–2.

l. We shift the discussion from *Craig,* a constitutional case, to *Newport News,* a case of statutory interpretation, because we believe that the Court is more likely to consider the preferences and likely actions of other political actors in statutory cases. This belief follows from the fact that Congress rarely invokes the tools it possesses to override constitutional decisions. The Court, therefore, may be *less* attentive (but not *inattentive*) to the other branches in constitutional disputes. We discuss this in detail in Chapter Five.

er's disability plan did not constitute sex discrimination.[m] Certainly, the Court recognized this fact, as Justice Stevens's majority opinion in *Newport News* made clear:

> When Congress amended Title VII in 1978, it unambiguously expressed its disapproval of both the holding and the reasoning of the Court in the *Gilbert* decision. . . . Proponents of the bill repeatedly emphasized that the Supreme Court had erroneously interpreted congressional intent and that amending legislation was necessary to reestablish the principles of Title VII law as they had been understood prior to the *Gilbert* decision. Many of them expressly agreed with the views of the dissenting Justices.[18]

And, according to scholars, the Court had little reason to believe that Congress's preferences had changed between then and the time it was considering *Newport News*.[19]

Let us assume that a majority of justices viewed the political situation the way we described it. What approach would a strategic Court take in *Newport News?* The Court may be unwise to vote its sincere preferences because, if it articulates its preferred approach to pregnancy, Congress may again try to override its decision by writing another, perhaps even more expansive, law or by resorting to other retaliatory measures. The Court, therefore, would have a strong incentive to compromise its preferences and adopt an interpretation that Congress would see was the best it could expect and leave undisturbed.

That was the course the justices chose in *Newport News.* Not only did the majority rule that an employer cannot give male employees a pregnancy benefit package for their spouses that is less inclusive than the package it gives to female employees, but also it recanted its earlier approach to pregnancy discrimination. As Justice Stevens wrote, "The Pregnancy Discrimination Act has now made clear that, for all Title VII purposes, dis-

---

m. One might ask why, if we are correct and the justices consider the preferences and likely actions of political actors, the Court ever puts itself in a position where its decisions would be overruled by Congress. We supply some answers in Chapter Five, but one that is relevant here centers on information: it is possible that in 1976 the Court did not know with certainty the preferences of other government actors on pregnancy discrimination. The justices could only form an estimate, which in this case turned out to be wrong. By 1983 the Court did not have to guess about Congress's preferences on pregnancy discrimination; its response to *Gilbert*—the PDA—made them clear.

crimination based on a woman's pregnancy is, on its face, discrimination because of her sex." [20]

By acting in such a sophisticated fashion, the Court's majority will not see its most preferred position (perhaps the *Gilbert* holding) become policy, but neither will its least preferred position, for example, further retaliation on the part of Congress, obtain. This course of action—the rational course of action under the circumstances—may lead to the best possible outcome for the majority.

Institutions

According to the strategic account, we cannot fully understand the choices justices make unless we also consider the institutional context in which they operate. By institutions, we mean sets of rules that "structure social interactions in particular ways." Under this definition, institutions can be formal, such as laws, or informal, such as norms and conventions.[21]

To see how central institutions are to this account of judicial decisions, consider two examples. First, think about how the norm governing the creation of precedent—a majority of justices must sign an opinion for it to become the law of the land—affected the resolution of *Craig.* Had Brennan believed that four other justices shared his preference for the strict scrutiny standard, he would have written an opinion that adopted that standard. However, only three justices at the most were firmly behind him. If a different threshold for the establishment of precedent had existed, if four justices were enough, perhaps Brennan would have pushed for strict scrutiny. But such was not the case, which may explain, in part, why he was willing to consider the heightened standard: given the norm for precedent, he thought heightened was the best he could do.

Second, another institution of some importance is Article III of the U.S. Constitution, which states that justices "hold their Offices during good Behaviour." What this phrase means is that, barring an impeachment by Congress, justices have life tenure; unlike members of legislatures and even judges in many states, they do not have to face the voters to retain their jobs. The institution of life tenure also influences justices' goals. Instead of acting to maximize their chances for reelection, justices act to maximize policy.[22] To understand the effect of this institution, one has only to think about the kinds of activities in which a justice running for office would engage as opposed to a justice attempting to influence policy. In deciding *Craig,* for example, rather than considering the preferences of his colleagues and Congress over what test to use in sex discrimination cases, Justice Brennan would have been taking the pulse of his "constituents," talking with lobbyists, holding press conferences, and otherwise behaving in the ways we associate with members of Congress, not justices of the Supreme Court.[23]

CONCLUSION

As we have set it out, the strategic account of judicial decisions has several implications for the way we think about the development of law in American society. We argue that it suggests that law, as it is generated by the Supreme Court, is the result of short-term strategic interactions among the justices and between the Court and other branches of government.[24] But before we think about the implications of the strategic account, we must consider whether it is plausible and whether it provides us with any real leverage to understand judicial decisions.

To accomplish these tasks, we follow essentially the same path that David Mayhew did in *Congress—The Electoral Connection:* we develop a "picture" of justices as strategic seekers of legal policy and explore how justices so motivated go about making choices.[25] The chapters to follow unpack the components of our argument. Chapter Two documents the importance of policy goals; Chapter Three discusses behavioral manifestations of strategic activity aimed at achieving policy ends; and Chapters Four and Five take up the institutions that structure such activity. In the concluding chapter, we consider the major implications of our argument, especially as they pertain to the development of law and to future research on the Court.

We attempt to make our main points with some degree of rigor, but we think of this book as only the first step toward a social explanation of Court decisions. It is a book about conceptions of decision making and mechanisms of strategic behavior, not about complete explanations of any substantive body of law. We are sure it will leave some questions unaddressed and alternative arguments unanswered. This does not trouble us as long as we can at least make a convincing case for the plausibility of our approach and show how pursuing its implications can lead to valuable insights into judicial decisions.

ENDNOTES

1. See Mark Wolfson, "The Legislative Impact of Social Movement Organizations: The Anti-Drunken-Driving Movement and the 21-Year-Old Drinking Age," 76 *Social Science Quarterly* (1995): 311–327.

2. The material in the next few paragraphs comes from *U.S. Supreme Court Records and Briefs*, BNA's Law Reprints, no. 75-628.

3. Susan Gluck Mezey, *In Pursuit of Equality* (New York: St. Martin's, 1992), 17.

4. The next few paragraphs draw on the papers, including case files, docket books, and transcriptions of conference discussions, of Justices William J. Brennan Jr., Lewis F. Powell Jr., and Thurgood Marshall. The Brennan and Marshall collections are located in the Library of Congress; the Powell papers, in the Law Library at Washington and Lee University.

5. Typically, Brennan's case files contain memos of the remarks he made at conferences. Unfortunately, his *Craig* conference memo was missing, so we rely on Bernard Schwartz, who writes that Brennan wanted to adopt the strict scrutiny approach (see Brennan's opinion for the Court in *Frontiero v. Richardson*), but at conference he offered the "in between" standard. See Bernard Schwartz, *The Ascent of Pragmatism* (Reading, Mass.: Addison-Wesley, 1990), 226. For now, the important point is that "strict scrutiny" represented Brennan's most preferred position.

6. See, for example, Lee Epstein and Jack Knight, "Documenting Strategic Interaction on the U.S. Supreme Court" (paper presented at the 1995 annual meeting of the American Political Science Association, Chicago). With the exception of vote shifts, we consider these other behaviors in the chapters to come. Vote shifts are already the object of extensive investigation. For the latest and best installment, see Forrest Maltzman and Paul J. Wahlbeck, "Strategic Considerations and Vote Fluidity on the Burger Court," 90 *American Political Science Review* (1996): 581–592.

7. Tracey E. George and Lee Epstein, "On the Nature of Supreme Court Decision Making," 86 *American Political Science Review* (1990): 325.

8. See Peter C. Ordeshook, *A Political Theory Primer* (New York: Routledge, 1992). We refer to nonparametric or strategic choice accounts, in which individuals make rational decisions, but the rational course of action is contingent upon their expectations about what other players will do. The exception is a dominant strategy; that is, a particular strategic choice that will produce the best outcome regardless of what the others do.

9. The rational choice paradigm has already been applied to the Court. As we noted in the Preface, in *Elements of Judicial Strategy* Walter Murphy paints a portrait of shrewd justices who know or anticipate the responses of their colleagues and of other relevant actors and take them into account in their decision making. They would rather hand down a ruling that comes close to their preferences than

see their colleagues take positions that move policy well away from their ideal or see another political institution (Congress, for example) completely reverse their decisions. *Elements,* in other words, elucidates the strategic nature of judicial decision making, as does *Choices.*

We also owe a good deal to a group of (mainly) law and business school professors who have, in recent years, adopted rational choice theory to study the role of the Court in the government system. For a list of citations, see endnote 1 of the preface.

10. Jack Knight, *Institutions and Social Conflict* (Cambridge: Cambridge University Press, 1992), 17.

11. Ordeshook, *A Political Theory Primer,* 10–11.

12. See, for example, John Ferejohn and Barry Weingast, "A Positive Theory of Statutory Interpretation," 12 *International Review of Law and Economics* (1992): 263–279.

13. Some jurists share this perspective. See, for example, Richard A. Posner, "What Do Judges and Justices Maximize? (The Same Thing Everybody Else Does)," 3 *Supreme Court Economics Review* (1993): 1.

14. See, generally, Ordeshook, *A Political Theory Primer.*

15. See Charles M. Cameron, "Decision-Making and Positive Political Theory (Or, Using Game Theory to Study Judicial Politics)" (paper presented at the 1994 Columbus Conference, Columbus, Ohio).

16. *Newport News Shipbuilding & Dry Dock v. EEOC,* 462 U.S. 669 (1983). We adopt this example from William N. Eskridge Jr., "Reneging on History? Playing the Court/Congress/President Civil Rights Game," 79 *California Law Review* (1991): 653.

17. *General Electric Co. v. Gilbert,* 429 U.S. 125 (1976).

18. *Newport News Shipbuilding & Dry Dock v. EEOC,* 462 U.S. 669 at 678 (1983).

19. See, for example, Eskridge, "Reneging on History?" 653; and Leslie Friedman Goldstein, *The Constitutional Rights of Women* (Madison: University of Wisconsin Press, 1988), 488–489. It is true, as Goldstein makes clear, that Congress's intent over the specific question at issue in *Newport News*—a question going to the reach of the PDA—was less clear than its overall preferences on pregnancy discrimination.

20. *Newport News Shipbuilding & Dry Dock v. EEOC,* 462 U.S. 669 at 684 (1983).

21. See Knight, *Institutions and Social Conflict,* 2–3.

22. See Jeffrey A. Segal and Harold J. Spaeth, *The Supreme Court and the Attitudinal Model* (New York: Cambridge University Press, 1993), 69–72.

23. See, generally, David Mayhew, *Congress—The Electoral Connection* (New Haven: Yale University Press, 1974).

24. Knight makes this argument in *Institutions and Social Conflict,* and we explore it in an essay on *Marbury v. Madison,* 1 Cr. 137 (1803). Jack Knight and Lee Epstein, "On the Struggle for Judicial Supremacy," 30 *Law and Society Review* (1996): 87–130.

25. After proclaiming that representatives and senators were "single-minded seekers of reelection," Mayhew (*Congress—The Electoral Connection,* 9) went on to develop a "picture of what the United States Congress looks like if the reelection quest is examined seriously."

CHAPTER TWO

Justices as Policy Seekers

In *Craig v. Boren,* Justice Brennan chose to advance the midlevel standard
of heightened scrutiny over two alternative standards, rational basis and
strict scrutiny. Rational choice theorists might say that Brennan did so to
maximize his preferences—that heightened scrutiny was the option
Brennan believed best served his goals. But such a statement would be
meaningless unless we specify *a priori* what Brennan's goals were.

To see why, suppose we thought Brennan's objective was to further his
political career, that he wanted to become president of the United States.
One might argue that his choice of the compromise position of the
midlevel standard was perfectly consistent with the pursuit of that goal.
After all, it was a position that would, in some sense, appease both sup-
porters and opponents of expanded rights for women. One could also
make the argument—as we did in the previous chapter—that heightened
scrutiny reflected the choice any rational justice concerned with policy,
and possessing Brennan's preferences, would make.

We could go on and show how Brennan's position in *Craig* was consistent with other goals, such as reaching principled decisions or ensuring the
integrity of the Court. But the general point would be the same: if we
want to explain—and not merely predict—why justices make the choices
they do, we should specify *a priori* the goals they are trying to attain. If we
do not, then the explanations we offer are a tautology: we can always say

that the goals of justices are to do precisely what we observe them doing. To move toward an explanation of judicial choices, we must therefore begin with the justices' goals and address these kinds of questions: What were Brennan's aims in *Craig?* More generally, what are the goals of most Supreme Court justices? What are they trying to accomplish?

We offer this answer: most justices, in most cases, pursue policy; that is, they want to move the substantive content of law as close as possible to their preferred position.[a] In what follows, we address three questions to which this assertion gives rise: (1) Is it reasonable to assume that justices pursue policy goals? (2) If it *is* reasonable to assume that justices pursue policy goals, does it make sense to focus on policy to the exclusion of other goals? (3) If justices, in the main, seek policy, are they in a position to realize their goal?[1]

REASONABLENESS OF POLICY ASSUMPTION

Throughout this book, we make many claims with which students of the Court might take issue. The minimal notion that it is *reasonable* to assume that justices pursue policy goals, however, is not among them. It is generally conceded, at least among social scientists, that members of the Court are by and large policy seekers.

That was not always the case. Prior to the 1940s, many scholars believed that justices were motivated to follow precedent rather than to pursue policy. According to this view, jurists are "mechanical" decision makers, who observe a similarity between cases, announce the rule of law inherent in the first case, and apply that rule to the second case.[2] In other words, because judges honor the doctrine of *stare decisis*—they abide by previously decided cases—their personal policy views are largely irrelevant, or so the argument went.

---

a. The concept of policy preferences can be construed to include (1) the justices' particular preferences about specific policy questions, such as the drinking age for alcoholic beverages, and (2) general preferences about society. For example, should the country have a laissez-faire economic system in which the judiciary defers to elected political actors or a heavily regulated system in which the judiciary plays an active role? The first type of preference correlates directly with the issues in a particular case, while the second translates indirectly into a decision about the effects of the case resolution on justices' general ideas about society. We note here that both conceptions of judicial motivation are consistent with our emphasis on policy preferences.

Figure 2-1   Proportion of U.S. Supreme Court Cases Containing at Least One Dissenting Opinion, 1800–1995 Terms

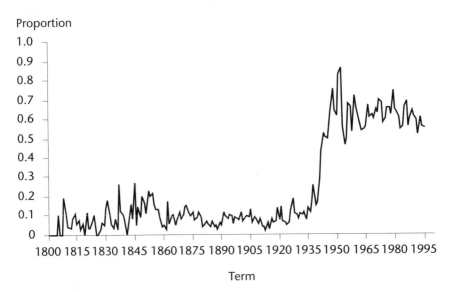

Data Sources: Lee Epstein, Jeffrey A. Segal, Harold J. Spaeth, and Thomas G. Walker, *The Supreme Court Compendium: Data, Decisions, and Developments,* 2d ed. (Washington, D.C.: Congressional Quarterly, 1996), Table 3-2. We thank Harold J. Spaeth for providing data for the 1995 term from his U.S. Supreme Court Judicial Database.

The initial debunking of the mechanical account came with the writings of C. Herman Pritchett in the 1940s.[b] His main insight was that dissent had become an institutionalized part of Supreme Court decision making (see Figure 2-1). If precedent drove Court rulings, as the mechanical view maintained, then why, Pritchett asked, did various justices interpreting the same legal provision consistently reach different conclusions? He concluded that justices were not following *stare decisis,* but were "motivated by their own preferences." [3]

---

b. See C. Herman Pritchett, *The Roosevelt Court* (New York: Macmillan, 1948). Many say the debunking of this myth started decades earlier with Oliver Wendell Holmes Jr.'s *The Common Law* (Boston: Little, Brown, 1881). On pages 1–2 the future Supreme Court justice wrote: "The life of the law has not been logic: it has been experience. The felt necessities of the time, the prevalent moral and political theories [and] intuitions of public policy have had a good deal more to do than the syllogism in

Over the years, students of the Court have amassed an impressive array of evidence to confirm Pritchett's intuition about the primary motivation of justices. They too infer from the continuing rise in dissensus that justices decide cases on factors other than precedent.[c] But they have also sought to determine whether justices manifest behavior, throughout the decision-making process, that is consistent with the "other factor" to which Pritchett pointed—pursuit of a policy goal.

Let us consider these assessments, along with some fresh data, as they pertain to four major aspects of the Court's work: case selection, conference discussion, the circulation of opinions, and the vote on the merits of cases. Each of these represents an important stage in the Court's decision-making process. (See Appendix A for a visual depiction.)

Selecting Cases

Each term, thousands of cases arrive at the Supreme Court's doorstep. A few have not been heard by another court, but come directly to the Court under its original jurisdiction. The vast majority of cases reach the Court under its appellate jurisdiction, which means that another court—state or federal—has already rendered a decision and one of the parties is asking the Court to review it. To invoke the Court's appellate jurisdiction, litigants can take one of three routes, depending on the nature of their dispute.

1. *Appeal as a matter of right.* Cases in this category are those Congress has determined are so important that a ruling by the Supreme Court is necessary. For most of the Court's history, these included cases in which a lower court declared a state or federal law unconstitutional or

---

determining the rules by which men should be governed." In the 1920s a group of law professors, now known as legal realists, picked up where Holmes had left off, arguing that rules based on precedents were nothing more than smoke screens and that it would be extraordinary to believe that judges were not susceptible to political and personal influences. See, for example, Jerome Frank, *Law and the Modern Mind* (New York: Coward-McCann, 1930). Pritchett brought legal realism to political science and equipped scholars with the arsenal necessary to evaluate its propositions.

c. Conversely, from the lack of dissensus during most of the Court's history (see Figure 2-1) can we infer that the early justices based their decisions on legal factors, such as *stare decisis?* Pritchett thought so. See his article, "Divisions of Opinion Among Justices of the U.S. Supreme Court," 35 *American Political Science Review* (1941): 890. Later in this chapter, we take issue with his claim.

in which a state court upheld a state statute challenged as violating the U.S. Constitution. Although the Court was obliged to decide such cases, it found ways to deal with most of them expediently, such as by issuing summary decisions—shorthand rulings made in the absence of oral arguments, briefs, and so forth. In 1988, at the Court's urging, Congress virtually eliminated mandatory appeals cases. Today, the Court is legally obliged to decide only those few cases, typically involving the Voting Rights Act, appealed from special three-judge courts.

2. *Certification.* The few certification cases are those in which lower appellate courts file writs of certification, asking the justices to respond to questions aimed at "clarifying" federal law. Only judges may use this route; and the justices are free to accept a question certified to them or dismiss it.

3. *Certiorari.* Cases in this category—the most common one—are those in which litigants request a writ of certiorari (Latin for "to be informed"). In a petition for a writ of certiorari, the litigants seeking Supreme Court review ask the Court, literally, to become informed about their cases by requesting the lower court to send up the record. The Court has complete discretion to determine which of these requests it will grant. The Court selects those it wants to "grant cert" via the Rule of Four, meaning that the Court will decide only those cases that at least four justices want to hear.

If justices are in fact the policy seekers that Pritchett and so many others say they are, do they pursue this goal when selecting the cases to hear or "deciding to decide"? We assume that they do, for it is at this agenda-setting stage when justices select the cases they will use to establish law.

Is this assumption reasonable? Substantial evidence suggests that it is. Some comes from the justices, who claim that policy is precisely what they have in mind. As Chief Justice Rehnquist once put it: "There is an ideological division on the Court, and each of us has some cases we would like to see granted, and on the contrary some of the other members would not like to see them granted."[4] Justices interviewed by H. W. Perry concurred. As one noted, a certiorari vote is a preliminary vote on the merits in a majority of cases and that "generally when people vote to grant, they feel that it is because [the case was] wrongly decided [below]."[5]

Further support comes from scholarly research grounded in the kind of response offered by Rehnquist and other Court members: the justices take cases they want to *reverse* in accordance with their policy preferences.[d] In other words, if justices pursue policy goals by agreeing to review decisions of lower courts with which they disagree, then we should see them reversing most of the cases they hear and decide.[e] That appears to be what happens: between the 1953 and 1994 terms, the Supreme Court reversed 61.3 percent of the 6,152 lower court decisions it reviewed.[6]

Finally, many studies have considered the effect of policy preferences while holding constant other factors that may affect the certiorari decision. For example, Gregory Caldeira and John Wright's work took into account nine variables (including whether conflict existed in the lower courts over the disposition of particular kinds of disputes and the presence of amicus curiae briefs) in addition to the ideological direction of the lower court. They wrote: "After Justice [Sandra Day] O'Connor's appointment in 1981, the Court had a decided . . . conservative ideological orientation. Thus the clear tendency for the Court to select cases decided liberally in the court below affirms that justices' ideological predilections affect their decisions in much the same way that other elite political actors are motivated by their personal ideological agendas." [7]

This is not to say that policy preferences alone drive certiorari votes. Many of the other variables that Caldeira and Wright considered, particularly conflict in lower courts and the presence of amicus curiae briefs, have bearing on the case selection decision, and we will return to them. Here, we simply note that Caldeira and Wright's work and many other studies suggest that our *de minimis* assumption—namely, justices pursue policy at the certiorari stage—is a reasonable one.[8]

---

d. Jeffrey A. Segal and Harold J. Spaeth provide the following justification for the reversal strategy: "Given a finite number of cases that can be reviewed in a given term, the Court must decide how to utilize its time, the Court's most scarce resource. Certainly, overturning unfavorable lower court decisions has more of an impact—if only to the parties to the litigation—than affirming favorable ones. Thus, the justices should hear more cases with which they disagree, other things being equal." See *The Supreme Court and the Attitudinal Model* (New York: Cambridge University Press, 1993), 191.

e. Even this evidence has implications for strategic interaction. For example, given the Rule of Four and the norm of a majority for precedent, policy-oriented justices who want to reverse, must—at the review stage—make a calculation about the fifth vote.

Discussing Cases

After a case is briefed and argued, the Court holds a conference to discuss it. During conference, the justices state their views on the case and, frequently, how they would dispose of it—reverse, remand, or affirm. As our discussion of *Craig v. Boren* reveals, the conference provides several opportunities for justices to pursue their goals. They can, for example, misrepresent their sincere preferences in their case statements, as Brennan did when he urged his colleagues to adopt a midlevel test rather than his most preferred standard. Or they can inject another dimension to a case to control the agenda in an effort to manipulate the outcome. Chief Justice Burger took this route in *Craig* when he attempted to steer the conference's attention toward a procedural dimension (standing) and away from sex discrimination policy.

Not only are these actions a type of strategic behavior, but also they demonstrate concern with policy goals: Brennan and Burger wanted to move sex discrimination law as close as possible to their preferred positions. Is this typical? Do justices generally pursue policy goals during conference discussion, or was *Craig* an anomaly?

To address these questions, we drew a random sample of cases that were orally argued during the 1983 term and characterized the remarks of each justice as involving the following: policy, precedent, fact-finding, or threshold issues.

- By *policy*, we mean statements concerning proposed courses of action or general plans the Court should advance, such as what Justice Stevens said in *Hishon v. King & Spaulding*. The case asked whether a lawyer can bring a discrimination suit under Title VII of the Civil Rights Act of 1964 against a law partnership for failure to invite her to become a partner. According to Justice Brennan's notes of the conference discussion, Stevens said: "A partner is not an employee. . . . But clearly prohibited is policy not to hire blacks or women."
- We coded statements as involving *precedent* when justices invoked previously decided cases in their remarks or referred to specific cases, as Burger did in conference discussion of *Secretary of State v. Munson Co.* The Court was asked to assess the constitutionality of a Maryland statute that prohibited a charitable organization, in connection with any fund-raising activity, from paying expenses of more than 25 percent of the amount raised. The statute authorized a waiver of this limi-

tation if it prevented the organization from raising contributions. Burger said, "*Schaumburg* makes it tough for states to do this." [f]

- *Fact-finding* occurs when conference comments center on lower court findings or the factual record of the case. Justice Marshall's remarks in *Schall v. Martin* are illustrative. The case involved a Fourteenth Amendment Due Process Clause challenge to a New York law authorizing pretrial detention of a juvenile if there is a "serious risk" that the juvenile will commit a crime. Marshall noted that the "finding below was that the statute was used to punish juveniles and that's enough to affirm."
- We take *threshold issues* to mean comments questioning whether the Court should formally decide the case because it may lack jurisdiction or because the case may not be properly before it. Justice White's question in *Board of Education v. Vail*, a job termination case that centered on the nature of property interests under the Due Process Clause, provides an example. White said: "Two years [have] now passed. . . . Isn't his claim moot therefore?" [9]

Table 2-1 displays the results of our content analysis. It shows that nearly half of the justices' conference comments involved policy concerns. In other words, the *Craig* conference was not anomalous in the sense that justices typically use conference statements to express their policy positions.

Interesting, too, is the degree to which the justices invoke precedent in their remarks: more than a quarter of their comments cited past cases. Often, a particular precedent was central to their statements, as when Justice Blackmun said with regard to *Munson* that he had sympathy for the state's effort but that "*Schaumburg* certainly controls." In others, however, justices were critical of particular precedents, with the chief justice's comments in *Schall* providing a good example: "[I] have always thought *Gault* would destroy juvenile system—[we] have to treat [juveniles] as adults. There are terrible problems of juvenile delinquency." [g] Some even went so

---

f. In *Village of Schaumburg v. Citizens for a Better Environment,* 444 U.S. 620 (1980), the Court held that an ordinance prohibiting door-to-door or on-street solicitation of contributions by charitable organizations that do not use at least 75 percent of their receipts for "charitable purposes" was unconstitutionally overbroad in violation of the First and Fourteenth Amendments.

g. *In re Gault,* 387 U.S. 1 (1966), concerned the application of procedural due process rights to juveniles charged with delinquency.

TABLE 2-1
Nature of Remarks in Conference Statements

Nature of Remarks	Number of Remarks (percent)
Policy	69 (47.6)
Precedent	37 (25.5)
Threshold	20 (13.8)
Facts	19 (13.1)
Total	145

Data Sources: Conference notes of Justices William J. Brennan Jr., Library of Congress; and Lewis F. Powell Jr., Washington and Lee University School of Law.

Note: This is a random sample of 1983 orally argued cases derived from the list of 1983 term cases in the register of the Papers of Justice William J. Brennan (Library of Congress) with the exception of original cases. The unit of analysis was citation. If two or more cases were combined under one U.S. cite, we included only the lead case. The number of cases in the sample = 16.

Data Note: We provide more detailed coding rules and the data at: *http://www.artsci.wustl. edu/~polisci/epstein/choices/*.

Because we use Brennan's notes, we have only his conference memoranda (a typed version of his conference statement)—not a transcription of his oral remarks. For comparability, we chose not to use those memos and, instead, relied on Powell's transcriptions to code Brennan's remarks.

far as to urge colleagues to alter particular precedents, as Blackmun did in *Copperweld Corporation v. Independence Tube Corporation,* which addressed whether a corporation and its wholly owned subsidiary are capable of conspiring with each other in violation of antitrust laws.[10] Blackmun said: "[The] time has come to overrule [the] doctrine that parent and subsidiary can conspire. Ever since *Sunkist* we've retreated from *Yellow Cab* and it's time to bury it." [h]

How should we interpret the results? Surely, they do not detract from our assumption that it is reasonable to suppose that justices pursue policy goals at the conference stage; the data displayed in Table 2-1 make this point clear. Nor do our results provide support for the view that justices are motivated to pursue other objectives, such as reaching decisions in line

---

h. *Sunkist Growers, Inc. v. Winckler & Smith Citrus Products Co.,* 370 U.S. 19 (1962), and *United States v. Yellow Cab Co.,* 332 U.S. 218 (1947). Both dealt with questions concerning the Sherman Anti-Trust Act.

with precedent. Blackmun's and the chief justice's remarks provide evidence to the contrary. However, the data do provide documentation of the use of precedent in the private deliberations of the Court. We return to this finding later in the chapter.

Circulating Opinions

Before the Court releases an opinion to the public, the justice assigned to write it circulates copies to the other members. Occasionally, the writer will send a draft to one or two justices—perhaps those who were tentative members of the majority conference coalition—to "preview" it. Justice Powell followed this course in *Akron v. Akron Center for Reproductive Health,* in which the Court considered an ordinance that placed restrictions on the ability to obtain an abortion.[11] Among other things, the ordinance required that all abortions performed after the first trimester be performed in a hospital and prohibited physicians from performing the procedure on an unmarried minor without the consent of one of her parents or unless the minor obtains a court order. Conference votes over the various provisions of the ordinance were close; one generated a 4-4 split, and others were 5-3 (the chief justice did not vote). Before Powell circulated his majority opinion to the full Court, he sent a copy to Stevens—apparently the weakest member of the majority, especially on parental consent—to solicit his views.[i]

More typically, the opinion writer circulates the initial draft to the entire Court. During this period, justices can request changes, and opinion writers can take these suggestions, follow them in part, or ignore them. In other words, justices bargain and accommodate. But over what? We suspect the answer is policy.

To explore this question, we examined the bargaining memoranda circulated in the same random sample of 1983 cases. By bargaining memos, we mean letters sent to the opinion writer by other members of the Court, which contained this sort of language:

---

i. At conference, Stevens joined a majority of five to strike down the parental consent provision. But he joined three others (White, Rehnquist, and O'Connor) to uphold a parental notification provision. The Court never issued a ruling on that question because, after conference, the justices decided that the provision was not before them. The court below had upheld it, and no party had sought Supreme Court review.

TABLE 2-2

Nature of Suggestions Raised in Bargaining Memoranda

Nature of Suggestion	Number of Suggestions (percent)
Policy	26 (65.0)
Precedent	11 (27.5)
Facts	3 (7.5)
Total	40

Data Sources: Case files of Justices William J. Brennan Jr. and Thurgood Marshall, Library of Congress; and Lewis F. Powell Jr., Washington and Lee University School of Law.

Note: This is a random sample of 1983 orally argued cases derived from the list of 1983 term cases in the register of the Papers of Justice William J. Brennan (Library of Congress) with the exception of original cases. The unit of analysis was citation. If two or more cases were combined under one U.S. cite, we included only the lead case. The number of cases in the sample = 16.

Coding Rules: We coded a bargaining statement as present when a justice explicitly hinged her "join" of the majority opinion on the writer's making a change(s) in the opinion. We excluded (1) memoranda in which justices asked for a change but stated that they joined the opinion regardless of whether the change was made and (2) various memoranda (as in "Memorandum of Justice Blackmun") that were actually opinions designed to set forth a view of the case, persuade tentative colleagues, and so forth. For the data, navigate to: *http://www.artsci.wustl.edu/~polisci/epstein/choices/.*

> I hope you will consider two suggestions in this case. . . . If you can see your way clear to making these changes, I would be pleased to join.
>
> I will join your opinion if you will make one change in it.

We then characterized the content of each request as involving policy, precedent, or the factual set up of the case.

As Table 2-2 shows, during the bargaining process the justices are largely concerned with policy. Of the forty suggestions contained in the seventeen bargaining memos, nearly two-thirds were requests for policy changes. For example, Stevens urged opinion writer White to "leave the policy choice whether to permit a probationer to remain silent or to prohibit silence but immunize the compelled answers to [the] Minnesota Supreme Court." [12] In a case involving whether Immigration and Naturalization Service agents can conduct "factory surveys"—enter workplaces to determine if illegal aliens are employed there—Stevens requested a change in the policy that Rehnquist's majority opinion draft had established:

The second full paragraph on page 7 states that people who are not illegal aliens have nothing to fear from these surveys and hence are not "seized." I am concerned about this argument. Legal aliens may have nothing to fear since they must have documentation on them at all times, so they can prove their legal status. But what of the Hispanic-looking American citizen? He or she has a lot to fear from these procedures, since if he or she states he is an American citizen, and is disbelieved, he or she may be detained.[13]

Even though policy dominated the suggestions in the bargaining memoranda, the data—once again—do not suggest that the justices neglect precedent. To the contrary: fully a quarter of the justices' concerns involved the interpretation the opinion writer gave to previously decided cases. A memorandum Brennan wrote to O'Connor is illustrative: "Is the sentence that begins on p. 8 and ends on p. 9 an accurate statement of what the Court said in *Ludecke v. Watkins?*[j] I'm inclined to doubt that it is."[14]

So, although we cannot dismiss the possibility that justices have things on their minds other than policy—a point we shall discuss—surely the data support our working assumption: it is reasonable to suppose that justices pursue policy at the circulation stage.

Voting on the Merits of Cases

Once Pritchett claimed that increasing dissent rates show that justices are not following a mechanical form of jurisprudence, but are pursuing policy goals, he sought to document his position by analyzing the votes of justices who served during the Roosevelt administration. Pritchett argued that if policy, rather than precedent, was motivating judicial behavior, then a good deal of variation in the ideological patterns of individual justices' votes should be evident. Indeed, some justices of the Roosevelt period, such as William Douglas, almost always took the liberal position on cases; others, such as James McReynolds, almost always voted in the conservative direction. Such variation, Pritchett said, substantiated his conclusion that political attitudes have a strong influence on judicial decisions.

---

j. *Ludecke v. Watkins,* 335 U.S. 160 (1948), challenged the attorney general's power to remove an alien under the Alien Enemy Act of 1798.

Figure 2-2 Percentage of Liberal Decisions in Civil Liberties and Economics Cases, 1953–1995 Terms

Proportion

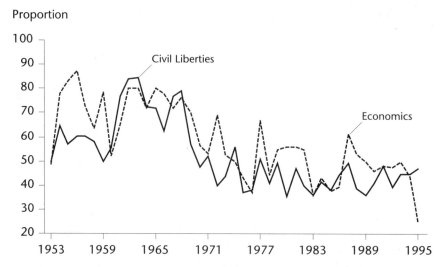

Data Sources: Lee Epstein, Jeffrey A. Segal, Harold J. Spaeth, and Thomas G. Walker, *The Supreme Court Compendium: Data, Decisions, and Developments,* 2d ed. (Washington, D.C.: Congressional Quarterly, 1996), Table 3-8. We thank Harold J. Spaeth for providing data for the 1995 term from his U.S. Supreme Court Judicial Database.

Note: The issue areas are defined as follows: **Civil Liberties** combines *Criminal Procedure, Civil Rights, First Amendment, Due Process, Privacy,* and *Attorneys* issue areas. *Criminal Procedure:* the rights of persons accused of crime except for due process rights of prisoners. *Civil Rights:* non–First Amendment freedom cases that pertain to classifications based on race (including Native Americans), age, indigence, voting, residence, military or handicapped status, sex, or alienage. *First Amendment:* guarantees contained in this constitutional provision. *Due Process:* noncriminal guarantees, plus Court jurisdiction over nonresident litigants and the Takings Clause of the Fifth Amendment. *Privacy:* abortion, contraception, the Freedom of Information Act and related statutes. *Attorneys:* attorneys' fees, commercial speech, admission to and removal from the bar, and disciplinary matters. **Economics:** commercial business activity, plus litigation involving injured persons or things, employee actions vis-à-vis employers, zoning regulations, and governmental regulation of corruption other than that involving campaign spending.

The term *liberal* represents the voting direction of the justices across various issue areas. It is most appropriate in the areas of civil liberties, criminal procedure, civil rights, First Amendment, due process, privacy, and attorneys, where it signifies pro-defendant votes in criminal procedure cases, pro-women or pro-minorities in civil rights cases, pro-individual against the government in First Amendment, due process, and privacy cases and pro-attorney in attorneys' fees and bar membership cases. In Takings Clause cases, however, a pro-government/anti-owner vote is considered liberal. The use of the term is perhaps less appropriate in economic cases, where it represents pro-government votes against challenges to federal regulatory authority and pro-competition, anti-business, pro-liability, pro-injured person, and pro-bankruptcy votes.

Figure 2-3   Support for Civil Liberties Predicted by Justices' Policy Preferences Plotted Against Actual Support

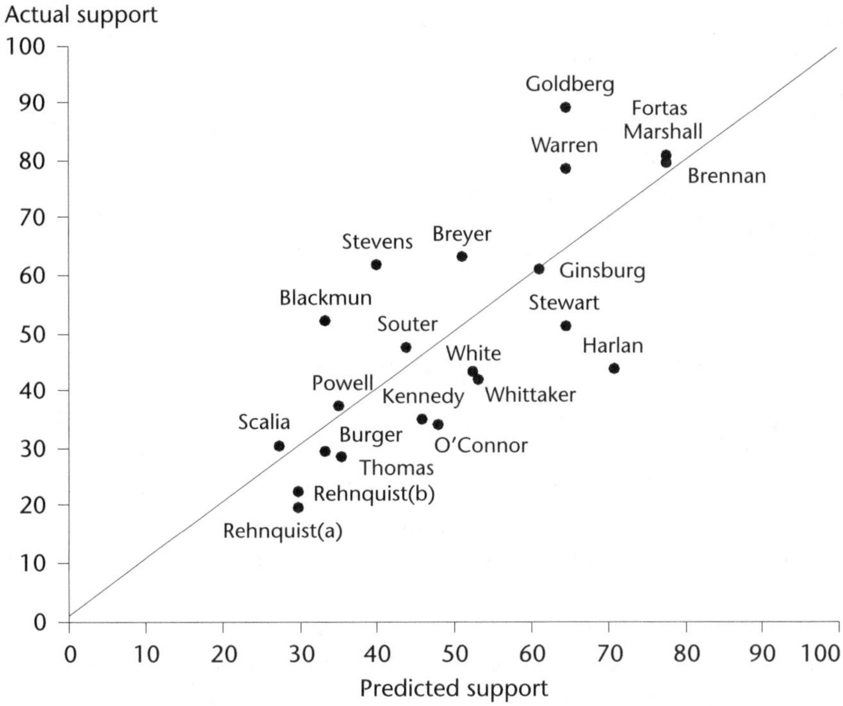

Actual support

Source: Updated (through the 1995 term) from Jeffrey A. Segal, Lee Epstein, Charles M. Cameron, and Harold J. Spaeth, "Ideological Values and the Votes of U.S. Supreme Court Justices Revisited," 57 *Journal of Politics* (1995): 816. The data are available at: *http://www. artsci.wustl.edu/~polisci/epstein/choices/.*

Note: Predicted support is based on $\hat{Y} = a + bX$. The equation is $\hat{Y} = 52.23 + 29.74X$. Rehnquist(a) represents his terms as associate justice (1971 through 1985); Rehnquist(b) represents his terms as chief justice (1986 through 1995).

Technical Note: The closer to the line the better the prediction. The prediction for Ginsburg of 61.1 almost exactly matched her actual support score of 61.4; the prediction for Goldberg (64.6), in contrast, missed the mark by nearly 25 percentage points (his actual support was 88.9).

Scholars following in Pritchett's footsteps have continued to observe dramatic ideological differences in the voting behavior of the Courts and justices since the Roosevelt era. To see this phenomenon at the Court level, consider the data depicted in Figure 2-2. It would be difficult to ignore the downward trend from the early 1960s through the 1990s, indicating increased conservatism of the Court in economics and civil liberties cases.

The same holds at the level of the individual justice, as work by Jeffrey Segal and his colleagues vividly shows. These political scientists analyzed editorial writers' comments on Supreme Court nominees to formulate a measure of the individual political preferences of justices. They then correlated this measure with votes to determine the degree to which they are related (see Figure 2-3). When it turned out that they could explain more than 60 percent of the variation in civil liberties votes based solely on the justices' policy preferences, the researchers concluded that justices come to the bench with a set of policy preferences, which they pursue through their votes, at least in civil liberties cases.[15]

EXCLUSIVE FOCUS ON POLICY GOALS

These vote data do not allow us to say much about strategic behavior on the part of justices, about the role of institutions in structuring their choices, or even about the ultimate policy that the Court articulates. *Craig* makes this last point abundantly clear: the decision to vote in support of or against the sex discrimination claim was less important than the choice of the standard of law to apply to future cases. We do maintain, however, that the vote data, along with the other information presented so far, provide sufficient ammunition to support the view that it is *reasonable* to assume that justices pursue policy goals.

But that conclusion alone does not answer a more fundamental question: Does it make sense to assume that policy is the *primary* goal justices pursue? We need to ask this question because there is evidence to support the existence of other motivations: (1) using the Court as a stepping-stone to higher political office; (2) reaching "principled" decisions; and (3) ensuring the integrity of the institution. But is this evidence sufficiently strong to undermine our working assumption that it is reasonable to focus our explanation primarily on policy goals? That question motivates our discussion below.

Using the Court as a Stepping-Stone

We usually think about the members of the Court and the members of elected institutions—legislators and executives—as wholly different. After all, they have distinct constitutional functions, represent different con-

TABLE 2-3
Pre-Court Political Activities of the Justices, 1997

Justice	Political Activities (Years)
Rehnquist	Assistant U.S. attorney general, 1969-1971
Stevens	Associate counsel to the U.S. House Judiciary Committee, 1951
O'Connor	Arizona legislator, 1969-1975
Scalia	Assistant U.S. attorney general, 1974-1977
Kennedy	Lobbyist, 1963-1974
Souter	Assistant/attorney general of New Hampshire, 1968-1978
Thomas	Director of the Equal Employment Opportunity Commission, 1982-1990
Ginsburg	None
Breyer	Counsel to the U.S. Senate Judiciary Committee, 1974-1980

Source: Lee Epstein, Jeffrey A. Segal, Harold J. Spaeth, and Thomas G. Walker, *The Supreme Court Compendium: Data, Decisions, and Developments,* 2d ed. (Washington, D.C.: Congressional Quarterly, 1996), Table 4-8.

stituencies, and attain their positions through different routes. But they are connected in at least one interesting way: 83 percent of the justices (89 of 107) had engaged in some sort of political activity before their appointment to the Court.[16] Indeed, the current justices, as Table 2-3 shows, are just as politically experienced as justices in any time in the nation's history—with one as state legislator and another as the head of the Equal Employment Opportunity Commission.

This finding is not so surprising because, to become a Supreme Court justice, one must come to the attention of a politician—a member of Congress, the attorney general, or even the president. What better way is there to become known to a senator than to have been a senator, as Hugo Black was, or to a president than to have worked on his campaign, as Byron White did for John Kennedy. The fact that most justices have some knowledge of politics indicates that they understand what it takes to succeed in that complex world. But do they use that knowledge to further their political ambitions? Is an elected office a primary goal for justices? Did Justice Brennan choose "heightened" scrutiny in *Craig* because it would help him to attain some higher office?

Histories of the Court tell us that some nineteenth century justices may have been motivated by political ambitions, with John McLean

(1830–1861) a prime example.[17] While serving on the Court, McLean actively (some say shamelessly) sought a presidential nomination three times from three different parties, the Free Masons, the Whigs, and the Republicans. It is hard to imagine that his political ambition did not affect the choices he made, especially since his jurisprudence evinced a major shift in the "politically correct" direction—from a Jacksonian view of constitutional law to a national stance. McLean was not the only justice to view the Court as a stepping-stone; scholars have long suspected that other early justices "were more anxious to be politicians than statesmen."[18]

That characterization may be applied to nineteenth century jurists, even though some question its accuracy.[19] But it is no longer apt for the motivations of most Supreme Court justices. First, even the early justices who resigned for "higher" political office may have done so because the Court lacked prestige—not because they were politically ambitious. John Jay, who left the Court in 1795 to become governor of New York, provides an example. In a letter to President Adams, turning down the president's offer to reappoint him to the bench in 1800, Jay wrote:

> [T]he efforts repeatedly made to place the [judicial branch] on a proper footing have proved fruitless. I left the bench perfectly convinced that under a system so defective it would not obtain the energy, weight, and dignity which was essential to its affording due support to the national government; nor acquire the public confidence and respect which, as the last resort of justice of the nation, it should possess. Hence I am induced to doubt both the propriety and the expediency of my returning to the bench under the present system.[20]

It is hard to imagine any contemporary justice writing such words because, today, it is hard to imagine any other position having more "power, prestige, and security than that of [a] Supreme Court justice."[21]

Second, we rarely observe contemporary justices engaging in the kinds of activities that we typically associate with those who are politically ambitious, such as advertising or attempting "to disseminate one's name among constituents in such a fashion as to create a favorable image but in messages having little or no issue content."[22] Not only do we lack evidence to support advertising and name-dissemination attempts among justices, but also, even if such evidence existed, we would be hard pressed to say that the justices were doing a particularly good job of it. A 1989 survey conducted by the *Washington Post* showed that far more Americans (54 percent) could

name the judge of the television show *The People's Court* than could identify the chief justice of the United States (9 percent).[23] A 1997 list of the
one hundred most important decision makers in the federal government
published in the *National Journal* included thirty-two members of
Congress, but only two Supreme Court justices (Kennedy and O'Connor).
The Defense Department comptroller, the Veterans' Affairs Department
chief of staff, and a staff aide to a Senate subcommittee rated mentions,
while Chief Justice Rehnquist did not.[24]

Third, although we believe that justices can harbor political ambitions
without actually advertising or engaging in the other activities we associate with the pursuit of public office—and the very fact that they have them
even if they do not act on them is important because it may affect their
choices—it seems implausible that justices would view the Court as a
political stepping-stone if there were not precedents for success. After all,
why would justices maintain a goal that they did not believe they could
attain? Yet, Charles Evans Hughes is the only twentieth century justice who
left the Court to seek a higher political office, a run for the presidency in
1916, only to return to the bench as chief justice in 1930.[k] Nearly 90 percent of the others either died in office or resigned in declining health.[25]

Our final argument against the importance of the stepping-stone goal is
that even in the case of Hughes available evidence suggests that his goal of
becoming president did not drive his judicial behavior prior to his campaign.[26] To put it more generally, we find it hard to imagine that a contemporary justice seeking higher political office, if such a justice exists,
could or would make choices in most cases with an eye toward accom-
plishing that goal. One reason is that most of what the Court decides has
little salience for the public. During its 1994 term, for example, the Court
decided eighty-four cases, and less than half (thirty-seven) involved "hot
button" issues, such as criminal procedure and civil rights.[27] The other
cases concerned questions about the exercise of the judiciary's own authority, commercial business activity, and the like—hardly the stuff of politics.
In short, although we cannot say that justices have never viewed the Court
as a political stepping-stone, it is not a goal that most pursued, especially
since the beginning of the twentieth century.

---

k. Others have left the Court for political positions but not higher office. For example, James Byrnes become director of the Office of Economic Stabilization, and Arthur
Goldberg became the U.S. ambassador to the United Nations.

Reaching Principled Decisions

Another motivation for justices' decisions centers on legal goals. Justices may desire to reach "principled" decisions—those based on impartial doctrines, such as *stare decisis* (deciding cases based on previously established precedent) or original intent (deciding cases according to the intent of those who drafted the particular constitutional provision or statute under review). These approaches are principled, their adherents say, because they are impartial as to the range of possible substantive results in a particular case. If justices looked only at previously decided cases, for example, their decisions would not reflect their own preferences over the substantive consequences of the case, but would be dictated by precedent.

Evidence in support of the importance of the impartial principle motivation is ambiguous. Consider arguments suggesting that justices do not exclusively pursue policy goals at the certiorari stage, that they have legal aims as well. The logic is as follows: because the Court's Rule 10 specifies that it will accept cases over which conflict exists in state and federal courts, when the Court follows this rule it is engaging in a principled, neutral form of analysis. (For Rule 10, see Appendix B.)

There is support for this proposition. Data collected and systematically analyzed by Caldeira and Wright, for example, suggest that—along with policy preferences—conflict goes a long way toward explaining the certiorari decision. In addition, Perry's interviews with several justices led him to conclude: "Without a doubt, one of the most important things to all the justices is when there is a conflict in the circuits. All of them are disposed to resolve conflicts when they exist and want to know if a particular case poses a conflict." [28]

But arguments against the principled perspective are equally impressive. First, if justices were *consistently* pursuing a legal goal, we would expect to see them *consistently* granting petitions with genuine conflict and rejecting those without it. But this is not the case. During its 1989 term, for example, the justices declined to review more than 200 petitions that in one way or another met the criteria stated in its rule, and, of the 184 cases the Court agreed to decide during its 1981 term, only 47 (25 percent) possessed real conflict. Moreover, in just 24 percent of the 4,787 cases decided on the merits between the 1953 and 1995 terms did the Court specifically mention conflict as a reason for granting certiorari. [29] Second, even if justices make decisions consistent with their internal rule, it does not necessarily mean that they are acting on legal goals. As Caldeira and Wright note,

Figure 2-4 Proportion of Unanimous U.S. Supreme Court Decisions, 1930–1995 Terms

Proportion

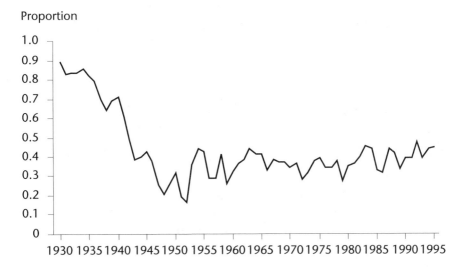

Data Sources: Lee Epstein, Jeffrey A. Segal, Harold J. Spaeth, and Thomas G. Walker, *The Supreme Court Compendium: Data, Decisions, and Developments,* 2d ed. (Washington, D.C.: Congressional Quarterly, 1996), Table 3-1. We thank Harold J. Spaeth for providing data for the 1995 term from his U.S. Supreme Court Judicial Database.

resolving conflict is a way for justices to set policy of some national importance. By following their own rule, they still may be seeking to further policy ends, not to mention those of institutional legitimacy.

If the evidence concerning the certiorari decision is unclear, what is the evidence for other parts of the process, such as the judicial vote? Scholars who argue that legal goals are important occasionally point to the continued existence of unanimous opinions. Recall that Pritchett inferred from the lack of consensus on the Court that the legal model was not operative. Surely, some argue, the reverse holds: we can infer that the legal model is operative when there is consensus. As Pritchett put it, "Presumably the facts and the law are so clear [in unanimous decisions] that no opportunity is allowed for the autobiographies of the justices to lead them to opposing conclusions." [30] In other words, because the justices continue to produce unanimous decisions in about a third of their cases, we cannot dismiss the legal model altogether. (See Figure 2-4.)

Despite the appeal of this claim, numerous historical and political accounts of early Court eras, when dissent was quite low, reveal its flaws. For example, research has shown that the justices who served on the Marshall Court (1801–1835), including the chief justice, were largely strategic actors who sought to move law as close as possible to their personal policy preferences; in fact, they may have been just as policy-motivated as their present-day counterparts.[31]

If these historical and political treatments are to be believed, then the lack of dissent cannot necessarily be taken to mean that early justices based their decisions solely on original intent or precedent. Rather, it provides an indication of the power of an institution disfavoring separate opinions. The justices may have tried to move law toward their preferred policy positions, but were constrained by the norm of consensus.[32] Data from the Waite Court (1874–1888) highlight this point: of the 205 cases the justices considered in conference during the 1874 term, 83 (40.5 percent) resulted in nonunanimous votes, but only 13.4 percent of the published decisions contained one or more dissenting votes or opinions.[33]

Even though this norm no longer exists on the Court (see Figure 2-1), research into earlier Courts has bearing on contemporary claims about meaning of unanimous opinions.[1] In particular, we would be hard-pressed to say that unanimous decisions of today are any more driven by legal goals than they were during the early periods. First, as Figure 2-5 shows, a close association exists between liberal unanimous and nonunanimous decisions.[34] In other words, a Court that reaches liberal decisions in divided

---

1. The norm of consensus may no longer exist, but literature on the Court is replete with examples of justices, especially chief justices, going to great lengths to produce unanimous opinions, especially in landmark cases. See, for example, Richard Kluger, *Simple Justice* (New York: Knopf, 1976); and Bernard Schwartz, *The Ascent of Pragmatism: The Burger Court in Action* (Reading, Mass.: Addison-Wesley, 1989). These efforts may reflect recognition by chief justices that other political actors are less like-ly to attempt to override and more likely to follow unanimous decisions than split decisions. See, for example, William N. Eskridge Jr., "Overriding Supreme Court Statutory Interpretation Decisions," 101 *Yale Law Journal* (1991): 331–417; and Charles A. Johnson and Bradley C. Canon, *Judicial Policies: Implementation and Impact* (Washington, D.C.: CQ Press, 1984). Lower court judges also may have higher rates of compliance and fewer complaints about consensual decisions. Burger made this point in a memo to Powell, dated June 5, 1980, in *Fullilove v. Klutznick,* 448 U.S. 448 (1980). Burger was trying to convince Powell not to write separately: "Would it not be better to try for a 'united front' instead of a cluster of concurring opinions—a practice of which I increasingly receive complaints from judges all over the country."

Figure 2-5   Percentage of Liberal Unanimous and Nonunanimous
Decisions in Civil Liberties Cases, 1953–1995 Terms

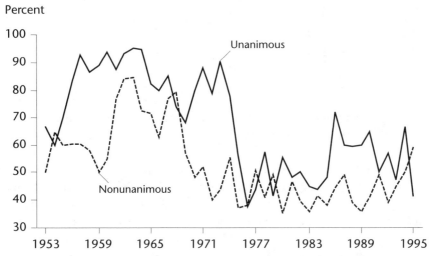

Percent

Data Sources: We thank Harold J. Spaeth for providing us with these data from his U.S. Supreme Court Judicial Database. To obtain the data, navigate to: *http://www.artsci.wustl.edu/ ~polisci/epstein/choices/.*

Note: **Civil Liberties** combines Criminal Procedure, Civil Rights, First Amendment, Due Process, Privacy, and Attorneys issue areas. *Criminal Procedure:* the rights of persons accused of crime except for due process rights of prisoners. *Civil Rights:* non–First Amendment freedom cases that pertain to classifications based on race (including Native Americans), age, indigence, voting, residence, military or handicapped status, sex, or alienage. *First Amendment:* guarantees contained in this constitutional provision. *Due Process:* noncriminal guarantees, plus Court jurisdiction over nonresident litigants and the Takings Clause of the Fifth Amendment. *Privacy:* abortion, contraception, the Freedom of Information Act and related statutes. *Attorneys:* attorneys' fees, commercial speech, admission to and removal from the bar, and disciplinary matters.

The term *liberal* represents the voting direction of the justices across various issue areas. In the areas of criminal procedure, civil rights, First Amendment, due process, privacy, and attorneys, it signifies pro-defendant votes in criminal procedure cases, pro-women or pro-minorties in civil rights cases, pro-individual against the government in First Amendment, due process, and privacy cases, and pro-attorney in attorneys' fees and bar membership cases. In Takings Clause cases, however, a pro-government/anti-owner vote is considered liberal.

cases is likely to reach liberal decisions in unanimous cases, and the same holds true for conservative decisions.

Second, justices seem as concerned with policy in unanimous decisions as they are in divided cases. *Kirby Forest Industries v. United States,* in which the Court considered the government's ability to take possession of property at the close of condemnation proceedings, illustrates the point.[35] The conference voted unanimously to affirm, and the published decision followed suit. But, during the circulation process, three justices (Stevens, White, and Rehnquist) threatened to write separately if the opinion writer—Marshall—did not make some rather important changes in the opinion's policy posture. Stevens objected to a statement in the original draft asserting that a reassessment of the value of property is "both necessary and sufficient." He wrote to Marshall, "I agree that the reassessment would be sufficient, but I hesitate to say that it is necessary for fear that it will become a standard part of every condemnation hearing in the future." Marshall made the change, along with many others, and preserved unanimity.[m]

We could describe the sequence of events in many other cases like *Kirby Forest* or, more generally, continue our investigation into how legal goals might affect other aspects of the Supreme Court's decision-making process. But we believe in the end the evidence would be equally ambiguous, serving only to reinforce the central result of the analysis so far: although there is support for the view that justices are more than occasionally motivated by impartial principles, reliance on legal goals fails to account for the large number of cases in which the justices' decisions are inconsistent with any measure of these goals. In other words, our analysis, which considered claims both for and against legal motivations, counsels against interpretations that suggest that the desire to reach principled decisions provides the *primary* reason for justices' choices. This result is significant because, ultimately, the answer to the question we pose in this section—Does it make sense to focus on policy goals to the exclusion of others?— turns on what goal does a better job in explaining the widest range of cases. We think the answer is now clear: the legal goal, like political ambition, lacks the generalizable quality that characterizes the policy objective.

---

m. *Kirby Forest* is not unusual. An examination of bargaining memoranda reveals that the average nonunanimous case generates about 1.1 memos; that figure is slightly lower (1.0) for the typical unanimous case. In other words, at least one justice attempts to bargain with another in most cases. Because roughly two-thirds of these memos involve policy (see Table 2-2), the data lend some support to the argument that unanimity does not mean that the law is so clear that policy preferences become irrelevant.

However—and this is just as important—the evidence seems to support another interpretation: legal factors can constrain justices from acting on their personal policy preferences, just as the norm of consensus did in the past. In other words, justices have a preferred rule that they would like to see established in the case before them, but they strategically modify their position to take account of a normative constraint—such as *stare decisis*—to produce a decision as close as possible to their preferred outcome.[36] The reason is simple: justices who wish to establish policy that will govern the future activity of the society in which their Court exists will be constrained to choose from among the set of rules (precedent and the like) that the members of that society will recognize and accept.[37] If Courts radically change existing rules, the community may not adapt. The result is a decision that does not produce an efficacious rule.

We expand on this idea in Chapters Four and Five, but here note that data presented earlier provide support for an interpretation of legal factors as norms. We found, for example, that 25 percent of the suggestions contained in bargaining memos and of the remarks made at conference centered on precedent. If reaching decisions in accord with *stare decisis* is not important to justices, why do they bother to bargain over how the opinion writer has invoked a particular case? Why, to return to the example we used above, did Brennan take issue with O'Connor's interpretation of *Ludecke v. Watkins* in her opinion for the Court? And why did Blackmun, in his conference comments, say that *"Schaumburg* certainly controls"?

We believe this sort of behavior lends support to the claim that a general norm favoring precedent exists in society at large. Justices who seek to establish legal rules that will engender compliance in the community will give priority to those rules that are consistent with a norm favoring respect for precedent, if they believe that such a norm exists. Therefore, justices might bargain and make accommodations over the interpretation of precedent because they believe that doing so enhances the probability that society will consider the resulting decision legitimate. The same logic applies with equal force to the invocation of precedent during conference.

What this means is that precedent, the intent of the Framers, and so forth play a role in Court decision making; respect for such factors is dictated by norms that structure judicial choices. What it does not mean is that the desire to reach principled decisions is a primary goal of justices. While some justices may be motivated to be "good" justices, we think it is difficult to maintain a proposition suggesting that this idea is in the minds of most justices in most cases.

Ensuring Institutional Legitimacy

A final goal that could be attributed to justices is maintaining institutional legitimacy. In the broadest sense, institutional legitimacy means that justices have an interest in making sure that the Court remains a credible force in American politics—both in the eyes of the public and public officials.

Concerns over institutional legitimacy manifest themselves in a number of ways. Consider again the stage at which justices must decide whether to accept a case for full review. If the Court is to maintain its position as an important policy maker, one would expect it to select cases with the potential to impact political, social, or economic policy. If the Court did not occasionally chime in on important matters of the day, the argument goes, it would not be regarded as a major player in the government process.

Some of the evidence in support of this proposition is anecdotal or spotty, such as the Court's own rule governing the certiorari process, which uses the word "important" five times. Or Alexis de Tocqueville's famous quip that "scarcely any political question arises in the United States that is not resolved, sooner or later, into a judicial question." [38] Or Chief Justice William Howard Taft's sentiment, endorsed by all nine justices in a 1982 letter supporting legislation to increase the Court's discretion, that the Court should devote its resources to cases that "involve principles, the application of which are of wide public importance or governmental interest, and which should be authoritatively declared by the final court." [39]

But there is systematic support as well, as shown by Caldeira and Wright's research on amicus curiae briefs filed at the certiorari stage.[40] These scholars posit that amicus briefs filed by organized interests on certiorari reduce the Court's uncertainty about the importance of cases—in other words, these briefs signal the presence of a significant case, thereby increasing the likelihood that the Court will hear it.[41] Their data, consisting of petitions the Court granted and denied during the 1982 term, support this prediction. When more than one amicus brief supports certiorari, the probability of review jumps from about .08 to .35. Even briefs filed against review increase the likelihood that the Court will review the case because they too signal that a case is sufficiently important to generate participation.

Despite these findings, each term the justices deny certiorari to many cases that seem to be deserving and grant certiorari to many that do not. For example, in October 1995 the Court refused to hear *American Life League v. Reno,* involving a constitutional challenge to a federal law that made it a crime to intimidate doctors or patients at abortion clinics. But several months earlier it agreed to decide *Commissioner of Internal Revenue v. Lundy,* an apparently trivial dispute concerning the U.S. Tax Court's interpretation of a section of the Internal Revenue Code.[42]

Do these cases, and many others we could cite, impinge on claims about the importance of ensuring institutional authority? We think they do not for two reasons. First, it is sometimes true that cases that seem trivial may actually be important. Take the issue in the *Lundy* dispute. Although it cannot compare in salience to *American Life League,* it led to conflicting rulings in the federal courts. Most affirmed the Tax Court's interpretation, but one, the U.S. Court of Appeals for the Fourth Circuit, reversed. By hearing the case, the Supreme Court attempted to resolve a conflict of legal importance and set policy for the nation's courts. Second, if we take amicus curiae activity on certiorari as an indicator of case importance, then we know from Caldeira and Wright's research that cases such as *American Life League* and *Lundy* (if we indeed believe this to be a trivial dispute) represent the exceptions, not the rules.

The motivation of protecting institutional integrity also may be evident at the merits stage, albeit in a somewhat different form. The landmark case *Marbury v. Madison* is illustrative.[43] At issue here were several judicial appointments that President John Adams had made but that the incoming president, Thomas Jefferson, refused to deliver. When William Marbury, who was denied his commission, brought suit, the Supreme Court, led by Chief Justice John Marshall, had to decide whether to force the new administration to deliver the commission.

Certainly, Marshall—himself an Adams appointee—wanted to give Marbury his appointment. But, at the same time, Marshall was well aware of the serious repercussions of ordering the administration to do so. Jefferson made no secret of his disdain for Marshall, and the chief justice's impeachment no doubt crossed the president's (and Marshall's) mind. Marshall was confronted with a dilemma: vote his sincere political preferences and risk the institutional integrity of the Court, not to mention his job, or act in a sophisticated fashion with regard to his political preferences and elevate judicial supremacy in a way that Jefferson could accept. Marshall chose the latter course.[44]

Marbury v. Madison may be the most famous example of pursuit of institutional goals, but it is surely not the only one. The decisions in a pair of cases, *Watkins v. United States* and *Barenblatt v. United States,* also nicely demonstrate that the justices occasionally eschew policy to protect the legitimacy of the Court.[45] In these cases, the Court considered similar questions pertaining to the rights of witnesses to refuse to answer questions put to them by congressional committees investigating subversive activities in the United States. In *Watkins* the Court ruled for the witness, but in *Barenblatt* it ruled against him. The majority in *Barenblatt* went to great lengths to indicate that its opinion amounted to nothing more than a clarification of *Watkins.* Many legal analysts (including the four *Barenblatt* dissenters), however, have suggested that, at the minimum, the justices backed away from *Watkins* and, at the maximum, the decision signaled a reversal from the earlier ruling.

If these analysts are right, how can we explain the shift, which occurred within a two-year period?[46] One possibility is that *Barenblatt* constituted a "strategic withdrawal." According to this line of thinking, *Watkins* and other "liberal" decisions, such as *Brown v. Board of Education,* had made the Court the target of numerous congressional proposals.[47] A few even sought to remove the Court's jurisdiction to hear cases involving subversive activities. The justices felt the heat and acceded to congressional pressure to protect the legitimacy of their institution.[n]

More support for the institutional integrity goal comes from research that has sought to assess the influence of public opinion on the Court's decision making. The argument is as follows: because the Court lacks the power to execute its decisions, it can never stray too far from the desires of the public if it wants to retain its legitimacy, to see its rulings implemented, and so forth. While considerable debate has ensued over the propriety of this premise, the most recent studies indicate that the Court does seem to respond, albeit modestly, to changes in public preferences.[48]

Together, these pieces of evidence form a picture of justices concerned with institutional integrity. But this concern does not necessarily lead to the conclusion that institutional integrity is a goal in and of itself. To the contrary: we would find it hard to imagine why justices would want to protect institutional authority unless they viewed it as a means to an end—

---

n. Another explanation for the *Watkins-Barenblatt* shift centers exclusively on the policy goal. In this view, the Court did not strategically withdraw from *Watkins;* rather, its policy preferences changed because the Court's membership changed. So *Barenblatt* simply represented a move "back toward a more conservative position" ushered in by President Dwight Eisenhower's appointments of Charles Whittaker and Potter Stewart. By way of support, scholars point to the voting alignments in the two cases and to the general trend in the disposition of civil liberties cases. As Murphy noted, during the 1956 term, which included *Watkins,* the Court ruled in favor of civil liberties claims in 74 percent of the cases; that figure fell to 59 percent and 51 percent in the 1957 and 1958 terms, respectively. See Walter F. Murphy, *Congress and the Supreme Court* (Chicago: University of Chicago Press, 1962), 246.

a policy end. We return to *Marbury v. Madison* to illustrate the point. We know that Marshall did not "vote" his sincere policy preferences in the case; instead, he dismissed Marbury's suit, claiming that Congress did not have the power, constitutionally speaking, to give the Court the jurisdiction necessary to hear it.

One could argue that the justices took the action they did in *Marbury to* protect their institution's integrity. But that does not mean policy was not also a factor; indeed, it may have been the prime motivation. The justices knew that if they ruled in favor of Marbury, the possibility of serious reprisal loomed large; Jefferson was threatening to impeach some justices or weaken the Court in other ways. Knowing that an impeached justice or a seriously deflated institution cannot make policy, effective or otherwise, the justices made the necessary concessions to Congress and the president. They acted against their short-term policy interests to protect long-term interests. We think the same could be said about *Barenblatt.*

We could discuss other cases in which concerns over institutional legitimacy served as the primary motivation for judicial decisions.[49] We could discuss other goals that scholars have posited.[50] And we could point to justices who not only seemed unconcerned with moving policy in the direction of their preferences but who also took steps to ensure that their policies were not etched into law.[51] But the general point would be the same: although justices occasionally pursue other goals and the occasional justice never pursues policy, most justices in most cases seek to establish law as close as possible to their own policy preferences. This is the lesson of Pritchett's writings, of the work that has followed in his path, and of our own investigation into the private papers of the justices.

And it is a conclusion that follows from the foregoing discussion. To put it simply, the policy goal has a certain "attractive universality" that the others lack. This is important to us as social scientists whose primary goal is to explain the usual, not the anomaly.[o]

---

o. Still, we think it important to reiterate a point we made in Chapter One about the relationship between the content of preferences and strategic action: one does not have to share our view about the nature of judicial goals to accept the argument that Supreme Court decision making involves strategic choice. Strategic actors can be, in principle, motivated by many things. As long as the ability of a justice to achieve her goals is contingent on the actions of others, her decision is interdependent and strategic. For an example of a strategic account of judicial decisions in which justices are motivated by jurisprudential principles, see John Ferejohn and Barry Weingast, "A Positive Theory of Statutory Interpretation," 12 *International Review of Law and Economics* (1992): 263–279.

ATTAINMENT OF GOALS

We are now ready to address the third question we asked at the beginning of the chapter: Are individual justices in a position to do anything about moving policy toward their preferred positions? If they are not, it makes little sense to talk about policy as a goal because justices would be unable to take steps to realize it.[52] We answer this question in the affirmative for two reasons. First, at the very least, individual justices *think* they can influence public policy. This is evident from their public comments, as this classic debate between Scalia and White, with White emerging as the clear winner, indicates:

> Scalia: I am not so naive (nor do I think our forebears were) as to be unaware that judges in a real sense "make" law. But they make it as judges make it, which is to say as though they were finding it—discerning what the law is, rather than decreeing what it today changed to, or what it will be tomorrow.

> White: [E]ven though the Justice is not naive enough (nor does he think the Framers were naive enough) to be unaware that judges in a real sense "make" law, he suggests that judges (in an unreal sense, I suppose) should never concede that they do and must claim that they do no more than discover it, hence suggesting that there are citizens naive enough to believe them.[53]

It is also evident from their actions. For example, during the circulation period the average opinion undergoes 3.2 drafts.[54] Why would justices bother recrafting their opinions if they believed that their writings would be ignored, if they thought their opinions would lack the force of law? Surely, given their heavy workloads, they would not. Even more to the point, they acknowledge that their words at the very least command attention and at most *can* become policy for the nation. An example is *Immigration and Naturalization Service v. Chadha,* in which the Court considered the constitutionality of the legislative veto, a device used by Congress to cancel policies enacted by executive agencies.[55] After the conference votes that rendered legislative vetoes unconstitutional, a worried Chief Justice Burger circulated six drafts of his opinion, knowing that it was going to get "microscopic—and not always sympathetic!—scrutiny from across the park." [P]

---

p. Memorandum from the Chief Justice to Brennan, 4/7/83. As it turned out, Burger was right to be worried. According to Louis Fisher, Congress has disregarded

But it is more than justices thinking they can influence policy, and this takes us to our second point: we know that they can do so. Data indicate that although Congress often scrutinizes their decisions, it rarely overturns them.[56] Research also shows that lower tribunals have a healthy respect for Supreme Court precedent.[57] Finally, we can provide example after example of justices—regardless of their particular ideology—having an enormous impact on the course of policy. One has only to consider Brennan's influence on sex discrimination law in *Craig:* although he was far from the middle in the Court on gender issues—Brennan was, in fact, one of the Court's most ardent advocates of women's rights—he was able to articulate policy that has yet to be overturned.[q]

So, if a justice's goal is to move the law as close as possible to his or her preferred position—as we maintain that it is—then this objective is clearly reachable. However, as *Craig* also illustrates, this does not mean that it is easy to reach. We know that Brennan could not have achieved his goal without acting strategically and without taking into account the rules, norms, and conventions that structure the decision-making process. It is to those two subjects—strategic interaction and institutions—that we now turn.

---

the Court's decision, passing more than two hundred new laws containing legislative vetoes since *Chadha.* See "The Legislative Veto: Invalidated, It Survives," 56 *Law and Contemporary Problems* (1993): 288. We have more to say about this in Chapter Five.

q. We do not mean to imply that justices can always attain their policy goals; an important body of literature suggests otherwise. See, for example, Gerald N. Rosenberg, *The Hollow Hope: Can Courts Bring About Social Change?* (Chicago: University of Chicago Press, 1991); and Rosenberg, "The Real World of Constitutional Rights: The Supreme Court and the Implementation of the Abortion Decisions," in *Contemplating Courts,* ed. Lee Epstein (Washington, D.C.: CQ Press, 1995). Indeed, we agree with the general conclusion reached by Rosenberg and others, namely, that the ability of justices to create efficacious policy—policy that other actors will respect and with which they will comply—depends, in some measure, on their ability to make accurate calculations about the preferences and likely actions of the relevant communities.

ENDNOTES

1. Mayhew raised similar questions about his working assumption that members of Congress were single-minded seekers of reelection. See David Mayhew, *Congress—The Electoral Connection* (New Haven: Yale University Press, 1974), 13–18. We think they are equally reasonable to raise about our assertion concerning the goals of justices.

2. See Edward H. Levi, *An Introduction to Legal Reasoning* (Chicago: University of Chicago Press, 1949), 4–5.

3. See C. Herman Pritchett, *The Roosevelt Court* (New York: Macmillan, 1948), xiii.

4. David M. O'Brien, *Storm Center,* 4th ed. (New York: Norton, 1996), 194.

5. H. W. Perry, *Deciding to Decide: Agenda Setting in the United States Supreme Court* (Cambridge: Harvard University Press, 1991), 194.

6. Lee Epstein, Jeffrey A. Segal, Harold J. Spaeth, and Thomas G. Walker, *The Supreme Court Compendium: Data, Decisions, and Developments,* 2d ed. (Washington, D.C.: Congressional Quarterly, 1996), Table 3-6.

7. Gregory A. Caldeira and John R. Wright, "Organized Interests and Agenda-Setting in the U.S. Supreme Court," 82 *American Political Science Review* (1988): 1120.

8. See, for example, Virginia Armstrong and Charles A. Johnson, "Certiorari Decision Making by the Warren and Burger Courts: Is Cue Theory Time Bound?" 15 *Polity* (1982): 141–150; Donald R. Songer, "Concern for Policy Outputs as a Cue for Supreme Court Decisions on Certiorari," 41 *Journal of Politics* (1979): 1185–94.

9. *Hishon v. King & Spaulding,* 467 U.S. 69 (1984); *Secretary of State v. Munson,* 467 U.S. 947 (1984); *Schall v. Martin,* 467 U.S. 253 (1984); and *Board of Education v. Vail,* 466 U.S. 377 (1984).

10. *Copperweld Corporation v. Independence Tube Corporation,* 467 U.S. 752 (1984).

11. *Akron v. Akron Center for Reproductive Health,* 462 U.S. 416 (1983).

12. Memorandum from Stevens to White, 11/30/83 in *Minnesota v. Murphy,* 465 U.S. 420 (1984).

13. Memorandum from Stevens to Rehnquist, 2/15/84 in *Immigration and Naturalization Service v. Delgado,* 466 U.S. 210 (1984).

14. Memorandum from Brennan to O'Connor, 5/16/84 in *Block v. Community Nutrition Institute,* 467 U.S. 340 (1984).

15. Jeffrey A. Segal, Lee Epstein, Charles M. Cameron, and Harold J. Spaeth, "Ideological Values and the Votes of U.S. Supreme Court Justices Revisited," 57 *Journal of Politics* (1995): 812–822. The original scores appeared in Jeffrey A. Segal and Albert D. Cover, "Ideological Values and the Votes of U.S. Supreme Court Justices," 83 *American Political Science Review* (1989): 557–565.

16. Epstein et al., *Supreme Court Compendium,* Table 4-8.

17. We draw the material on McLean from Clare Cushman, ed., *The Supreme Court Justices: Illustrated Biographies, 1789–1995,* 2d ed. (Washington, D.C.: Congressional Quarterly, 1995), 103–104.

18. Russell Wheeler, "Extrajudicial Activities of the Early Supreme Court Justices," *Supreme Court Review* (1973): 123.

19. Ibid.

20. Cushman, *Supreme Court Justices,* 4.

21. Jeffrey A. Segal and Harold J. Spaeth, *The Supreme Court and the Attitudinal Model* (New York: Cambridge University Press, 1993), 70.

22. Mayhew, *The Electoral Connection,* 49.

23. *Washington Post Weekly Edition,* June 26–July 2, 1989.

24. "The Washington 100," *National Journal,* June 14, 1997. We thank Charles Cameron for bringing this article to our attention.

25. See Epstein et al., *Supreme Court Compendium,* Table 5-7.

26. See Merlo J. Pusey, *Charles Evans Hughes* (New York: Macmillan, 1951).

27. Epstein et al., *Supreme Court Compendium,* Table 2-9.

28. Perry, *Deciding to Decide,* 127.

29. For the 1989 term, see Lawrence Baum, *The Supreme Court,* 6th ed. (Washington, D.C.: CQ Press, 1998), 114. For the 1981 term, see O'Brien, *Storm Center,* 215. We thank Harold J. Spaeth for providing us with the data on the more recent terms from his U.S. Supreme Court Judicial Database.

30. C. Herman Pritchett, "Divisions of Opinion Among Justices of the U.S. Supreme Court," 35 *American Political Science Review* (1941): 890.

31. See Jack Knight and Lee Epstein, "On the Struggle for Judicial Supremacy," 30 *Law and Society Review* (1996): 87–130; Robert Lowry Clinton, "Game Theory, Legal History, and the Origins of Judicial Review: A Revisionist Analysis of *Marbury v. Madison,*" 38 *American Journal of Political Science* (1994): 285–302; and Walter F. Murphy, *Elements of Judicial Strategy* (Chicago: University of Chicago Press, 1964).

32. Thomas G. Walker, Lee Epstein, and William J. Dixon, "On the Mysterious Demise of Consensual Norms in the United States Supreme Court," 50 *Journal of Politics* (1988): 361–389.

33. We collected the conference vote data from the docket books of Chief Justice Morrison Waite, located in the Library of Congress; Jeffrey A. Segal amassed the final vote data from *U.S. Reports.*

34. The correlation between the two series is .66 (p < .001).

35. *Kirby Forest Industries v. United States,* 467 U.S. 1 (1984).

36. See Jack Knight, *Institutions and Social Conflict* (Cambridge: Cambridge University Press, 1992); Jack Knight and Lee Epstein, "The Norm of *Stare Decisis,*" 40 *American Journal of Political Science* (1996): 1018–35.

37. Jack Knight, "Interpretation as Social Interaction" (typescript, Washington University, St. Louis, Mo., 1994).

38. Alexis de Tocqueville, *Democracy in America* (New York: American Library, 1956), 72.

39. Quoted by Chief Justice Burger in a letter to Rep. Robert Kastenmeier, re: H.R. 2406, June 17, 1982.

40. Caldeira and Wright, "Organized Interests and Agenda Setting."

41. Justice Stevens, however inadvertently, confirmed Caldeira and Wright's contention that amici on certiorari signal that a case is important. In a dissenting opinion in *United States v. Dalm,* 108 L.Ed. 2d 548 at 564 (1990), Stevens argued that the case was a trivial one that the Court should not have agreed to decide. By way of evidence, Stevens noted that "not a single amicus curiae was filed." Cited in Segal and Spaeth, *The Supreme Court and the Attitudinal Model,* 197.

42. *American Life League v. Reno,* 116 S.Ct. 55 (1995); *Commissioner of Internal Revenue v. Lundy,* 116 S.Ct. 647 (1996); *cert. granted,* 115 S. Ct. 2244 (1995).

43. *Marbury v. Madison,* 1 Cr. 137 (1803).

44. Actually, the situation was a bit more complex than we describe here. For the details, see Knight and Epstein, "On the Struggle for Judicial Supremacy."

45. *Watkins v. United States,* 354 U.S. 178 (1957); *Barenblatt v. United States,* 360 U.S. 109 (1959).

46. We draw this discussion from Lee Epstein and Thomas G. Walker, *Constitutional Law for a Changing America: Institutional Powers and Constraints,* 2d ed. (Washington, D.C.: CQ Press, 1995), 156. See also C. Herman Pritchett, *Congress versus the Supreme Court* (Minneapolis: University of Minnesota Press, 1961), 12.

47. *Brown v. Board of Education,* 347 U.S. 483 (1954).

48. See James A. Stimson, Michael B. Mackuen, and Robert S. Erikson, "Dynamic Representation," 89 *American Political Science Review* (1995): 556; Bradford S. Jones and Valerie J. Hoekstra, "Dynamic Representation and the Attitudinal Model" (paper presented at the 1997 annual meeting of the American Political Science Association, Washington, D.C.); Roy B. Flemming and B. Dan Wood, "The Public and the Supreme Court: Individual Justice Responsiveness to American Policy Moods," 41 *American Journal of Political Science* (1997): 469–498.

49. See, for example, Lee Epstein and Thomas Walker's essay on *Ex parte McCardle* (1869), "The Role of the Court in a Democratic Society," in *Contemplating Courts,* ed. Lee Epstein (Washington, D.C.: CQ Press, 1995).

50. See Lawrence Baum, "What Judges Want: Judges' Goals and Judicial Behavior," 47 *Political Research Quarterly* (1994): 749–768. Among the goals Baum lists are achieving harmony with other judges, maximizing judicial salaries, and holding power within the court.

51. For examples, see Bernard Schwartz, *The Ascent of Pragmatism: The Burger Court in Action* (Reading, Mass.: Addison-Wesley, 1990).

52. See Mayhew, *Electoral Connection,* 17–18.

53. Concurring in judgment in *James M. Beam Distilling Company v. Georgia,* 501 U.S. 529 at 549 and 546 (1991).

54. Lee Epstein and Jack Knight, "Documenting Strategic Interaction on the U.S. Supreme Court" (paper delivered at the 1995 annual meeting of the American Political Science Association, Washington, D.C.).

55. *Immigration and Naturalization Service v. Chadha,* 462 U.S. 919 (1983).

56. See, for example, William N. Eskridge, "Overriding Supreme Court Statutory Interpretation Decisions," 101 *Yale Law Journal* (1991): 331–417.

57. See, for example, Jeffrey A. Segal, Donald R. Songer, and Charles M. Cameron, "Decision Making on the U.S. Courts of Appeals," in *Contemplating Courts.*

CHAPTER THREE

Strategic Interaction

Three years before the Court's decision in *Craig v. Boren,* Justice Brennan had made known his preferences on the subject of sex discrimination. His judgment for the Court in *Frontiero v. Richardson* (1973) provided a strong indication that he believed sex should be treated as a suspect class.[1] But in *Craig* Brennan wrote an opinion forgoing his most preferred standard and adopting a midlevel approach to sex discrimination cases. Why? The answer we offered in Chapter One was that Brennan acted strategically. He thought an opinion advancing strict scrutiny would have been unacceptable to a majority of his colleagues and that they would have pushed for a rational basis standard. On our account, Brennan chose heightened scrutiny because—based on his beliefs about the preferences of other justices and his knowledge of Court norms—it allowed him to avoid rational basis, his least preferred position, and not because it was his first choice.

Brennan took the course of action that any rational actor, concerned with maximizing his policy preferences, would take. In other words, for Brennan to set policy as close as possible to his ideal point, strategic behavior was essential. In this instance, he needed to act in a sophisticated fashion, given his beliefs about the preferences of the other actors and the choices he expected them to make.

Was Brennan exceptional in this regard? Surely, as the previous chapter demonstrated, he was not unusual in pursuing a policy goal, which is an

56

objective of most justices in most cases. But was Brennan atypically strategic in *Craig*? Do justices pursue their policy goals with regard to the positions of their colleagues and other actors, such as Congress and the president? Or was there something unique about Brennan, about the case, or
about the circumstances surrounding it?

We believe the answer to these questions is clear. For the reasons we set
out in Chapter One, justices must act strategically if they wish to see the
law reflect, as closely as possible, their preferred positions. The task of providing documentation for this intuition, however, is not an easy one
because of the problem of behavioral equivalence: accounts that acknowledge strategic interaction and those that do not occasionally predict the
same behavior for many of the activities in which justices engage, making
it difficult to distinguish between the two approaches. To see this point,
recall that in *Craig* Chief Justice Burger cast his final vote against the sex
discrimination claim. In Chapter One we argued that this action was perfectly consistent with a strategic account of judicial decision making. But
one could just as easily claim that Burger's vote was nonstrategic, that
Burger—being relatively conservative—preferred the state's position and
voted without regard to the preferences of other actors and the actions he
expected them to take.

So, the task, as we see it, is to identify *distinct* and *discrete* kinds of activities in which justices would engage if they were seeking to advance policy goals in a strategic fashion. In our view, there are at least four such activities: bargaining, forward thinking, manipulating the agenda, and engaging
in sophisticated opinion writing. While we do not claim that these activities exhaust all the possibilities, we contend that they are types of behavior
that are most likely to be associated with strategic decision making. As
such, we maintain that they are phenomena that perspectives that do not
take strategic behavior into account cannot readily (or do not attempt to)
explain.[a]

---

a. The attitudinal model is one such approach: justices' votes are solely a function
of their values and the facts of cases. See Jeffrey A. Segal and Harold J. Spaeth, *The
Supreme Court and the Attitudinal Model* (New York: Cambridge University Press, 1993).
Therefore, according to October 25, 1996, correspondence from Segal, this model
(1) does not attempt to explain choices other than the vote on the merits of cases and
(2) does not contemplate strategic interaction over votes.

BARGAINING

In many social and political situations, actors want to reach one of several possible agreements, but they may disagree over which agreement is the best. Bargaining is one of the primary methods of resolving such differences.[2] Seen in this way, bargaining is inherently strategic. Parties involved in a bargaining situation—whether they are the leaders of two nations attempting to form an alliance or employers and employees trying to hammer out a benefits agreement—must, in making their own choices, consider the preferences of the other relevant actors and the actions they expect them to take. Only by recognizing their interdependency can the actors hope to be successful in the bargaining process.

Do the justices of the Supreme Court bargain? We would certainly expect them to do so, as they know that their ability to set authoritative policy depends not just on their own choices but on those of other actors and that those others—their colleagues—often disagree over the best policy. Moreover, justices have ample opportunities to engage in bargaining throughout the process, from the decision to hear a case to publication of the final opinion.

In what follows, we consider whether the evidence supports this expectation; in particular, we examine the degree to which justices bargain over the certiorari decision and over the policies articulated in majority opinions. Because bargaining is a form of strategic behavior, evidence that it is widespread would go some distance toward documenting at least one manifestation of interdependent interaction among the justices and its impact on the development of the law.

Bargaining over the Decision to Decide

As much of the scholarly literature acknowledges, the decision over certiorari presents a strategic situation.[3] Given the Rule of Four, justices realize that the outcome—granting or denying review—depends not on the decision of one justice but on four or more. What treatments often neglect, however, is that the cert decision contains all the makings of a classic bargaining problem.[4] First, justices want to reach an agreement over whether to hear a case; if they are consistently unable to reach such agreements, they will fail to attain their main goal of issuing policy proclamations. Second, justices often disagree over which agreement—to grant or deny—is better. Available data suggest that at least one justice votes to grant certiorari in nearly 50 percent of the cases the Court discusses and denies, and at least

Figure 3-1   The Threat to Dissent from a Certiorari Denial: A Typical
Path of Play

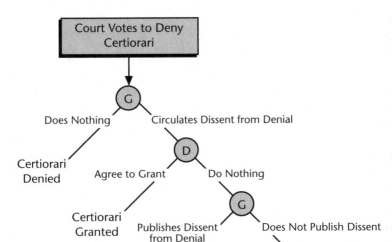

Note: G = justice wanting to grant certiorari; D = justices wanting to deny certiorari.

one votes to deny cert in 98 percent that the Court grants.[5] Finally, justices have various tools at their disposal to enable them to bargain with
their colleagues, with a potentially powerful one being the threat to issue
an opinion dissenting from a denial of certiorari. Although such a threat
can occur at various points in the review process, Figure 3-1 depicts a typical path: the Court votes against hearing a case, and a justice circulates a
dissent from the denial.[b]

---

b. There are at least two alternative routes. First, justices can circulate an opinion
dissenting from a cert denial, along with a memorandum stating that they will publish
it if the Court denies review; in other words, they pose their threat *before* the Court
decides. Second, justices can circulate dissents from a recommendation of a cert denial
made by the writer of a "hold" memorandum. Suppose the Court receives ten petitions that raise the same issue, say, speedy trials. The justices may group these petitions
together, select one for full review, and hold the rest. Once the Court issues its decision in the selected case, the majority opinion writer circulates a hold memo, detailing what she thinks her colleagues should do with the held cases: grant or deny cert
or issue a summary order (for example, a grant, vacate, and remand order). Justices who
disagree with a recommendation against granting cert may circulate a dissent.

We look at these circulated dissents as bargaining tools because their primary purpose is to force justices to change their votes from denies to grants.[c] Justice Stevens said as much in a rather odd opinion in which he complained about the practice:

> Admittedly these dissenting opinions may have some beneficial effects. Occasionally a written statement of reasons for granting certiorari is more persuasive than the Justice's oral contribution to the Conference. For that reason the written document sometimes persuades other Justices to change their votes and a petition is granted that would otherwise have been denied. That effect, however, merely justifies the writing and circulating of these memoranda within the Court; it does not explain why a dissent which has not accomplished its primary mission should be published.[6]

Other justices and their clerks concur: "After [the cert] conference . . . there were certainly attempts at persuasion. . . . The major vehicle for this was a dissent from denial; I mean, those were addressed to the Court as much as they are to the public. The justices get a little more vituperative if it's something where they want to see people swayed." Another simply said that dissents from denials "are often attempts to persuade other justices— at least threats of denials are." [7]

The justices have also supplied reasons for the effectiveness of this form of bargaining. Most important is that these dissents represent threats to the institutional integrity of the Court. As Stevens put it:

---

c. There are other motivations: signaling the legal community that the Court is divided over a particular issue, explaining the rationale behind the denial, or merely taking a policy stance. See H. W. Perry, *Deciding to Decide* (Cambridge: Harvard University Press, 1991), 170–179.

One or more of these factors may help to explain why Brennan and Marshall used to issue "boilerplate" dissents in all death penalty cases that the Court refused to hear: "Adhering to my view that the death penalty is in all circumstances cruel and unusual punishment prohibited by the Eighth and Fourteenth Amendments. . . , I would grant certiorari and vacate the death sentence in this case." Some scholars suggest that they wrote these dissents because they strongly opposed the death penalty, but that may not have been the only reason. As one clerk told Perry: "Brennan and Marshall's dissents from denial [in capital cases] are not necessarily arguments to persuade the Supreme Court to take [them], but they become briefs for the lawyers." (Page 176).

It can be argued that publishing these dissents enhances the public's understanding of the work of the Court. But because they are so seldom answered, these opinions may also give rise to misunderstanding or incorrect impressions about how the Court actually works. Moreover, the selected bits of information which they reveal tend to compromise the otherwise secret deliberations in our Conferences. There are those who believe that these Conferences should be conducted entirely in public or, at the very least, that the votes on all Conference matters should be publicly recorded. The traditional view, which I happen to share, is that confidentiality makes a valuable contribution to the full and frank exchange of views during the decisional process; such confidentiality is especially valuable in the exercise of the kind of discretion that must be employed in processing the thousands of certiorari petitions that are reviewed each year. In my judgment, the importance of preserving the tradition of confidentiality outweighs the minimal educational value of these opinions.[8]

Rather than see a dissent go unanswered or a private vote published, justices may succumb to the threat and join the dissenter. That may be what happened in *Bowers v. Hardwick,* in which the Court considered the constitutionality of a Georgia law outlawing sodomy.[9] When an insufficient number of his colleagues voted to hear the case, Justice White circulated a rather pointed dissenting opinion.[d] His major claim was that the circuit court's decision, which held that the Georgia law infringed on Hardwick's constitutional rights, conflicted with decisions in other circuits—especially a case out of the District of Columbia holding that no constitutional right to engage in homosexual activity exists. "Given this lack of consistency among the Circuits on this important constitutional question," White wrote, "I would grant the petition."[10]

White's threat of going public with the dissent worked. Within a week of its circulation, White had picked up a sufficient number of votes to grant cert. The Brennan, Marshall, and Powell files were difficult to interpret, but the following events seem to have transpired. After White filed his dissent, Rehnquist and Brennan joined it. Rehnquist felt so strongly about hearing the case that he told White he "anticipate[d] writing a little something" himself. At the next day's conference, White picked up a fourth vote, Marshall's. But six days later Brennan changed his vote to a deny. Chief Justice Burger saved White's cause by agreeing to a grant. Later, White gar-

---

d. Only White voted to grant cert. Rehnquist wanted to reverse summarily; the rest voted to deny.

nered enough votes to write a landmark majority opinion reversing the lower court's decision.[e]

Is *Bowers* an anomaly? Or do justices attempt to bargain this way on a regular basis? On the one hand, we would not expect to find justices filing dissents in every case in which they disagree with the Court's decision to deny the cert petition. It may be that another justice has already written such an opinion, which they can join. Or they may not wish to spend precious time writing a dissent if they think they will ultimately fail to pick up four votes. We should also keep in mind the risk justices take in circulating dissents. If they do not convert a sufficient number of justices, they face the choice, as Figure 3-1 shows, of retracting their writing or publishing it. On occasion, they must publish so that their future threats will be credible. But therein lies the risk. For the reasons provided by Stevens, justices may be less than keen to make public their private disagreements. On the other hand, because a dissent from a cert denial is one of the few bargaining mechanisms available to the justices during this stage, we should find some evidence of its use—and, *occasionally,* of its successful uses. This follows from the fact that the primary reason justices file such dissents is to change votes; they would have no reason to circulate them if they thought they would never have such an effect.

With these expectations noted, let us turn to the data. We began the collection process by consulting the case files of several justices and the publicly available records for two terms of the Burger Court, 1982 and 1983. We could obtain data on "successes"—those instances in which dissents pick up three or more votes—only from the private files because, if a justice converts a deny to a grant via a dissenting opinion, that dissent is never made public. To gather information on failures, we relied on Harold J. Spaeth's U.S. Supreme Court Judicial Database, which contains information on published dissenting opinions.[11] We also consulted the private records of Justices Brennan and Marshall, where we found unpublished dissents—those that were retracted by writers when they did not succeed in converting a sufficient number of votes.

Table 3-1 displays the results yielded by these procedures. As indicated, the justices invoked this particular bargaining tool with some selectivity. In only 19 percent of the cases in which they desired to see cert granted, but

---

e. But not without difficulty. The initial vote on the merits was 5-4 to affirm. Only after Powell changed his vote did White have a Court to reverse.

TABLE 3–1

Dissents from Denials of Certiorari

Justice	N of Conference Votes Cast to Grant Cert when the Court Initially Denies	N of Opinions★ Dissenting from Denial of Cert that Did Not Get Fourth Vote	N of Opinions Dissenting from Denial of Cert that Got Fourth Vote
Burger	20	4	0
Brennan	22	2	0
White	50	14	6
Marshall	14	11	0
Blackmun	36	0	0
Powell	23	1	1
Rehnquist	80	10	4
Stevens	17	1	1
O'Connor	23	0	0
Total	285	43	12

Data Sources: We thank Gregory A. Caldeira for supplying the vote data in column 1. Data on published and unpublished dissents are from the U.S. Supreme Court Judicial Database and the case and administrative files of Justices William J. Brennan Jr. and Thurgood Marshall, Library of Congress; and Lewis F. Powell Jr., Washington and Lee University School of Law.

★Published and unpublished.

Note: Data on conference votes and the number of published opinions are from the 1982 term; all other data are from the 1983 term. The rationale for the difference in years is that almost all 1982 term dissenting opinions that succeeded in picking up a fourth vote were eventually decided on their merits in the 1983 term.

Data Note: Column 1 includes only cases in which a vote was taken; column 2 includes only dissenting opinions (not votes) and excludes stock dissents, such as those Brennan and Marshall issued in all death penalty cases that the Court refused to hear. For an explanation, including the data and more detailed coding rules, navigate to: *http://www.artsci.wustl.edu/ ~polisci/epstein/choices/*.

the Court denied, did they circulate a written dissent. For the reasons we have discussed, this finding is not unexpected. What is interesting, however, is that some justices use this tool far more frequently than others: Rehnquist circulated fourteen dissents—only five fewer than the number of majority opinions he wrote during the 1983 term, and White and Marshall issued them in more than a third of the cases in which they disagreed with the Court's denial.

Equally intriguing is that this form of bargaining occasionally has the desired results: about 23 percent of the fifty-five dissents succeeded in picking up four votes. To put it another way, of the 150 or so cases decided with an opinion during the 1983 term, 9 started as denials of cert.[f] These included two significant cases, *New York v. Quarles* and *Bose Corp. v. Consumers Union of the United States.*[12]

Quarles began in 1980 with a woman reporting to two New York police officers that she had been raped by a tall black man who was armed. When the officers drove to the site they spotted the alleged assailant, Benjamin Quarles, ordered him to stop, and asked him where his weapon was. Quarles responded, "The gun is over there." At this point the officers placed Quarles under arrest and read him his Miranda rights. But a trial court judge excluded Quarles's statement concerning the gun because he had spoken before hearing his rights.

The case made its way to the Supreme Court, but on April 14, 1983, the justices voted to deny cert. In response, Burger filed a short statement saying that he dissented from the denial and would prefer to reverse summarily the decision of the court below. About a month later, Rehnquist circulated a dissenting opinion in which he not only urged his colleagues to hear the case but offered his view on *how* the Court should decide it. Rehnquist believed that the state's argument, namely that the justices should adopt a public safety exception to the Miranda rule, was entitled to "careful consideration. If there are ever to be 'exigent circumstances' justifying a refusal to exclude evidence because of a technical *Miranda* violation, the circumstances of this case would seem to be as likely a candidate as any." [13]

On May 23 the Court took another vote on cert, which resulted in a success for Rehnquist: he picked up a sufficient number of votes (Burger, Powell, and O'Connor) for a grant. About a year later, the Court followed the course of action Rehnquist had suggested in his dissent and carved out a public safety exception to *Miranda;* in fact, Rehnquist wrote the majority opinion.

Bose Corporation v. Consumers Union followed a similar path, at least initially. This suit involved a maker of stereo speakers, the Bose Corporation, which believed that *Consumer Reports* magazine had reviewed one of its products with "reckless disregard" for the truth. In mid-April 1983, when

---

f. Table 3-1 shows that there were twelve opinions dissenting from denial of cert that succeeded in picking up a fourth vote. Two of those, one by Powell, the other by Rehnquist, were filed in the same case.

the Court voted on whether to hear the case, only Rehnquist and White cast clear votes to grant. O'Connor voted to reverse summarily or to deny; the chief justice voted to "Join 3," meaning—in all likelihood—that he would go along with a grant if three others voted for it, and the rest voted to deny. His colleagues' votes prompted White to file a dissent a week later, which Rehnquist, Brennan, and O'Connor joined. In the dissent, White— like Rehnquist in *Quarles*—freely offered his opinion on how the case should come out on the merits. He believed that the court of appeals had applied the wrong standard of review and would have vacated its judgment. Unlike Rehnquist in *Quarles,* however, White failed to prevail on the merits. The Court went on to affirm the decision of the lower court, resulting in a victory for the Consumers Union.

From these cases and the data displayed in Table 3-1, what do we learn about bargaining at the cert stage? The first and most obvious lesson is that the decision over cert does indeed present the justices with opportunities for bargaining. Granting cert is an inherently strategic decision, and Court members seem well aware of their mutual dependencies. Second, justices take advantage of at least one tool—dissent from a denial of cert—that enables them to bargain with their colleagues. Although they circulate them selectively, just as we expected, they do circulate them, and with a modicum of success. Finally, because bargaining is a form of interdependent interaction, we can begin to understand the importance of such strategic behavior for the course of the law. One has only to consider *Bowers, Quarles, Bose,* and many other cases that the Court never would have decided had it not been for the threat of going public with an opinion dissenting from the denial of cert.[g]

Bargaining over Policy at the Merits Stage

Like the cert process, the merits stage offers opportunities for justices to bargain. These can begin directly after conference, even before opinions begin to circulate, as *Pulliam v. Allen* illustrates.[14] Richmond Allen was arrested for using abusive and insulting language, a nonjailable misde-

---

g. While our analysis answers a number of important questions, it also leaves many unaddressed. For example: Under what conditions are justices most likely to initiate the bargaining process by threatening to dissent from a cert denial? Under what conditions will such threats fail or succeed? We hope to address these questions in future research.

meanor offense in Virginia. The magistrate, Gladys Pulliam, imposed bail and, when Allen could not pay, Pulliam had him jailed. He then brought suit against the magistrate, claiming that her practice of imposing bail on persons arrested for nonjailable offenses and incarcerating those who could not pay was unconstitutional. A federal district court agreed; it enjoined the practice and awarded Allen $7,691.09 in costs and attorney's fees. A U.S. court of appeals rejected Pulliam's claim that the award of attorney's fees should have been barred by principles of judicial immunity, and the case went to the Supreme Court.

Conference produced something short of consensus: four (Burger, Marshall, Powell, Rehnquist) voted to reverse, four (Brennan, White, Blackmun, Stevens), to affirm, and one (O'Connor) to dismiss the writ of certiorari as improvidently granted (known as a "DIG"). O'Connor broke the deadlock about a week later, when she circulated a memo noting that she tentatively cast her vote to reverse. With "reverse" now representing the majority position, the chief assigned Justice Powell the task of writing the majority opinion.

Powell and O'Connor had a "brief discussion" about the case, which O'Connor followed up with a private memo (that is, a memo sent only to Powell), dated December 1, 1983, outlining her views in some detail and describing the sort of opinion she could join. On December 21 Powell sent O'Connor—and O'Connor only—a draft of his majority opinion, with this memo:

> Here is the first draft . . . of the opinion in this case. As I need you for a Court, and also because of your experience and special interest, I send the draft to you before circulating it.
>
> I had in mind, of course, the two concerns that you have expressed to me.

Believing that she was critical to his ability to establish policy (and she being fully aware of this belief), Powell sought out O'Connor's opinion. O'Connor bargained with Powell, Powell accommodated O'Connor, and she agreed to join his opinion—all before it was circulated to the rest of the Court.[h]

---

h. Powell's ploy ultimately failed because after Marshall, who had voted to reverse, joined Blackmun's dissenting opinion, Blackmun's draft became the majority opinion, and Powell's became a dissent.

Also interesting to note is that bargaining justices occasionally attempt to persuade

More typically, however, bargaining on the merits begins after the opinion writer sends a first draft of an opinion to the full Court. From there, the justices may attempt to bargain over the language of the opinion, including the rationale it invokes and the policy it adopts.

To see how this process works, consider *United Jewish Organizations of Williamsburgh v. Carey,* which involved a highly salient issue—the use of racial factors in redistricting and apportionment.[15] The dispute began in 1972, when New York, in accordance with Section 5 of the Voting Rights Act of 1965, submitted a legislative reapportionment plan to the U.S. attorney general for approval. The Voting Rights Act of 1965 is the most comprehensive statute ever enacted to enforce the guarantees of the Fifteenth Amendment. Not only was it aimed at eliminating various devices, such as literacy tests, that some states had designed to exclude blacks from voting, but also it gave the federal government extraordinary power to regulate elections. If a state or political subdivision had erected any barriers to voting prior to 1964 or if less than 50 percent of its voting age population was registered to vote or had voted in the 1964 election— conditions known as the "triggering formula"—then, under Section 5, the state had to obtain "preclearance" from the federal government before it could enact new voting laws, including reapportionment. Because certain New York counties had once used a discriminatory literacy test and had

---

their colleagues to change their votes after conference but before circulation of opinions. For example, after a sharply divided conference vote in *Board of Education v. Vail,* 466 U.S. 377 (1984), Powell, who had voted to reverse, wrote a private memo to Burger, who had voted to DIG or affirm. The memo was carbon copied to Rehnquist and O'Connor, who also had voted to reverse. In the memo, Powell tried to show Burger why an affirmance would lead to the expansion of several earlier Court holdings, an outcome that Burger would find unattractive. The memo had the desired effect: Burger changed his vote to a reverse. O'Connor attempted a similar move in *Patton v. Yount,* 467 U.S. 1025 (1984). The same day that the conference had divided 4-4 (Marshall did not participate), O'Connor sent the following memo to Powell:

> I write because you are always willing to listen and because it seems most unfortunate to resolve this case by an equally divided Court. You qualified your vote to affirm as being "tentative" and I hope you might be persuaded to consider a reversal.

Powell was indeed open to persuasion: not only did he change his vote but also he wrote the majority opinion reversing the lower court. These examples may demonstrate out-and-out lobbying rather than bargaining, but they serve to highlight strategic interaction on the Court.

low voter participation levels, the state was subject to monitoring. The controversy arose when a community of Hasidic Jews claimed that redistricting had diluted their voting power.

At their initial conference, the justices expressed a wide range of views. According to Brennan's and Powell's transcriptions of the discussion, Justice Stewart said, "No case at all here. Courts cannot get into legislative apportionment unless there's a violation of one-man, one-vote or of Section 5." [i] He wanted to DIG the case. Stevens was at the opposite end of the spectrum, believing that the Court should decide the case and do so in favor of New York because it is "not impermissible to take into account race in drawing district lines." Others debated the degree to which the issue here was similar to affirmative action questions that they had failed to resolve in an earlier case, *DeFunis v. Odegaard*. As White put it, "What we ducked in *DeFunis* is here." [j] But he thought they could again evade the issue by tying the opinion "as closely as possible to Section 5," thereby limiting its application. Powell disagreed with at least the first part of White's statement, noting that he could not see the "rub off" from the affirmative action cases. "This is legislative reapportionment," Powell declared, "and that's different." He also took issue with White's approach: "I don't need to rely on Section 5 where legislative reapportionment is involved." At the end of the day, Brennan recorded the initial vote in the case as 5 (Stevens, Powell, Blackmun, White, and Burger) to uphold the New York plan, 2 (Stewart and Rehnquist) to DIG, 1 (Brennan) to remand, and 1 (Marshall) not participating. [k]

---

i. In previous reapportionment cases the Court made it clear that "as nearly as is practicable one man's vote in a congressional election is to be worth as much as another's." See *Wesberry v. Sanders*, 376 U.S. 1 at 8 (1964). This principle is widely known as "one person, one vote."

j. In *DeFunis v. Odegaard*, 416 U.S. 312 (1974), the Court had "ducked" DeFunis's claim that the University of Washington Law School engaged in reverse discrimination because it denied him, a white male, a place in its program, but accepted statistically less qualified minority students. The Court said the case was moot because DeFunis had almost finished law school by the time his case was heard. The justices finally dealt with the affirmative action question in *Regents of the University of California v. Bakke*, 438 U.S. 265 (1978), but that decision came down a year after *Carey*.

k. Powell's vote tallies are the same as Brennan's, with one notable exception. Powell showed Burger initially passing, then changing to an affirm, a move that enabled the chief to assign the majority opinion. As we discuss in Chapter Four, *Carey* was not the only case in which Burger used the "pass" strategy.

Burger assigned White the difficult task of writing an opinion for the Court. White's first draft, circulated on November 22, 1976, held true to his conference position:

> This is not a case, as petitioners would have it, of "affirmative action."... It is rather a case involving the application of the screening procedures of the Voting Rights Act to ensure that a change in voting procedures—here a new reapportionment statute—does not discriminate against racial minorities.

In other words, White rested his opinion on the fact that New York was subject to the Voting Rights Act, a law the Court had previously upheld as a valid exercise of congressional power.[16] The state was merely complying with the wishes of the U.S. attorney general, who, in turn, was acting in a way consistent with the act.

Because this draft, as White later put it, adopted a "rationale for which there was little enthusiasm at conference," not one justice joined it.[17] Stevens circulated a concurring opinion suggesting that a state may, without relying on the Voting Rights Act, use racial considerations in districting as New York did in its plan. To put it another way, Stevens disagreed with White's assumption that the act, "which was enacted to implement the Fourteenth Amendment—may authorize conduct which would violate that amendment if it were not so authorized." Stewart also circulated a concurring opinion, asserting that the petitioners had no basis to bring suit because they "failed to show that the legislative reapportionment plan had either the purpose or the effect of discriminating against them on the basis of their race." And Brennan wrote the following memorandum to White:

> I've mentioned to you that I favor your approach to this case and want if possible to join your opinion. If you find the following suggestions ... acceptable, I can, as stated in the enclosed concurrence, join you. I'm not generally circulating the concurrence until you let me have your reaction.[18]

Brennan was attempting to strike a bargain with White: if White would change his opinion in accordance with Brennan's suggestions, Brennan would join the opinion and suppress his concurrence. And, apparently, Stevens was attempting to do roughly the same thing with his separate writing because, after White circulated a substantially revised opinion that adopted the logic of Stevens's concurrence, Stevens withdrew his opinion and joined White.

The *Carey* episode, then, illustrates two forms of bargaining in which justices can engage during the circulation stage: *issuing bargaining statements,* as Brennan did, and *circulating separate writings* that they hope to have incorporated in the final version of the opinion, as Stevens did. Are these types of bargaining behavior widespread, or is *Carey* an isolated example? To address these questions, we consider the frequency with which the justices invoke the two tools.

BARGAINING STATEMENTS. All circulated opinions of the Court produce responses from the justices, as Court members must eventually tell the conference what they plan to do—join the Court's opinion, file a dissent, or join a concurrence. Opinions also can generate, as we now know, more substantive memos: suggestions for opinion revision or descriptions of future actions, to name just two.[1] Brennan's memo to White in *Carey* provides an example of the first type, while one Burger wrote to White before he circulated his substantially revised draft illustrates the second:

> I hope to circulate a memo articulating my problems with any fixed "numbers" which seem to give tacit approval to a "quota" concept. We unanimously rejected racial balance in school desegregation . . . and I fear the proposed disposition seems counter to that in spirit. I will have my thoughts ready this week.[19]

Such substantive memos, as Figure 3-2 shows, are the norm. In only 16 percent of the cases we examined were no memoranda circulated. Moreover, for two reasons, this figure probably underestimates the amount of communication among the justices. First, as we know from *Pulliam v. Allen,* justices occasionally circulate private memoranda to one or more colleagues, but not to the whole Court. If private memoranda were not

---

1. A third type of substantive memo is a justice's explanation for an action. A memo Powell sent to White, also in *Carey,* is illustrative. After White had circulated his revised draft, Powell told White why he was planning to join Stewart's concurrence: "I have concluded that Potter's concurring opinion best reflects my thinking about this troublesome case. It also leaves me with more options for the future." Memorandum from Justice Powell to Justice White, 2/16/77, re: 75-104, *United Jewish Organizations v. Carey.*

Figure 3-2   Substantive Memoranda

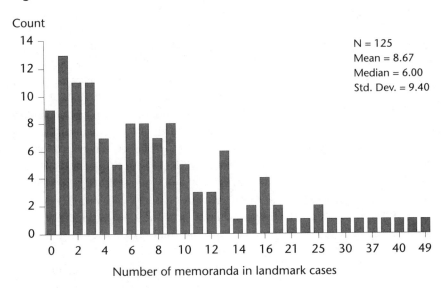

N = 125
Mean = 8.67
Median = 6.00
Std. Dev. = 9.40

Number of memoranda in landmark cases

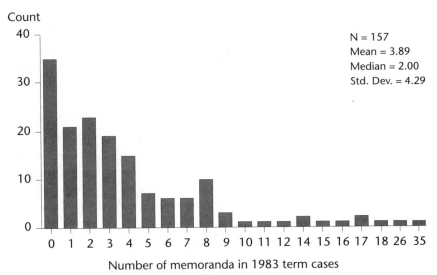

N = 157
Mean = 3.89
Median = 2.00
Std. Dev. = 4.29

Number of memoranda in 1983 term cases

Data Sources: Case files of Justices William J. Brennan Jr. and Thurgood Marshall, Library of Congress; and Lewis F. Powell Jr., Washington and Lee University School of Law.

Note: The data are from cases decided during the 1983 term and those that led to landmark rulings during the Burger Court era. We included all 1983 cases listed on the register of the Papers of Justice William J. Brennan, located in the Library of Congress.

sent or carbon copied to Douglas, Brennan, Marshall, or Powell, naturally we have no record of them. However, private memos tend to be written by those in the majority: a justice who voted in conference with the prevailing coalition is more likely to write to the opinion writer and to carbon copy such memoranda only to other members of the majority. Because it was a rare occasion when at least one of these four justices was not on the "winning" side, we are probably not missing that many memos.[m] But this does not help us with the second reason for underestimation: even if we had access to the papers of all the justices, verbal communication would remain undetected. Snippets from their memoranda reveal statements such as, "At the luncheon conference, we discussed . . ." or, "As I said to you orally. . . ."

These problems—really sources of underestimation—noted, the data still lead to the inescapable conclusion that it is the rare opinion draft that fails to generate a response from the justices. Indeed, the average case generated not one but six memos.

Taken on their face, these data convey important information about the nature of Supreme Court decision making: they indicate that the justices respond to one another's opinions. What they cannot reveal is whether these communications represent explicit bargaining attempts. Note the difference between the memo Brennan sent to White in *Carey* and the one written by Burger. Burger was merely declaring his intention of writing a separate opinion because he disagreed with a particular aspect of White's writing; Brennan, however, provided White with a list of suggestions—suggestions that he framed as an explicit bargaining statement: he would consider joining the opinion only if White made them.

The distinction between the two memos takes us back to the question we asked at the beginning of this section: To what extent are private communications between the justices attempts at bargaining (the Brennan memo) or mere declarations of intention (the Burger memo)? This question is important because regular use of the sort of statements Brennan made would challenge those views of the Court that do not contemplate interdependent interaction. A justice who fails to consider the preferences of others and the actions she expects them to take would have *no* reason to make bargaining statements, whether they reflect real intentions to

---

m. For example, data from Harold Spaeth's U.S. Supreme Court Judicial Database show that in only 2.2 percent (69 of 3,170) of the orally argued cases in which Brennan and Powell both participated were both in the minority.

change behavior or not. In a very real sense, documentation of the widespread existence of bargaining statements would provide support for our assumption of strategic interaction.

To gauge the frequency of this practice, we examined the substantive memoranda circulated during the 1983 term and in landmark cases. Our goal was to identify the number of cases in which justices made explicit bargaining statements—those in which they offered to join if the opinion writer made changes.[n]

Table 3-2 displays the results. In more than two-thirds of the most important cases of the 1970s and 1980s, at least one justice attempted to bargain with the opinion writer—with a good deal of the negotiation done through private memos. *Milliken v. Bradley,* involving a school desegregation plan devised by a federal district court, supplies an example.[20] After the Court voted 5 (Burger, Stewart, Blackmun, Powell, and Rehnquist) to 4 (Douglas, Brennan, White, and Marshall) to strike down the district court's plan, the chief justice assigned the opinion to himself. Even before he circulated his first draft, he began to receive private communications from some of the members of the majority. Powell, for instance, wrote to tell him about a story he "recalled" in the press recently "to the effect that Senator Ervin was then holding hearings of a subcommittee on the proposed anti-busing constitutional amendment." [21] Powell wondered if the chief might want to get a hold of some of the testimony from school officials who had experienced the effect of school desegregation programs. Then, after Burger circulated two drafts of his opinion, he was barraged with a flood of private memos. Powell's list of suggested changes ran more than ten pages; Stewart's six; Rehnquist's, which was sent to the chief justice, with a blind copy circulated to Powell, and Blackmun's, two pages each. It was apparently going to be difficult to keep the majority coalition intact. But, by the third draft, it became clear that Burger would pull it off. As Rehnquist put it in a memo sent to the chief and carbon copied to Stewart, Blackmun, and Powell: "I think you have made very substantial changes to accommodate the view expressed by the rest of us who voted with you at Conference on this case. . . . I sincerely hope that we can come out with an opinion for the Court." Yet, the four members of the minority saw none of this "accommodation"; all

---

n. The Table 3-2 note and web site provide information about our coding procedures. Here we note that we would not have coded Burger's memo to White in *Carey* as a bargaining statement; rather, as we mention in the text, it was a declaration of intent.

TABLE 3-2
Bargaining Statements

	Landmark Cases		1983 Term Cases		Total	
	n	%	n	%	n	%
No bargaining statements	37	29.6	83	52.9	120	42.6
One or more bargaining statements	88	70.4	74	47.1	162	57.4
Total	125		157		282	

Data Sources: Case files of Justices William J. Brennan Jr. and Thurgood Marshall, Library of Congress; and Lewis F. Powell Jr., Washington and Lee University School of Law.

Note: We included all 1983 cases listed on the register of the Papers of Justice William J. Brennan, located in the Library of Congress, with two exceptions: original cases and non-orally argued cases. Landmark cases are those listed in Elder Witt, *Guide to the U.S. Supreme Court,* 2d ed. (Washington, D.C.: Congressional Quarterly, 1990), 915-926, that were decided during the 1969-1985 terms. For both samples, the unit of analysis was citation: if two or more cases were combined under one U.S. cite, we included only the lead case.

Coding Rules: We coded a bargaining statement as present when a justice explicitly hinged her "join" of the majority opinion, per curiam, and so forth on the writer's making a change(s) in the opinion. We excluded (1) memoranda in which justices asked for a change but stated that they joined the opinion regardless of whether the change was made and (2) various memoranda (as in "Memorandum of Justice Brennan"), which are typically opinions circulated at the request of the chief justice. For the data, navigate to: *http://www.artsci. wustl.edu/~polisci/epstein/choices/.*

they received were the end results of the bargaining process—the various opinion drafts.

As Table 3-2 shows, the justices also make bargaining efforts in the more typical sorts of cases, here represented by suits resolved during the 1983 term. Although the figure is smaller than it is for landmark litigation, one cannot help but conclude that bargaining is a regular feature of the process by which justices reach their decisions. The justices even use the language of bargaining in their memos, as these excerpts reveal:

- From Rehnquist to Burger, Powell, and O'Connor: "I have been *negotiating* with John Stevens for considerable time in order to produce a fifth vote in my *Bildisco* opinion. I have agreed to make the following changes in the currently circulating draft, and he has agreed to join if I do."

- From Burger to Powell: "I have your memo re the above. . . . With all deference to your right to express views separately in any way you wish, may I suggest that we accomplish a good deal by exchange of memos—*one-on-one*—rather than by concurring opinions which tend to get people '*locked in*'? After *consultation* on the points of your concern, I may well be able to embrace them!"
- From Brennan to Burger: "I share your hope that we may reach an *accommodation* and common position in these important cases. The approach taken in your draft, however, differs considerably from that which I believe is required." [22]

It is also worth noting that this sort of bargaining is not a phenomenon exclusively associated with the Burger Court. Other scholars have noted evidence of negotiation and accommodation on earlier Courts.[23] Our examination of William O. Douglas's case files confirms their findings for as early as 1939, when Douglas sent a memo to the opinion writer, Harlan Fiske Stone, in *United States v. Morgan*. The case involved the meaning of certain provisions of the Packers and Stockyards Act, enacted to secure services to stockyard patrons at "just and reasonable rates." Douglas wrote:

> It is my view that your opinion is superb and magnificent. You have done a perfectly grand job. I have only two suggestions to make. The first is somewhat minor, the second perhaps more important.[24]

Felix Frankfurter apparently expressed the same sentiments to Stone, who the next day sent a letter to both Douglas and Frankfurter: "As your criticisms . . . are substantially the same, I will call your attention to a difficulty in the case which gives me some trouble, and which I had hoped to avoid discussing very specifically one way or the other." After outlining possible ways to deal with his "difficulty," Stone ended with the following:

> Please compare notes on these suggestions and let me know whether they are acceptable or, if not, make a counter-suggestion which will avoid foreclosing the point I have in mind.

Frankfurter and Douglas wrote a joint letter back to Stone that very day. They made a counterproposal, which Stone wrote into the opinion verbatim. This accommodation enabled both to join the majority opinion—from which three other justices (Roberts, McReynolds, and Butler) dissented.

And bargaining continues—has even escalated—into the current Court era. Of nine landmark cases handed down during the first term of the Rehnquist Court (1986), eight generated at least one bargaining statement.[25] In several of those, the opinion writer was confronted with the task of negotiating with more than one justice at the same time. Such was Brennan's problem in two affirmative action cases, *United States v. Paradise* and *Johnson v. Transportation Agency*. In *Paradise* the question was whether a "one-black-for-one-white" promotion plan violated the Fourteenth Amendment; *Johnson* asked whether an affirmative action plan that allowed sex to be taken into account in deciding on promotions violated Title VII of the Civil Rights Act of 1964. Collectively, Brennan had to deal with "suggestions" from O'Connor, Stevens, and Powell about ways to "improve" his initial drafts.

These and other findings lead us to conclude that bargaining has been and still is a fundamental part of the Supreme Court decision-making process. They are also suggestive of something else that is quite important: justices believe that bargaining can lead to favorable outcomes. If they thought that their bargaining statements never had an effect, there would be no reason to make them—and to make them in more than half of their cases, at least on the Burger and Rehnquist Courts. Given the findings of other scholars, coupled with our reading of the Douglas case files, we have no reason to believe that we cannot make the same inference for earlier Court periods.

SEPARATE WRITINGS. As we saw in *Carey*, once the opinion writer has released a first draft, the other justices are free to issue their own writings. These may be (1) concurrences in judgment, (2) regular concurrences, (3) concurrences in part and dissents in part, (4) dissents, or (5) memoranda opinions.° But *Carey* also shows that not all of these writings are published, nor do they necessarily remain in the same form as they were when the writer initially circulated them—for example, dissents sometimes become concurrences and vice versa.[26]

Why changes of this sort occur is a matter of speculation. But our suspicion, as we have mentioned, is that the justices occasionally use these

---

o. Typically, memoranda opinions come at the request of the chief justice. If the conference discussion produces an ambiguous result, the chief may ask one or two justices with opposing points of view to circulate opinions containing their views on the case. Such opinions would be labeled as memoranda.

writings as bargaining tools. They demonstrate to the writer that she cannot count on support if she does not adjust her opinion in ways suggested in the dissent or concurrence. By this logic, a writing circulated by the non-opinion writer that is never published or that changes in form when it is published provides some evidence of strategic interaction.[p] This, at the very least, is the lesson of *Carey:* both Brennan and Stevens circulated (or threatened to circulate) concurring opinions with the hope of convincing White to adjust his position.

Again, we must ask: Is *Carey* anomalous or do justices regularly use their writings as bargaining tools? One way to address this question is to count dissenting and concurring opinions. The problem with this approach, however, is that justices circulate separate writings for reasons other than to convince the writer to adjust her opinion. For example, they may use them to persuade justices who have not joined the majority opinion to change their vote or to adopt a different rationale. Chief Justice Burger clearly intended to affect White's vote when he asked Stewart to write a dissent in *County of Washington v. Gunther.*[q] Burger wrote to Stewart: "Are you willing to take on the dissent in this case? You recall Byron [White] said his vote to affirm was 'tentative.' A swift dissent might 'shake' the case." [27]

Or justices may use separate writings as a way to alert external political communities to alternatives to the majority's policy. Burger may have had this in mind in his dissent in *Furman v. Georgia,* a well-known death penalty case.[28] While a five-person majority agreed that *existing* death penalty statutes were unconstitutional, Burger was quick to point out that three of the five (Douglas, Stewart, and White) had not ruled capital punishment unconstitutional and that it may be possible for states to rewrite their laws to meet their objections—an invitation that many states quickly accepted. Or justices may—viewing the resolution of particular policy matters as an ongoing game—see dissents, in particular, as appeals "to the brooding spir-

---

p. We should also point out that both the threat of publication of alternative opinions and their actual publication provide evidence of the importance justices attach to the content of legal opinions—evidence that lends indirect support to the centrality of the most fundamental manifestation of strategic interaction: changes in the policy articulated in majority opinions. We discuss this manifestation toward the end of the chapter.

q. *County of Washington v. Gunther,* 452 U.S. 161 (1981). The question was whether 703(h), known as the Bennett Amendment, of Title VII of the Civil Rights Act of 1964 restricts Title VII's prohibition of sex-based wage discrimination to claims of equal pay for equal work.

TABLE 3-3
Changes in Opinion Status

	Landmark Cases		1983 Term Cases		Total	
	n	%	n	%	n	%
Absence of change	92	73.6	140	89.2	232	82.3
Presence of change	33	26.4	17	10.8	50	17.7
Total	125		157		282	

Data Sources: Case files of Justices William J. Brennan Jr. and Thurgood Marshall, Library of Congress.

Note: By changes in opinion status, we mean that the writing was retracted or transformed from, say, a dissent to a concurrence during the circulation period. We included all 1983 cases listed on the register of the Papers of Justice William J. Brennan (Library of Congress) with two exceptions: original cases and nonorally argued cases. Landmark cases are those listed in Elder Witt, *Guide to the U.S. Supreme Court,* 2d ed. (Washington, D.C.: Congressional Quarterly, 1990), 915-926, that were decided during the 1969-1985 terms. For both samples, the unit of analysis was citation: if two or more cases were combined under one U.S. cite, we included only the lead case.

Coding Rules: We coded a change in opinion status as present when justices, other than the justice assigned to write on behalf of the Court, (1) circulated a dissent, concurrence, or unlabeled opinion ("Memorandum of Justice Brennan") that they eventually retracted or (2) circulated a dissent, concurrence, or unlabeled opinion that eventually changed in status (*e.g.,* from a dissent to a concurrence). We excluded opinions that were never circulated to the full Court. For the data, navigate to: *http://www.artsci.wustl.edu/~polisci/epstein/choices/.*

it of the law, to the intelligence of a future day, when a later decision may possibly correct the error into which the dissenting judge believes the Court to have been betrayed." [29]

To eliminate these possibilities (that is, other motivations behind separate writings) we focus here only on those instances when an opinion written by a justice other than the assigned opinion writer changed in form or was retracted. Table 3-3 reports the results. As noted, in 17.7 percent of the cases justices suppressed their writings or changed them during the circulation period. The figure again was significantly higher for landmark cases such as *Carey* (26.4 percent) than for those decided during the 1983 term (10.8 percent).

How should we interpret these results? On the one hand, we would be hard-pressed to say that justices regularly write opinions that go unpublished or unchanged. At the very least, they do not do so as frequently as they issue explicit bargaining statements. On the other hand, the fact that such writings are produced and then retracted or altered in nearly 20 percent of the cases is not easy to ignore in light of the workload complaints registered by many contemporary justices.[30]

Nor should we overlook the finding that this form of bargaining occurs in more than a quarter of landmark cases, for it suggests that some of the most important decisions of the era may have expressed a very different rationale had it not been for separate writings. We have only to recall the original logic of White's opinion in *Carey* to see the potential effect on the Court's policy proclamations.

FORWARD THINKING

The overall contention of this chapter is that we cannot understand the choices justices make—from the decision on certiorari through the choice of policy in the majority opinion—without taking into account the strategic nature of the decision-making context. Justices, we argue, do not make their choices in isolation; they must and do pay some heed to the preferences of others and the actions they expect others to take.

Important support for our argument, we believe, would come from evidence demonstrating that justices are "forward-thinking" actors, meaning that they make a particular choice based on what they think will happen in the future. Consider the decision to grant cert. If justices think prospectively, we would expect them to vote to deny or grant review based on what they think will happen at the merits stage. These votes would provide evidence of strategic behavior because, given the Rule of Four and the requirement of a majority for establishing precedent, it would be hard to believe that justices could make such calculations without considering the preferences and expected actions of their colleagues and other relevant actors. After all, why would a policy-oriented justice vote to review a case if she did not think her side could muster the support of at least four others at the merits stage?

In fact, data suggest that justices do not behave in this fashion; rather, they think prospectively before they agree to hear a case. By way of evidence, in Chapter Two we discussed reversal rates, providing support for the proposition that justices grant cert to cases that they want to *reverse* in accordance with their policy preferences.[31] One could argue, therefore, that reversal rates provide clear evidence of strategic calculations: a justice would vote to hear only those cases she thinks the majority will reverse.[32] But one could just as easily argue that such rates are the product of pure preference-driven behavior: a justice votes to hear cases she wants to reverse, regardless of how she thinks the Court will vote.[33]

To overcome this problem of behavioral equivalence, let us turn to two kinds of conduct that would be difficult to explain if justices did not think prospectively at the cert stage: aggressive grants and defensive denials. A grant of certiorari is described as *aggressive* when the justices take a case that may not warrant review "because they have calculated that it has certain characteristics that would make it particularly good for developing a doctrine in a certain way, and the characteristics make it more likely to win on their merits." [34] Typically, scholars have suggested that such grants occur when a justice *agrees* with a lower court ruling and believes that the majority of the Court will go along. By this logic, she votes to grant cert because she hopes to give the ruling the weight of a Supreme Court affirmance to make it the policy of the nation. When justices deny cert to cases that they would like to hear because they believe that they will not prevail at the merits stage, they are issuing a *defensive denial*. Many analysts interpret this action as a clear form of sophisticated behavior.[35] On this account, a defensive denial is most likely to occur when a justice votes against cert, even though she disliked the lower court decision, because she believes that the Court will probably affirm the decision.[r]

Do justices regularly engage in these forms of strategic behavior? They say they do. As one put it, "I might think that the Nebraska Supreme Court made a horrible decision, but I wouldn't want to take the case, for if we take the case and affirm it, then it would become precedent." [36] The classic logic of a defensive denial. By the same token, the justices' clerks—who are charged with making recommendations on cert to the justices—occasionally couch their memoranda in strategic terms. Consider the

---

r. It is also true that justices sometimes defensively deny cases with lower court decisions with which they agree. In *Bowers v. Hardwick* Brennan initially joined White's dissent from a denial of cert, but, after Rehnquist also joined, Brennan changed his mind and voted to deny. Why? One might speculate that once Rehnquist, who was unlikely to adopt Brennan's preferred position to strike down sodomy laws, joined White, Brennan began to believe that he would lose on the merits and decided that a favorable lower court ruling was better than an unfavorable Supreme Court precedent.

advice Marshall's clerk offered to his boss in *Wiegand v. United States.*[37] In this case the U.S. Court of Appeals for the Ninth Circuit had upheld a search warrant that agents had used to seize child pornography from a man's house, a decision contrary to Marshall's preferences:

> Petitioner argues that the terms of the warrant are so broad that they per- mit the seizure of materials protected by the First Amendment. . . . The First Circuit seemed to be troubled by a similar argument . . . noting that "the question of whether a warrant authorizing seizures of films depicting sexual activity by children under 18 violates the particularity requirement of Fourth Amendment is a significant one of current interest." Thus, there is an incipient split [among] the Circuits here on an important question. Nonetheless I would not vote to grant on this issue, because I think that this Court will not find any First Amendment problem with such a war- rant. *Seems to me that a defensive denial is in order.*[38]

More systematic evidence comes from a recent investigation of cert vot- ing during the Court's 1982 term.[39] Unlike many other research efforts in this area, this study went to great lengths to include variables to account for the ideological preferences of the individual justices *along with* those of their colleagues. The results are clear. While the authors find strong evi- dence of policy voting, defined as voting to grant or deny based on ideo- logical preferences, they show that there is equally strong support for strategic behavior, defined as voting to grant or deny inconsistently with one's ideal policy point.[s] They also find that such strategic behavior takes the form of both aggressive grants and defensive denials.[t]

---

s. It is worth reiterating that both types of behavior, policy voting and aggressive grants/defensive denials, may be forms of strategic voting. But only the second type can be explained solely in strategic terms.

t. One might take issue with this research, and our account more generally, by mak- ing the following claim: if we are correct, we should never find justices voting to grant cert and then losing on the merits of cases; but, in fact, this series of events happens frequently.

We offer the following responses: the first comes from the research by Gregory A. Caldeira and his colleagues in "Strategic Voting and Gatekeeping in the Supreme Court," showing that justices who are ideologically distant from the majority of their colleagues tend to cast fewer votes in favor of cert. During the 1982 term, a period of relative conservatism, Marshall voted to grant cert in only 12 percent of the cases on

Consideration of the Preferences and
Expected Behavior of External Actors

Most claims about the existence (or lack thereof) of forward thinking at the cert stage assess the extent to which justices base their decision to deny or grant cert on what they think will happen at the merits stage. On our account, strategic justices do more than consider the preferences and expected actions of their colleagues; they also take into account the likely reactions of other relevant actors, such as Congress and the president. The logic here, as we laid it out in Chapter One, is straightforward: if the objective of justices is to see their favored policies become the ultimate law of the land, then they must take into account the preferences of other major actors and the actions they expect them to take. If they do not, they risk seeing massive noncompliance with their rulings, meaning that their policy fails to take on the force of law; or having Congress replace their most preferred position with their least; or other forms of retaliation, such as removing the Court's jurisdiction to hear cases, keeping judicial salaries constant, and impeaching justices.

Translating this claim to the cert stage, we would expect a strategically oriented justice to engage in two kinds of behavior: (1) declining to hear a case if she believed a merits decision favorable to her preferred policy position would anger relevant external actors and (2) agreeing to hear a case that relevant actors wanted the Court to resolve, even if she would be unable to place policy on her ideal point.

DECLINING TO DECIDE CASES. The first expectation—refusing to decide certain disputes—flows directly from our claims about the importance of the policy goals and the existence of strategic interaction on the Court: justices would be loath to take cases, even if they believed they could obtain the necessary support for their position inside the Court, if they simulta-

---

which the Court took a vote; that figure was 43 percent for Rehnquist. Second, as we noted in Chapter Two and as a large body of literature makes clear, policy may be the most important goal that justices pursue at the cert stage, but it is not the only goal. If a justice votes to grant cert because she believes it is important for the Court's institutional legitimacy to resolve a conflict between federal courts, she would not necessarily expect to win on the merits. Finally, justices will not always know with absolute certainty what their colleagues will do at the merits stage; they may only be able to formulate a guess, which may be wrong.

neously believed that political actors would move policy far from their ideal points.

Anecdotal support for this "dispute-avoidance" proposition abounds. There are, for example, many salient and, seemingly, certworthy petitions that the Court has denied over the years at least in part because it wanted to avoid collisions with Congress and the president. The justices never resolved the question of the constitutionality of the Vietnam War, despite its obvious importance and many requests to do so.[40] In addition, Supreme Court clerks occasionally point out the political consequences of accepting petitions. Sociolegal scholar Doris Provine provides a nice example. After the Court issued its highly controversial decision in *Brown v. Board of Education* in 1954, it was asked the very next year to resolve a challenge to a miscegenation law (*Naim v. Naim*).[41] Justice Harold Burton's clerk made the following recommendation to his boss:

> In view of the difficulties engendered by the segregation cases it would be wise judicial policy to duck this question for the time being . . . [but] I don't think we can be honest and say that the claim is unsubstantial. . . . It is with some hesitation . . . that I recommend that we NPJ ["note probable jurisdiction," the functional equivalent of granting review]. This hesitation springs from the feeling that we ought to give the present fire a chance to burn down.[42]

Burton declined to take his clerk's advice, voting instead to dismiss. But four others (Douglas, Stanley Reed, Hugo Black, and Earl Warren) wanted to resolve the dispute. Although there were enough votes to review, the Court put the case on hold. On the next vote, only Douglas, Reed, and Black agreed to note jurisdiction and, at the final conference, the justices unanimously agreed to issue a vacate and remand order. Why the change? According to Justice Tom C. Clark, the author of the published order in the case, the probability of a negative reaction to a decision on the merits "had been an important consideration in the decision."[43]

There is also more systematic evidence to support the existence of a dispute-avoidance strategy. Provine shows that between 1954 (after *Brown*) and 1957, the Court received at least five petitions involving "major" segregation issues, in addition to *Naim;* it granted cert in just one, *Holmes v. City of Atlanta,* only to vacate the lower court's ruling without a full hearing on the merits.[44] We supply further evidence from more recent data on cases involving equal employment practices. As Table 3-4 shows, during the

TABLE 3-4
Review of Cases Involving Race/Sex Equal Employment Practices

	1978 Term[a]		1982 Term[b]	
	n	%	n	%
Cases granted certiorari	5	13.2	7	28.0
Cases denied certiorari	33	86.8	18	72.0
Total	38		25	

Data Source: CCH Supreme Court Bulletin.

[a] Republican Court, Democratic President and Congress.

[b] Republican Court, Republican President and Senate.

Note: We included cases listed under the subject "Equal Employment Practices," subheading "Race" and "Sex," listed in the index of the *CCH Supreme Court Bulletin*. For coding rules and the data, navigate to: *http://www.artsci.wustl.edu/~polisci/epstein/choices/*.

1978 term, when the Republican Court was more conservative than the Democratic Congress and president, the justices rejected nearly 90 percent of these petitions, although many presented important issues.[u] Why? On our account, the Republican majority on the Court, while believing it could prevail on the merits, thought that the Democratic president and Congress would override the Court's decision. Rather than see its holdings reversed, it avoided the dispute. When the political landscape changed in the early 1980s with the election of Ronald Reagan and a Republican Senate, the Court also moved in a more conservative direction. During the 1982 term, it agreed to hear 28 percent of the employment cases—nearly 15 percent more than it did in 1978 and more than four times its average acceptance rate (6 percent) for that term.[v]

---

u. *Westinghouse v. State Human Rights Appeal Board*, 439 U.S. 1073 (1979), is a case in point. It involved a highly salient issue, the exclusion of pregnancy-related benefits from an employer's disability plan, an issue that had created conflict in state courts. The International Union of Electrical, Radio, and Machine Workers filed an amicus curiae brief at the review stage, further underscoring the case's significance. The brief urged the Court to deny cert, but, as Caldeira and Wright show, amicus briefs in opposition increase the chances that the Court will hear the case because they signal the importance of the petition, just as briefs in support of cert do.

v. The percentage of employment cases granted during the 1978 term (13.2) was also higher than the average acceptance rate that term (about 9 percent). But it is worth

More broad-based support comes from a recent study by Epstein and Segal that considered agenda-setting behavior during the 1953 through the 1993 terms of the Court.[45] These researchers begin with the basic dispute-avoidance hypothesis: justices avoid placing policies on their agenda when they believe that members of the other branches will move policy far from their ideal points. To this hypothesis, they add the following: justices behave in this way unless they also believe that they can insulate their holdings from reversal by reaching consensual decisions. This claim, Epstein and Segal argue, flows from the comments of scholars, legislators, and the justices themselves that suggest the more authoritative a holding (for example, a unanimous decision) the less likely that Congress will attempt to overturn it.[46]

To test this prediction, the researchers considered the percentage of constitutional cases the Court decides each year, arguing that the percentage should increase when the justices and external political actors are far apart in policy terms, but that this effect is mitigated when the Court is relatively homogeneous.[w] Because the data largely confirm this hypothesis, they lend even more support to the notion that justices are not only forward thinking with regard to the preferences and likely actions of their colleagues but also of other relevant political actors.

AGREEING TO DECIDE CASES. Just as justices are loath to take cases that may ultimately lead to the creation of "unfavorable" policy or collisions with Congress, we suspect that they are equally reluctant to ignore disputes that the government wants them to resolve—even if they believe that they would be unable to set policy on their ideal points. Avoiding such cases

---

noting that the (Democratic) federal government played a role in four of the five petitions the 1978 Court accepted. For reasons we discuss in the next section, the (Republican) Court may have felt compelled to review those cases. So, if we eliminate those four from consideration, justices serving during the 1978 term granted only one of the remaining thirty-four equal employment petitions—for a review rate of 2.9 percent compared with 4.5 percent, which is about the average rate for cases in which the United States does not participate either as a petitioner or amicus curiae. Thanks to Gregory Caldeira for providing that last figure.

w. Epstein and Segal hinge this argument on the notion that Congress can far more readily overturn the Court's construction of its statutes than it can constitutional provisions. Accordingly, justices are freer to make decisions in line with their sincere preferences in constitutional disputes. We discuss this argument in some detail in Chapter Five.

might generate a backlash just as great as deciding cases against the interests of other government actors.

   This proposition follows from the fact that perceptions that the Court is
dodging its responsibilities may generate attacks on its institutional authority—attacks that, in turn, could affect the ability of policy-oriented justices
to achieve their goals. To see this, we have only to recall that during the
mid-1930s, when the Court was under siege from Congress and the president, one of the charges against it was that it "was using its discretionary
jurisdiction to duck important cases." [x] The justices responded to this allegation by assuring Congress that they follow the nonmajority Rule of
Four precisely because they prefer "to be at fault in taking jurisdiction
rather than to be at fault in rejecting it." [47]

   The justices' reply quelled this particular congressional concern, and it
may have helped to stave off dramatic plans to change the fundamental
nature of the Court.[y] Still, this historical episode and several others indicate that the justices occasionally open themselves up to criticism by duck-
ing cases, even if the critics are using the dispute-avoidance charge as a ruse
to accomplish other objectives.[z] More systematic data suggest that the justices may be responding to these criticisms or, at the very least, hoping to

---

   x. We base this discussion on a memorandum titled "The Rule of Four" that
Thurgood Marshall circulated to conference September 21, 1983. Marshall was
responding to a call by Justice Stevens that the Court consider changing the Rule of
Four to a majority rule. Marshall adamantly opposed the plan, at least in part because
he thought the justices could not change the rule without congressional approval.

   The supporting citation Marshall provides for the quote is 81 Cong. Rec. 2809-
2812 (1939). Marshall, however, was quick to note that "this criticism may have been
a stalking horse for the [Roosevelt] administration's 'court-packing' plan."

   y. As Justice Marshall put it, "Although the Rule of Four did not play a decisive role
in stemming the anti-Court sentiment of the 1930s, a fair reading of the legislative
debate of that period shows that allies of the Court relied upon the Rule as an example of the responsible manner in which the Court was exercising its discretionary jurisdiction." Marshall, "The Rule of Four," 3-4.

   z. Charges that the Court "ducks" its constitutional responsibilities surfaced again
in the 1950s, when the Court was under heavy fire from Southern Democrats for its
Brown decision. Sen. Herman E. Talmadge, D-Ga., expressed his "grave concern [with]
the increasing tendency of the Supreme Court . . . to act upon lower court decisions
without hearing oral arguments on the points at issue." Talmadge requested that a list
of the cases with which the Court dealt in a summary fashion be printed in the
Congressional Record, and proposed a law forbidding the Court to "affirm, modify,

deter them by taking cases the government wants them to decide, even if that is not their desire. For example, of the five employment cases (see Table 3-4) that the Republican 1978 Court agreed to decide, the Democratic federal government played a role in all but one. More general analyses demonstrating the phenomenal success of the United States at the cert stage also shore up the point. Provine shows that during the 1947–1957 terms the government submitted 554 petitions for review, and the justices granted cert in 66 percent of them, a figure well above their overall rate of grants for the period (9.6 percent).[48] Caldeira and Wright's research, which took into account a range of explanations for the cert decision including whether the United States was a petitioner, reaches a similar conclusion: even if a government petition presents no evidence of real conflict and no amici file in its support, the likelihood of Court review is a staggering 37 percent, compared with an average review rate of 8 percent for the term Caldeira and Wright examined.[49]

There are many possible explanations for these findings. Provine writes, "Because of their quality, the clerks and justices probably read [U.S.] petitions with special care." [50] Caldeira and Wright focus on the solicitor general, who represents the United States in Court. They suggest that the "solicitor general's expertise is evidently highly respected by the justices."[51] But neither these reasons nor others that scholars have offered preclude the possibility that a fear of retaliation plays some role in explaining the Court's unusual willingness to resolve government disputes.[52] Even more to the point, they provide support for it. After all, why would the justices read U.S. petitions with "special care" if they were not concerned with the response a denial might engender?

We end our discussion of forward thinking where we began it: the data lead to the inescapable conclusion that this type of strategic behavior is a fundamental part of the process by which justices reach cert decisions. When deciding whether to hear cases, not only do Court members take

---

vacate, set aside, or reverse any judgment" without hearing oral arguments. See *Congressional Record,* 1959, 86th Cong., 1st sess., vol. 105, pt. 2, 1479.

Talmadge probably had more than Court procedure on his mind. Indeed, we suspect that he was sending the same sort of warning to the justices that his predecessors did in the 1930s: start ruling our way or face serious institutional penalties. If this was a warning, it was not lost on the justices. Less than three weeks after Talmadge's statement, Brennan circulated a memo to conference containing a breakdown of the cases on Talmadge's list. Memorandum from Justice Brennan to the conference, 3/11/59.

into account the preferences of their colleagues and the actions they expect them to take at the merits stage, but also they consider the likely reactions of other political actors, most notably members of Congress. Such calculations, as we have argued, occasionally lead them to avoid taking disputes that they may want to resolve and, at times, to take cases that they may not want to decide.

MANIPULATING THE AGENDA

Most judicial specialists use the term "agenda setting" to refer to the process the Court uses to make decisions over which disputes to hear and resolve. But that is not the only type of agenda setting; another occurs after the Court has heard oral arguments and then must decide on the particular issues it will address in its opinion. This process is agenda setting because justices can engage in "issue suppression"; that is, after they agree to decide a case, they may (and often do) neglect to resolve questions that the parties have raised in their briefs.[53] In other words, justices are free to pick and choose among the issues to address.

The fact that justices engage in issue suppression opens the door to another form of strategic behavior: agenda manipulation. Chief Justice Burger, recall, engaged in this sort of behavior during the conference over *Craig* when he tried to steer attention toward standing and away from sex discrimination policy. He was attempting to develop another dimension of the case to control the agenda as a way to manipulate the outcome.[54]

Burger failed in his effort to convince the Court to dismiss *Craig* on standing grounds, but under a different set of circumstances he might very well have succeeded. Suppose, for the sake of simplicity, that the chief was operating on a three-person court in which the members had the following preferences over the standard to use in sex discrimination cases (P = "preferred to"):

Justice 1: higher level of scrutiny P rational basis test
Justice 2: higher level of scrutiny P rational basis test
Chief justice: rational basis test P higher level of scrutiny

If this court took a vote between the two alternatives, the chief would lose 2-1. But suppose the chief introduces a third alternative—dismiss on standing—and the new choice alters the preference orderings in the following way:

Justice 1: higher level of scrutiny P dismiss on standing P rational basis test
Justice 2: dismiss on standing P higher level of scrutiny P rational basis test
Chief justice: rational basis test P dismiss on standing P higher level of scrutiny

Further suppose that this court must first decide the procedural question, whether to dismiss on standing, before it turns to the more substantive issue of what standard to invoke. Surely, Justice 1 would vote against dismissal. She knows that if the court gets to the substantive question, she will see her most preferred position etched into law because Justice 2 also supports a higher level of scrutiny over rational basis. Equally clear is Justice 2's vote. He would vote to dismiss on standing because that is his most preferred position; he also knows that if the court reaches on the merits of the case, his least desired policy would not be adopted. Finally, the chief justice would vote for dismissal. Even though this is not his first choice, it is—given his beliefs about the preferences of the other justices and his own desires—his best possible outcome, which is why our chief introduced this option to begin with.

The example shows that the interjection of an additional dimension to a case can be a rational course of action for policy-oriented justices, especially if they believe they lack support for their most preferred substantive policy outcome. This form of agenda setting is also a type of sophisticated behavior: on our account, the chief justice—either in our hypothetical example or in *Craig*—would not have pushed the standing alternative had he believed his most preferred position enjoyed sufficient support. But, perceiving that he lacked a majority, he gave up his ideal policy in an effort to avoid adoption of his least favored alternative.

How common are these sorts of attempts at agenda manipulation? To address this question, we focus on sophisticated behavior during the conference discussions that took place in the 1983 term and in landmark cases decided by the Burger Court. We take evidence of agenda manipulation at the discussion stage as an attempt to interject a procedural dimension into case discussion or to avoid, suppress, or narrow the range of issues. *Craig* provides an example of the former, while *Bob Jones University v. United States* illustrates the latter.[55] After the United States revoked Bob Jones University's tax-exempt status on grounds that the school operated on racist policies, the university challenged the decision, asserting that its policies reflected religious, not racial, beliefs. At conference, Burger said, "Does . . . [the tax] statute embody this? I think it does. [But I] wouldn't reach on equal protection argument." In other words, the chief did not want the

Court to decide the case on the basis of the discrimination claim because, we suspect, he believed that he and the majority would part company on precisely what policy to adopt. Seen in this way, Burger's attempt at issue suppression represents yet another form of agenda manipulation.

Finally, our focus in this analysis of agenda manipulation is on the chief justice, even though conference discussions provide opportunities for any justice to manipulate the agenda. But, as Rehnquist once said, "What the conference shapes up like is pretty much what the chief justice makes it."[56] In other words, chiefs—perhaps because of the Court norm that they speak first at conference—have a unique opportunity to engage in this form of strategic behavior.

To what extent did Burger attempt to manipulate the agenda during conference? The data in Table 3-5 show that he did so in nearly 20 percent of the cases, with many mirroring his *Craig* effort. In *Wallace v. Jaffree*, for instance, Brennan's conference notes record Burger as attempting to inject a procedural dimension into the case, which involved the constitutionality of a moment of silence in public schools, along with some remarks on the merits.[57] According to Brennan, Burger said:

> Is there a case or controversy here? Assert they [are] telling students they may have a moment of silence. On merits, moment of silence completely neutral. Reference to "prayer" in statute doesn't change this for me. Statute serves secular purpose since students can use moment of silence for anything they please.

And we suspect that he did so for precisely the same reason as in *Craig:* realizing that the majority of his colleagues would disagree with his substantive position on the merits, he thought that a procedural dismissal was the best he could do.

In other cases Burger pressed for the avoidance of certain issues, typically as a way to attain his policy goals. *United States v. Leon* provides an interesting example. Here the U.S. government asked the Court to carve out a "good faith" exception to the exclusionary rule, which holds that evidence gathered illegally may not be admitted into court.[58] This exception would enable prosecutors to admit evidence police seized "in reasonable, good-faith reliance on a search warrant that is subsequently held to be defective."[59]

When the Court agreed to take *Leon,* there was little doubt that Burger would support the establishment of the good faith exception; in fact, many

Table 3-5
Agenda Manipulation Attempts by the Chief Justice

	1983 Term		Landmark Cases		Total	
	n	%	n	%	n	%
Attempt made	27	17.5	18	15.5	45	16.7
Attempt not made	127	82.5	98	84.5	225	83.3
Total	154		116		270	

Data Sources: Conference notes of Justices William J. Brennan Jr., Library of Congress; and Justice Lewis F. Powell Jr., Washington and Lee University School of Law.

Note: We included all 1983 cases for which either Brennan or Powell recorded a remark made by the chief justice and that were listed on the register of the Papers of Justice William J. Brennan, Library of Congress, with two exceptions: original cases and nonorally argued cases. Landmark cases are those listed in Elder Witt, *Guide to the U.S. Supreme Court,* 2d ed. (Washington, D.C.: Congressional Quarterly, 1990), 915-926, that were decided during the 1969-1985 terms, and for which Brennan or Powell recorded a remark made by the chief justice. For both samples, the unit of analysis was citation: if two or more cases were combined under one U.S. cite, we included only the lead case.

Coding Rules: We coded an agenda manipulation attempt by the chief justice as occurring when Brennan or Powell recorded in their notes of conference discussion the chief as attempting (1) to inject a procedural element such as standing or mootness into the discussion or (2) to avoid an issue or narrow the range of issues. For detailed coding rules and the data, navigate to: *http://www.artsci.wustl.edu/~polisci/epstein/choices/.*

thought he would go further and adopt a position that several states had urged on the Court: eradicate the exclusionary rule altogether.[60] Surely, this was the chief's preference, as he had implied in a 1971 dissent.[61] He had also made his thoughts clear in a concurrence in judgment in *Stone v. Powell,* which he had circulated to the full Court but modified significantly before publishing as a regular concurrence:

> [I]t seems clear to me that the exclusionary rule has been operative long enough to demonstrate its futility and that the time has come to modify its reach if no more. Over the years, the strains imposed by reality have led the Court to vacillate as to the rationale for deliberate exclusion of truth from the fact-finding process. The rhetoric has varied with the rationale, to the point where it has become a doctrinaire result in search of validating reasons. . . .

> The exclusionary rule had its genesis in the natural desire to protect private papers. From this origin, the rule has now been carried to the point of excluding evidence from the body of a homicide victim.
> It is time to change. [62]

Yet, at the conference at which the justices discussed *Leon,* Brennan recorded Burger as saying:

> Adopt good faith. [But] would be disaster to write anything that might be read as wiping out [the] exclusionary rule. [We] must write tightly to avoid that.

Why would Burger take a position in the *Leon* conference discussion so at odds with his sincere preference over the exclusionary rule? The answer, we believe, is obvious: Burger thought that he could attract sufficient support for the establishment of a good faith exception only by taking the eradication of the rule off the table. Creating that exception was less preferable to Burger than simply eradicating the rule, but, given the preferences of the other justices and the actions he expected them to take, it was the best he could do. He therefore engaged in sophisticated behavior to manipulate the agenda as a way of achieving a more preferred outcome.

Certainly, as the data in Table 3-5 suggest, this behavior was not unusual for Burger, nor was the chief the only justice who attempted to manipulate the agenda. The others, as we noted, also have opportunities to engage in agenda manipulation, and several seemed prone to take advantage of them. Consider, for example, Brennan's efforts in *Hudson v. Palmer,* in which the Court addressed whether the guarantees in the Fourth Amendment against illegal searches and seizures apply to prisoners.[63] Brennan's clerk prepared a conference memorandum on the substance of the case, but at the bottom of the memo, the justice typed a note to himself: "If other [justices] want to reach the substantive due process allegations raised by the inmate before this Court, it should be noted that the issue was never presented below." Brennan was attempting to engage in some issue manipulation of his own; because he believed that the Court would adopt a position adverse to his on the due process allegation, he wanted to eliminate it from consideration.

Such efforts do not always work, as Burger's lack of success in *Craig* and *Wallace* indicate. But when they do, the implications for public policy can be significant, as demonstrated by Burger's efforts in *Leon* and Brennan's in

Palmer. Had Burger *not* attempted to suppress the exclusionary rule issue in *Leon,* it might not have been possible (as he probably suspected) to secure a Court in favor of the good faith exception. By strategically narrowing the agenda to eliminate an issue that would have caused splintering among the justices, Burger paved the way for a fundamental change in search and seizure law: the establishment of a major exception to the exclusionary rule. Brennan's efforts also affected the development of law. While the substantive due process issue apparently did not arise during conference discussion of *Palmer,* it did come up during the circulation stage. Burger's initial opinion for the Court held that "an unauthorized intentional deprivation of property by a State employee does not constitute a violation of the Fourteenth Amendment if a meaningful postdeprivation remedy for the loss is available." Brennan asked Burger to revise the sentence by inserting the following phrase before the words *Fourteenth Amendment:* "the procedural requirements of the Due Process Clause of the. . . ." "By adding [these] words," Brennan wrote to the chief, "it will be clearer that we are not addressing privacy or other due process guarantees of the Fourteenth Amendment that do not depend upon procedural requirements." [aa] The chief made the requested change, giving Brennan a small victory in a case otherwise decided against his interests.[bb]

Finally, it is worth noting, our analysis has focused on the discussion stage, but there is evidence indicating that justices occasionally continue their efforts to interject procedural dimensions after conference to manipulate the final opinion. Two examples, one from the Burger Court, the other from the Rehnquist Court, make the point. The first case, *Board of*

---

aa. Brennan gave Burger another reason for making the change—Burger could possibly lose the signature of Blackmun if he did not. As Brennan put it, "You will recall that [the substantive due process issue] was one of the concerns that led Harry [Blackmun] to write separately in *Parratt"* [*v. Taylor,* 451 U.S. 527 (1981)]. Memorandum from Justice Brennan to chief justice, 6/7/84, re: 82-1630, *Hudson v. Palmer.*

bb. The Court held that although some constitutional guarantees apply to prisoners, others do not because imprisonment by its very nature necessitates the loss of rights, among them the guarantees contained in the Fourth Amendment. Brennan, along with Stevens, Marshall, and Blackmun, agreed with the majority that "the imperatives of prison administration require random searches of prison cells." But they disagreed with the view that prisoners lose their Fourth Amendment protection altogether. See *Hudson v. Palmer,* 468 U.S. 517 at 541 (1984).

Education, Island Trees Union Free School District v. Pico, asked whether the First Amendment prohibits a school board from removing books from a school library that it deems inappropriate or vulgar.[64] When Brennan—the author of the Court's opinion from which Burger had prepared a dissent—told the chief justice that he wanted to announce the decision before the plaintiff graduated from high school, he reminded Burger of a possible procedural "loophole": mootness. Indeed, in response to Brennan's request, Burger wrote, "Is it not a bit odd that the Court strains so mightily to get down a plurality opinion on an important constitutional question 24-40 hours before it is mooted?" Burger also added a footnote in his circulating dissent, noting the mootness problem, which elicited an uncharacteristically harsh response from Brennan:

> As for the potential question of mootness in this case, we have *all* known about that question since at least March 2, the date of oral argument. And it has been perfectly plain from the onset that this case was one of those important ones that normally come down in the last week of our Term—that is, in June. In short, we have all possessed all of the information pertinent to this case for many months, and we resolved to decide the case based on that information. *In my view, nothing has changed since then except that time has passed—and that you, who voted to grant, are now in dissent.*[65]

In the example from the Rehnquist Court, Justice Marshall's attempt to interject a procedural dimension into *United States v. Salerno* mirrored Burger's effort in *Pico.*[66] At issue in *Salerno* was the Bail Reform Act of 1984, which authorizes federal judges to deny bail to defendants to "assure . . . the safety of any other person and the community." The conference vote was 6 (Rehnquist, White, Blackmun, Powell, O'Connor, and Scalia) to 3 (Brennan, Marshall, and Stevens) to uphold the law, but Chief Justice Rehnquist, who was writing the opinion, had a difficult time keeping the majority coalition together. At one point, O'Connor threatened to concur in judgment, and Scalia wanted changes as well. Just when it appeared that Rehnquist had his Court—all members of the majority vote coalition joined the chief's third draft—Marshall circulated the following memo:

> In connection with my research for the dissent in this case, I have been informed that in affidavits filed in the United States District Court . . . the Government discloses that appellee Vincent Cafaro became a cooperating witness in September 1986. Furthermore . . . "the Government consented to Mr. Cafaro's temporary release *on bail.*" This statement is difficult to

reconcile with the statement in the Government's Reply Brief in this Court . . . that "Cafaro was temporarily released for medical treatment" but was "still subject to the pretrial detention order."

    These recent disclosures by the Government . . . suggest to me that there may not have been a live controversy in this case at the time of the argument.[67]

Stevens immediately chimed in, suggesting that the Court look into this situation, while Rehnquist responded with his own memo, expressing his belief that there is no "substantial question of mootness or collusion presented in this case."[68] The matter was settled a few days later when Powell expressed agreement with Rehnquist's view. But Marshall did raise the procedural issue in his dissent, and the chief justice added a footnote to respond to Marshall's claim that "only by flatly ignoring [the live controversy issue] is the majority able to maintain the pretense that it has jurisdiction to decide the question which it is in such a hurry to reach."

STRATEGIC OPINION WRITING

In *Keyes v. Denver School District,* involving a school desegregation plan, Brennan circulated a majority opinion that distinguished between de jure segregation, which occurs as a result of law or government action, and de facto or actual segregation.[69] But, in an uncirculated memo, perhaps meant for his clerks, Brennan wrote:

> At our original conference discussion of this case, Lewis [Powell] first expressed his view that the de jure/de facto distinction should be discarded. I told him then that I too was deeply troubled by the distinction. Nevertheless, it appeared that a majority of the Court was committed to the view that the distinction should be maintained, and I therefore drafted *Keyes* within the framework established in our earlier cases. . . . I would be happy to recast the opinion and jettison the distinction if a majority of the Court was prepared to do so.[70]

In light of this memo, Brennan's first draft in *Keyes* provides an example of another form of strategic behavior: sophisticated opinion writing. Brennan sincerely wanted to write an opinion that would have eradicated the distinction between de facto and de jure segregation, but did not believe he could marshal a Court for that position. *Craig* provides another.

There Brennan wrote in sophisticated fashion to attain the best possible outcome (heightened scrutiny) and to avoid his least favored alternative (rational basis).

That Brennan engaged in sophisticated writing in these cases is not a surprise. Given the requirement of a majority for the establishment of precedent and the fact that it would be difficult to imagine any case in which the opinion writer fully agreed with the majority on every point, all opinions of the Court are, to greater and lesser degrees, the product of strategic calculations.

Indeed, Powell made this point explicit in a private memo he sent to Chief Justice Burger after conference on *Nixon v. Fitzgerald,* a case asking whether the president had absolute immunity from civil damage suits for official actions taken during his term.[71] The justices met twice to discuss this case, but remained divided on how to dispose of it. Powell nicely summed up the situation in a memo to the chief justice: "Bill Brennan and Harry [Blackmun] would DIG the *Nixon* case. Byron [White] and Thurgood [Marshall] would dispose of it narrowly as a case in which no private cause of action could be implied, limiting the analysis to the special relationship of government employment." Burger, Rehnquist, and O'Connor wanted to hold that the president has absolute immunity from damage suit liability. Stevens and Powell agreed with Burger, Rehnquist, and O'Connor, but also wanted to address the cause of action question. As Powell put it, "It is evident that a Court opinion is not assured if each of us remains with our first preference votes." He went on to say, "As I view the *Nixon* case as uniquely requiring a Court opinion, I am now prepared to defer to the wishes of you, Bill Rehnquist, and Sandra [O'Connor] and prepare a draft opinion holding that the President has absolute immunity from damage suit liability." [72] Powell, then, was willing to give up his sincere preference for the sake of obtaining an opinion of the Court—an outcome he viewed as essential, but one that would have been difficult to obtain given the various divisions of opinion.

When there is a conference consensus and opinion writers attempt to diverge substantially from it by attempting to write their sincere preferences into law, however, rebuffs can be swift—as Burger found out in *Palmore v. Sidoti.*[73] Among the questions this case presented was whether trial court judges can take race into account when deciding on child custody arrangements. The Court could have offered the following responses: (1) it is permissible to take race into account; (2) it is permissible to take race into account so long as race is not the dispositive factor; or (3) it is never permissible to take race into account. Stressing during conference that the "racial factor was [the] dominant if not exclusive" grounds on which the trial judge had rested his order, Chief Justice Burger seemed to favor the second approach. The majority, however, was closer to the third. Nonetheless, Burger circulated an opinion reflecting his sincere preferences—to which Brennan quickly responded:

> My recollection of the consensus reached at Conference differs slightly from that reflected in your draft opinion. . . . As I understood the discussion, it was agreed that race would be an improper consideration in the child custody context, irrespective of whether it was the "dispositive" factor in the Court's decision.
>
>   To this end, I hope you can make some minor revisions so that I could join your opinion.[74]

Burger conceded the point, thereby preserving the unanimity that had prevailed at conference.[cc]

Palmore, Keyes, Craig, and many other cases illustrate the extent to which opinion writers will put aside their most preferred position to generate a definitive ruling of the Court—and one that represents the best they feel they can do under the circumstances.[dd]

---

cc. Justices *can* succeed in thwarting conference consensus; if that were not the case, they would never attempt to do so. An example is *Goldfarb v. Virginia State Bar,* 421 U.S. 773 (1975). The conference agreed that the holding—namely, the Sherman Anti-Trust Act applies to the legal profession—should not be applied retroactively. Before he circulated the first draft of his opinion, however, Burger had a change of heart. In a long memorandum to conference, he outlined the reasons why the antitrust act "requires there be a no 'prospective-only' limitation." Memorandum from Chief Justice Burger to conference, 4/24/75, re: 74-70, *Goldfarb v. Virginia State Bar.* And this was enough to convince his colleagues to go along.

   Why did Burger succeed in this case but fail in others? More generally, under what circumstances and through what kinds of appeals can justices persuade their colleagues to change their minds? These are important questions that Walter F. Murphy started to address in *Elements of Judicial Strategy* (Chicago: University of Chicago Press, 1964) and that we hope to reopen in future research.

   dd. *Segura v. United States,* 468 U.S. 796 (1984), a case involving the exclusionary rule, is perhaps the quintessential example of sophisticated opinion writing. After Burger circulated the first draft of his majority opinion, he watched as three members of the majority coalition defected to the other side and knew that a fourth (O'Connor) was considering a concurrence in judgment only. To keep a Court, he produced *two* new drafts—one that was close to the first version and another that

More systematic data also shore up the frequency of strategic writing during the circulation process: opinion writers produce 3.2 drafts in the average case and nearly 4 in disputes that lead to landmark rulings.[75] These figures suggest that justices are willing to recast their opinions in ways that do not necessarily reflect the preferences revealed in the initial draft of their writing, but they do not tell us whether sophisticated opinion writing has any importance for the policy that the Court produces. Do many opinions undergo significant change in their rationale or in the policy they generate? Or are *Palmore, Keyes,* and *Craig* exceptions?

To answer these important questions—after all, the most fundamental and significant manifestations of strategic interaction are the major alterations in the policy the Court produces or in the rationale the majority uses to decide a case—we compared the policy and rationale adopted in the opinion writer's first circulation with that contained in the published opinion. The samples are those we used throughout this chapter: cases decided during the 1983 term and those that led to landmark rulings during the Burger Court era. Table 3-6 displays the results. As we can see, in more than 50 percent of the cases a significant change—from the first draft through the published version—occurred in the language of the opinion. Changes were more likely to occur in landmark cases than in less important cases (65 percent versus 45 percent). This finding is especially interesting because it suggests that precedents set in a fair share of the Burger Court's most important cases would have been quite different in the absence of sophisticated opinion writing.

Table 3-7 drives home the point by detailing policy changes that occurred in landmark cases. Some of the alterations are not as dramatic as others, and the kinds of changes differ from case to case, as do the reasons for the shifts. Nevertheless, virtually all reflect strategic calculations by opinion writers about the preferences of their colleagues and the actions they expected them to take and, occasionally, about the preferences of other relevant actors and their expected actions. *Swann v. Charlotte-Mecklenburg Board of Education* (1971) is a good example. From the beginning of this case, which concerned a school desegregation plan, Burger had

---

advanced a theory "perhaps preferred by Sandra, with whom I have conferred"—that he circulated only to the remaining members of the majority. Although he said in the memo that he preferred Draft A, he also expressed the view that he was "willing to abide by the wishes of 'four.' " With some minor adjustments, Draft B became the judgment of the Court.

TABLE 3-6
Major Changes in Opinions

	1983 Term		Landmark Cases		Total	
	n	%	n	%	n	%
Absence of change	86	54.8	44	35.2	130	46.1
Presence of change	71	45.2	81	64.8	152	53.9
Total	157		125		282	

Data Sources: U.S. Reports; case files of Justices William J. Brennan Jr. and Thurgood Marshall, Library of Congress; and Justice Lewis F. Powell Jr., Washington and Lee University School of Law.

Note: We included all 1983 cases listed on the register of the Papers of Justice William J. Brennan, Library of Congress, with two exceptions: original cases and nonorally argued cases. Landmark cases are those listed in Elder Witt, *Guide to the U.S. Supreme Court,* 2d ed. (Washington, D.C.: Congressional Quarterly, 1990), 915-926, that were decided during the 1969-1985 terms. For both samples, the unit of analysis was citation: if two or more cases were combined under one U.S. cite, we included only the lead case.

Coding Rules: We compared the drafts of the opinion (majority, plurality, per curiam) contained in the Brennan case files, double checked against the Marshall/Powell files, with the final opinion published in the *U.S. Reports.* (The justices indicate the pages on which they made changes and whether the changes were merely "stylistic," which facilitated the coding process.)
Virtually all opinions undergo changes in language. Because we were interested in major changes in rationale or policy, we noted the presence of change if (1) a case was overruled in the first draft but not in the final opinion (or vice versa); (2) the case was reassigned to a member of the minority conference vote coalition after the first draft was circulated; (3) the case was summarily disposed of but later was decided by a full opinion; (4) a major section of the opinion was deleted or added between the first draft and final publication; (5) the published opinion articulated a test, policy, or standard of law different from what appeared in earlier drafts; or (6) the published opinion invoked a rationale or justification different from what appeared in earlier drafts. We excluded minor or stylistic changes and changes that occurred during the circulation process but were omitted in the final version. For the data, navigate to: *http://www.artsci.wustl.edu/~polisci/epstein/choices/.*

imparted to his colleagues the need for unanimity, as a memo accompanying his first opinion draft makes clear:

> I am sure it is not necessary to emphasize the importance of our attempting to reach an accommodation and a common position, and I would urge that we consult or exchange views by memorandum or both.
> Separate opinions, expressing divergent views or conclusion will, I hope,

TABLE 3-7
Policy Changes in Select Landmark Cases

Case	Policy in First Draft	Reaction to First Draft	Policy in Published Opinion
Argersinger v. Hamlin, 407 U.S. 25 (1972)	Douglas's first draft held that individuals accused of a crime that carries with it the possibility of imprisonment are entitled to an attorney, even if imprisonment is virtually never imposed for the crime.	The first draft garnered almost no immediate support from the members of the conference majority. Burger said he could not join it. Stewart wrote a memo to Douglas setting out a few "difficulties," including the standard Douglas adopted. Stewart wanted to adopt an "actual imprisonment" approach.	The published opinion enumerated the actual imprisonment standard: no person can be imprisoned "for any offense . . . unless he was represented by counsel at his trial."
Ballew v. Georgia, 435 U.S. 223 (1978)	Blackmun's original draft included a long section on why the Court's decision—holding unconstitutional five-person juries—would not be applied retroactively.	Three members of the eight-person conference majority took issue with the retroactive holding. Blackmun wrote to Stewart: "Bill Brennan and John [Stevens] have now indicated a preference to say nothing about retroactivity. You are inclined to feel that we should decide in *Ballew* that the decision is retroactive. This is enough of an indication for me to drop [that portion] of the opinion."	The final opinion deleted the section on retroactivity, meaning that the Court chose not to address the issue.

Garcia v. SAMTA, 469 U.S. 528 (1985)	The conference split 4–4; Burger eventually cast his vote to affirm and assigned the opinion to Blackmun. Blackmun produced a first draft that reversed but did not overturn *National League of Cities v. Usery*, 426 U.S. 833 (1976), in which the Court struck down an amendment to the Fair Labor Standards Act.	After Blackmun circulated his draft, Burger wrote a memo to Blackmun and to conference saying that he thought the case should be reargued. This generated a long response from Stevens, who had voted to reverse: "Your motion to reargue this case prompts me to suggest that perhaps it would be useful to have a conference discussion of the standard that should be applied to such motions." He gave "four alternative grounds for reargument," none of which covered *Garcia*. But Stevens did not prevail, and the case was reargued.	After the case was reargued, Blackmun wrote a new draft that overturned *National League of Cities*.
H. L. v. Matheson, 451 U.S. 398 (1981)	In his draft majority opinion, Marshall struck down a Utah law requiring doctors to "notify if possible" a minor's parents prior to performing an abortion. He asserted that a pregnant minor always has the right to decide for herself whether to obtain an abortion free from any parental notification.	When Stewart and Powell (two of the five who had voted with the majority in conference) wrote a draft of a proposed opinion for the Court, which upheld the Utah law.	Burger's draft became the majority opinion.

(Table continues)

TABLE 3-7 (Continued)

Case	Policy in First Draft	Reaction to First Draft	Policy in Published Opinion
Michelin Tire Corporation v. Wages, 423 U.S. 276 (1976)	Brennan's first draft discussed the question of whether a nondiscriminatory ad valorem property tax was prohibited by the Import and Export Clause. Allowing the tax would require a reexamination of *Low v. Austin*, 13 Wall. 29 (1872), which held that it was prohibited. Brennan thought that overruling *Low* would "have far-reaching consequences," although he was prepared to do so.	After a majority of the justices expressed interest in Brennan's notion of overruling *Low*, Brennan circulated a "completely rewritten" opinion, taking that step.	The final opinion overruled *Low v. Austin*.
Roe v. Wade, 410 U.S. 113 (1973)	Blackmun's first draft struck the Texas abortion ordinance on the narrowest possible grounds, vagueness, asserting that the law's "sole criterion for exemption as 'saving the life of the mother' is insufficiently informative to the physician." The draft avoided the core constitutional questions of	Upon reading Blackmun's first draft, Brennan and Douglas asked him to recast it. But Burger reinitiated efforts to have the case (along with *Doe v. Bolton*, 410 U.S. 179) reargued. After considerable debate, the Court went along with Burger's suggestion. In the meantime, Blackmun continued to revise his initial circulation.	The final opinion struck the Texas law as an infringement of the Fourteenth Amendment's concept of personal liberty, which "is broad enough to encompass a woman's decision whether or not to terminate a pregnancy."

individual liberty and "freedom from bodily restraint," that the conference majority had framed.

Swann v. Charlotte-Mecklenburg Board of Education, 402 U.S. 1 (1971)

Despite the fact that only Justices Black and Blackmun fully agreed with his position—that a lower court had gone too far in attempting to remedy a segregated school system—Burger assigned the majority opinion to himself. His first draft reflected his conference position and remanded the case.

A memorandum Douglas wrote for his own records says: "When [Burger's] opinion at last came around reversing the District Court, the six [of us] were astounded. I wrote a separate opinion. Brennan did; Marshall did; and finally Stewart did. Brennan and I saw Stewart and made several changes, indicating that if he made them he'd have a court opinion. So he made the changes. Instead of circulating, he went to the Chief Justice saying he thought he had a court for the opposed view. That started a slow turn-around that eventually ended in the unanimous opinion of April 20, 1971." Brennan's case files substantiate Douglas's account. The one major exception is that Burger's first draft remanded rather than reversed the cases.

The published opinion fully repudiated Burger's original approach and disposition and provided judges with a great deal of remedial power to dismantle segregated school districts.

(Table continues)

TABLE 3-7 (Continued)

Case	Policy in First Draft	Reaction to First Draft	Policy in Published Opinion
Tennessee v. Garner, 471 U.S. 1 (1985)	White's original draft held that police may shoot a fleeing suspect if the suspect is "armed with a lethal weapon or if there is probable cause to believe the suspect has committed a violent crime."	Shortly after the draft was circulated, Brennan asked White to modify the holding. At the time Brennan requested the change, only three justices had joined White's opinion; a dissent was circulating; and Burger, who had voted with the majority at conference, informed White that he was, for the moment, deferring a decision to join.	The final opinion for the Court adopted a modified version of Brennan's suggestion and held that reason to believe that the suspect is armed is not in itself sufficient grounds to use deadly force to prevent escape.
United States v. Nixon, 418 U.S. 683 (1974)	During conference discussion, the justices agreed that some form of an executive privilege exists, but that it is neither absolute nor unreviewable by courts. Yet Burger's first draft was closer to the interests of the executive than the conference had desired: it suggested that presidents might win their claims of executive privilege if "core functions" are shown to be at stake.	The other justices would not go along with the "core functions" notion because they believed it could be used to support Nixon's executive privilege claim. Stewart redrafted this portion of Burger's decision; other justices worked on the balance of the Burger draft, which they also viewed as weak.	The published version—largely Stewart's draft—dropped the "core functions" notion.

| *Wallace v. Jaffree*, 472 U.S. 38 (1985) | Stevens's initial drafts for the majority in this case, involving the constitutionality of a moment of silence in public schools, held that "the First Amendment requires that a statute must be invalidated if it is entirely motivated by a purpose to advance religion." | When a member of the five-person conference majority—O'Connor—circulated an opinion concurring in judgment, Stevens was worried about losing his opinion of the Court; without O'Connor's support, his opinion would amount to a mere judgment or even a dissent if O'Connor joined with the opposing camp. So when Powell, who had been in the conference minority, suggested a change in the Stevens circulation, Stevens jumped at the chance of converting his vote. He wrote in a memo to those who had already joined his opinion: "Although there is nothing definite at this point, I think there is a strong possibility that this change would enable Lewis to change his vote and to join our opinion." | The final opinion for the Court modified the language the way Powell wanted: "For even though a statute that is motivated in part by a religious purpose may satisfy the first criterion [that the statute have a secular legislative purpose], the First Amendment requires that a statute must be invalidated if it is entirely motivated by a purpose to advance religion." |

Data Sources: Case files of Justices William J. Brennan Jr., William O. Douglas, and Thurgood Marshall, Library of Congress; and Justice Lewis F. Powell Jr., Washington and Lee University School of Law; and Bernard Schwartz, *The Ascent of Pragmatism* (Reading, Mass.: Addison–Wesley, 1990).

be deferred until we have exhausted all other efforts to reach a common view. I am sure we must all agree that the problems of remedy are at least as difficult and important as the great Constitutional principle of *Brown*.[76]

In fact, it was not "necessary to emphasize" the point: Burger's colleagues understood that a unanimous opinion in such a major case would have a greater chance of remaining undisturbed by external political actors than a divided opinion. The value of unanimity was one of the lessons of *Brown v. Board of Education;* and it is also the moral of scholarly research on the Court, suggesting that rulings on which the entire Court agrees are less susceptible to overturning and more likely to be followed.[77]

Nonetheless, the reaction to Burger's first draft did not bode well for a unanimous outcome. As Douglas later put it, most of the justices were "astounded" by Burger's rationale, which reflected the position that Burger and only two other justices, Blackmun and Black, had expressed at conference, and four others (Douglas, Stewart, Marshall, and Brennan) began to draft separate opinions. Finally, after Stewart went to Burger to inform him that he had more support for his view than did the chief, Burger circulated new drafts designed to avoid division—including, as he put it, adopting "points that [are] in conflict with my own position."[78]

Seen in this way, *Swann* provides a quintessential example of sophisticated opinion writing. It is difficult, we think, to read about this case or to examine Tables 3-6 and 3-7 and fail to reach the conclusion that this form of strategic behavior exists, as do the others we have considered. Simply put, the data we have presented and the cases we have recounted throughout this chapter show that the justices are, in fact, strategic actors—they bargain and accommodate, they think prospectively, and they alter their opinions—and that these behaviors have a nontrivial effect on the policy the Court ultimately produces.

We also hope that the material in this chapter has begun to make an important point about the context in which justices make their strategic calculations: it is shaped by rules, norms, and conventions. To see this, we only have to recall the role of:

- the rule requiring a majority for precedent in inducing strategic opinion writing, as in *Keyes v. Denver School District;*
- the norm that the chief justice speaks first at conference in creating opportunities for agenda manipulation, as exemplified by *United States v. Leon;*

- the convention of unanimity in important cases in limiting the range of choices and in encouraging strategic opinion writing, with *Swann v. Charlotte-Mecklenburg Board of Education* one illustration.

These are just a sample of the many institutions that structure the context in which justices make their choices—choices that we have now seen reflect their strategic calculations. In the next chapter, we consider others, along with a more general look at institutions and the critical role they play in the decision-making process.

ENDNOTES

1. *Frontiero v. Richardson,* 411 U.S. 677 (1973).

2. See James D. Morrow, *Game Theory for Political Scientists* (Princeton, N.J.: Princeton University Press, 1994), 5, 112.

3. See, for example, Gregory A. Caldeira, John R. Wright, and Christopher J. W. Zorn, "Strategic Voting and Gatekeeping in the Supreme Court" (paper presented at the 1996 annual meeting of the American Political Science Association, San Francisco). The authors suggest that justices occasionally cast votes against hearing cases they would sincerely like to decide—a clear example of sophisticated behavior.

4. An important exception is H. W. Perry, *Deciding to Decide* (Cambridge: Harvard University Press, 1991).

5. We thank Gregory A. Caldeira for supplying these figures.

6. Opinion of Justice Stevens respecting the denial of the petition for writ of certiorari in *Singleton v. Commissioner of Internal Revenue,* 439 U.S. 940 at 945 (1978).

7. Quoted in Perry, *Deciding to Decide,* 171, 177. Perry went on to note, "Sometimes they are published as a way of communicating to future litigants."

8. Opinion of Justice Stevens respecting the denial of the petition for writ of certiorari in *Singleton v. Commissioner of Internal Revenue,* 439 U.S. 940 at 945 (1978).

9. *Bowers v. Hardwick,* 478 U.S. 186 (1986).

10. The D.C. case was *Dronenburg v. Zech,* 741 F. 2d 1388 (1984). Justice White, dissenting from denial of certiorari in *Bowers v. Hardwick,* 85-150. Unpublished opinion, circulated to the conference 10/17/85.

11. Harold J. Spaeth, *United States Supreme Court Judicial Database* (Ann Arbor, Mich.: Inter-University Consortium for Political and Social Research, 1997, updated annually). Published as study no. 9422.

12. *New York v. Quarles,* 467 U.S. 649 (1984); and *Bose Corp. v. Consumers Union of the United States,* 466 U.S. 485 (1984).

13. Justice Rehnquist, dissenting from denial of certiorari in *New York v. Quarles,* 82-1213. Unpublished opinion, circulated to the conference 5/11/83.

14. *Pulliam v. Allen,* 466 U.S. 522 (1984).

15. *United Jewish Organizations of Williamsburgh v. Carey,* 430 U.S. 144 (1977).

16. See *South Carolina v. Katzenbach,* 383 U.S. 301 (1966).

17. Memorandum of Justice White to the conference, 12/2/76, re: 75-104, *United Jewish Organizations v. Carey.*

18. Memorandum from Justice Brennan to Justice White, 12/9/76, re: 75-104, *United Jewish Organizations v. Carey.*

19. Memorandum from Chief Justice Burger to Justice White, 1/3/77, re: 75-104, *United Jewish Organizations v. Carey.*

20. *Milliken v. Bradley,* 418 U.S. 717 (1974).

21. Memorandum from Justice Powell to Chief Justice Burger, re: *Detroit School Case.*

22. Our emphasis. Memoranda of 12/13/83, re: nos. 82-818 & 82-852, *NLRB v. Bildisco & Bildisco;* 6/5/80, re: no. 78-1007, *Fullilove v. Klutznick;* and 12/30/70, re: no. 281, *Swann v. Charlotte-Mecklenburg* and no. 349, *Charlotte-Mecklenburg Board v. Swann.*

23. See, for example, Walter F. Murphy, *Elements of Judicial Strategy* (Chicago: University of Chicago Press, 1964); J. Woodford Howard, "On the Fluidity of Judicial Choice," 62 *American Political Science Review* (1968): 43–56; David J. Danelski, "The Influence of the Chief Justice in the Decisional Process of the Supreme Court," in *American Court Systems,* ed. Sheldon Goldman and Austin Sarat (San Francisco: Freeman, 1978).

24. *United States v. Morgan,* 307 U.S. 183 (1939). Memorandum from Justice Douglas to Justice Stone, 5/8/39, re: no. 221, *United States v. Morgan.*

25. The 1986 term landmark cases are: *Tison v. Arizona* (481 U.S. 137), *McCleskey v. Kemp* (481 U.S. 279), *Tashijan v. Republican Party* (479 U.S. 208), *United States v. Paradise* (480 U.S. 149), *Johnson v. Transportation Agency* (480 U.S. 616), *Edwards v. Aguillard* (482 U.S. 578), *Shaare Tefila v. Cobb* (481 U.S. 615), *Saint Francis College v. Al-Khazraji* (481 U.S. 604), and *United States v. Salerno* (481 U.S. 739). *Edwards* was the only case that failed to generate a bargaining statement. List compiled by Elder Witt, *Guide to the U.S. Supreme Court,* 2d ed. (Washington, D.C.: Congressional Quarterly, 1990), 927–928.

26. See also Bernard Schwartz, *The Unpublished Opinions of the Warren Court* (New York: Oxford University Press, 1985); and Schwartz, *The Unpublished Opinions of the Burger Court* (New York: Oxford University Press, 1988).

27. Memorandum from Chief Justice Burger to Justice Stewart, 4/4/81, re: 80-429, *County of Washington v. Gunther.*

28. *Furman v. Georgia,* 408 U.S. 238 (1972).

29. Charles Evans Hughes, *The Supreme Court of the United States* (New York: Columbia University Press, 1928), 68.

30. Stephen L. Wasby, *The Supreme Court in the Federal Judicial System* (Chicago: Nelson-Hall, 1993), 196–197.

31. That evidence came largely from Gregory A. Caldeira and John R. Wright, "Organized Interests and Agenda-Setting in the U.S. Supreme Court," 82 *American Political Science Review* (1988): 1109–27.

32. See Robert L. Boucher Jr. and Jeffrey A. Segal, "Supreme Court Justices as Strategic Decision Makers: Aggressive Grants and Defensive Denials on the Vinson Court," 57 *Journal of Politics* (1995): 824–837.

33. See John F. Krol and Saul Brenner, "Strategies on Certiorari Voting on the U.S. Supreme Court," 43 *Western Political Quarterly* (1990): 335–342.

34. Perry, *Deciding to Decide,* 208.

35. See, for example, Boucher and Segal, "Supreme Court Justices as Strategic Decision Makers," 825–826.

36. Quoted in Perry, *Deciding to Decide,* 200.

37. *Wiegand v. United States,* 484 U.S. 856, *cert. denied* (1987).

38. Our emphasis. Certiorari memorandum from unnamed clerk to Justice Marshall in 87-310, *Wiegand v. United States.*

39. Caldeira, Wright, and Zorn, "Strategic Voting and Gatekeeping in the Supreme Court."

40. See, for example, *Mora v. McNamara,* 389 U.S. 934 (1967). Example cited in Doris Marie Provine, *Case Selection in the United States Supreme Court* (Chicago: University of Chicago Press, 1980), 54.

41. *Brown v. Board of Education,* 347 U.S. 483 (1954); *Naim v. Naim,* 350 U.S. 891 (1955).

42. Quoted in Provine, *Case Selection,* 59–60.

43. Quoted in ibid., 61.

44. *Holmes v. City of Atlanta,* 350 U.S. 879 (1955). See also Gerald N. Rosenberg, *The Hollow Hope* (Chicago: University of Chicago Press, 1991), 74–75. He notes: "In the wake of congressional hostility the Court did not vigorously follow the logic and power of *Brown.* While not backtracking . . . it avoided cases and sidestepped issues."

45. Lee Epstein and Jeffrey A. Segal, "Assessing Cross-Institutional Constraints on Supreme Court Agenda Setting" (paper presented at the 1997 Conference on the Scientific Study of Judicial Politics, Atlanta, Ga.).

46. See William N. Eskridge, "Overriding Supreme Court Statutory Interpretation Decisions," 101 *Yale Law Journal* (1991): 331–417; Charles A. Johnson and Bradley C. Canon, *Judicial Policies: Implementation and Impact* (Washington, D.C.: CQ Press, 1984); and Thomas R. Marshall, *Public Opinion and the Supreme Court* (Boston: Unwin Hyman, 1989).

47. Hearings on S. 2176 before the Senate Judiciary Committee, 74th Cong., 1st sess., 9–10 (1935) (statement of Justice Van Devanter).

48. Provine, *Case Selection,* 85.

49. Caldeira and Wright, "Agenda Setting," 1121.

50. Provine, *Case Selection,* 82.

51. Caldeira and Wright, "Agenda Setting," 1121.

52. See Steven Puro, "The Role of Amicus Curiae in the United States Supreme Court, 1920–1966" (Ph.D. diss., State University of New York at Buffalo, 1971); Jeffrey A. Segal, "Courts, Executives, and Legislatures," in *The American Courts,* ed. John B. Gates and Charles A. Johnson (Washington, D.C.: CQ Press, 1991).

53. Kevin T. McGuire and Barbara Palmer show that issue suppression takes place in about 50 percent of all cases. See "Issue Fluidity on the U.S. Supreme Court," 89 *American Political Science Review* (1995): 691–702.

54. For more on this general point, see Nancy Maveety, *Justice Sandra Day O'Connor: Strategist on the Supreme Court* (Lanham, Md.: Rowman & Littlefield Publishers, 1996).

55. *Bob Jones University v. United States,* 461 U.S. 574 (1983).

56. Quoted by David M. O'Brien in *Storm Center,* 4th ed. (New York: Norton, 1996), 228.

57. *Wallace v. Jaffree,* 472 U.S. 38 (1985).

58. *United States v. Leon,* 468 U.S. 897 (1984). *Mapp v. Ohio,* 367 U.S. 643 (1961), established the exclusionary rule.

59. Petition for a writ of certiorari, filed by the United States in *United States v. Leon,* no. 82-1771.

60. See brief of amici curiae filed by Kansas, Missouri, South Dakota, Wisconsin, and the Gulf & Great Plains Legal Foundation, in *United States v. Leon,* 82-1771.

61. See, for example, Chief Justice Burger's dissent in *Bivens v. Six Unknown Named Agents of the Federal Bureau of Narcotics,* 403 U.S. 388 (1971).

62. *Stone v. Powell,* 428 U.S. 465 (1976). The published concurrence reads as follows:

> [I]t seems clear to me that the exclusionary rule has been operative long enough to demonstrate its flaws. The time has come to modify its reach, even if it is retained for a small and limited category of cases.
>
> Over the years, the strains imposed by reality, in terms of the costs to society and the bizarre miscarriages of justice that have been experienced because of the exclusion of reliable evidence when the "constable blunders," have led the Court to vacillate as to the rationale for deliberate exclusion of truth from the fact-finding process. The rhetoric has varied with the rationale to the point where the rule has become a doctrinaire result in search of validating reasons. . . .
>
> From its genesis in the desire to protect private papers, the exclusionary rule has now been carried to the point of potentially excluding from evidence the traditional corpus delicti in a murder or kidnapping case.

Expansion of the reach of the exclusionary rule has brought Cardozo's grim prophecy in *People v. Defore* nearer to fulfillment [opinion ends with Justice Benjamin Cardozo's quote].

63. *Hudson v. Palmer,* 468 U.S. 517 (1984).

64. *Board of Education, Island Trees Union Free School District v. Pico,* 457 U.S. 853 (1982).

65. Our emphasis. Memorandum from Justice Brennan to Chief Justice Burger, 6/22/82, re: 80-2043, *Board of Education v. Pico—Possible Mootness Issue.*

66. *United States v. Salerno,* 481 U.S. 739 (1987).

67. Memorandum from Justice Marshall to the conference, 3/26/87, re: no. 86-87, *United States v. Salerno.*

68. Memorandum from Chief Justice Rehnquist to the conference, 3/26/87, re: no. 86-87, *United States v. Salerno.*

69. *Keyes v. Denver School District,* 413 U.S. 189 (1973).

70. Undated writing located in Brennan's *Keyes* case file.

71. *Nixon v. Fitzgerald,* 457 U.S. 731 (1982).

72. See memorandum from Justice Powell to Chief Justice Burger, 12/17/81, re: 78-1738, *Nixon v. Fitzgerald.*

73. *Palmore v. Sidoti,* 466 U.S. 429 (1984).

74. Memorandum from Justice Brennan to Chief Justice Burger, 3/20/84, re: 82-1734, *Palmore v. Sidoti.*

75. Lee Epstein and Jack Knight, "Documenting Strategic Interaction on the U.S. Supreme Court" (paper delivered at the 1995 annual meeting of the American Political Science Association, Chicago). For more on this general topic, see Paul J. Wahlbeck, James F. Spriggs II, and Forrest Maltzman, "Marshaling the Court: Bargaining and Accommodation on the U.S. Supreme Court," *American Journal of Political Science* (forthcoming).

76. Memorandum from the chief justice to conference, 12/8/70, re: 281, *Swann v. Charlotte-Mecklenburg Board of Education.*

77. See Eskridge, "Overriding Supreme Court Statutory Interpretation Decisions"; Johnson and Canon, *Judicial Policies;* and Marshall, *Public Opinion and the Supreme Court.*

78. Memorandum from the chief justice to conference, 1/11/71, re: 281, *Swann v. Charlotte-Mecklenburg Board of Education.*

CHAPTER FOUR

The Institutional Context I

In *Craig v. Boren* the specific question before the Court was whether an Oklahoma law that set different minimum ages for males and females for the purchase of beer constituted impermissible discrimination on the basis of sex. The more general question, however, was what would be the appropriate constitutional standard to apply in sex discrimination cases. This duality is a regular feature of Supreme Court cases. The justices must dispose of the particular conflict between the parties *and* establish general legal standards that will apply to society at large. The Court's decision in *Craig*, as we have documented, was a product of strategic bargaining among the nine justices, each of whom had his own preference as to how to resolve both the specific dispute and the general constitutional question.

The bargaining that occurred in *Craig*, however, was not unfettered. Rather, it took place within a *complex institutional framework*, meaning that sets of rules—institutions—structured the social interactions. To put it in more concrete terms, the policy-oriented justices involved in this dispute—indeed, in any dispute—needed to take account of three different sets of rules governing three different strategic relationships: (1) among the justices themselves, (2) between the Court and the other branches of government, and (3) between the Court and the American people.

Let us consider the first set of rules or institutions structuring the relations among the justices. That *Craig* came before the Court at all was due to the fact that at least four justices had agreed to hear it, a threshold for consideration set by an agenda-setting norm, the Rule of Four. After the case had been argued and the justices sat down in conference to consider it, the initial discussion was structured by a norm establishing the order in which the justices reveal their preliminary positions on the case. The opening discussion revealed a clear majority favoring Craig's position, but an array of opinions on the question of the most appropriate standard by which to adjudicate sex discrimination cases.

Once the discussion was over and the justices learned the preliminary preferences of their colleagues, they started the process of arriving at a collective resolution of the case. This process is also structured by the norms of the Court. One of the justices has to take initial responsibility for drafting an opinion that attempts to reconcile the various individual positions. A norm provides a method for selecting that justice: the first draft is assigned to someone who holds the preference of the majority of justices on the question of the specific disposition of the case. If the chief justice is in the majority, he assigns the case; if he is not in the majority, the senior justice on the majority side makes the assignment. In *Craig*, Justice Brennan, the senior justice in the majority, assigned the writing of the initial draft to himself, which gave him the chance to reconcile the various positions on the general constitutional question in terms as close as possible to his own preferred position.

Brennan's strategic task was structured by the differing institutional thresholds for resolving specific and general questions before the Court. If his only goal was to say whether the Oklahoma statute was constitutional, he need not obtain majority agreement on the larger question of what standard to apply. The Court could settle the case if a majority of justices voted in favor of one party, even if they disagreed over the reason why. If disposition were his only goal, therefore, Brennan could have written a first draft that strictly reflected his preference on the general constitutional question without worrying about the preferences of the other justices. If, however, he wanted to establish a general standard to govern future questions of the constitutionality of laws that distinguish between men and women, the norms for the establishment of precedent required him to craft his opinion so that at least four other justices would be willing to agree with him on the legal rationale of the case.

Seen in this way, *Craig* highlights some of the norms that govern the relations among Court members, but they are not the only institutional influences on justices' choices. Because justices seek to create general standards to govern society, they must also take account of the potential effects of other relevant actors, including elected officials and those outside of government. To understand the relationship between the Court and other government actors, recall the Chapter One discussion of the separation of powers/checks and balances system. We described how each branch can affect the attempts of the others to establish general rules of behavior. This is so because the efforts of actors within the branches are structured by both the explicit constitutional provisions governing the separation of powers and the implicit set of norms that have evolved to flesh out the details of this division of political authority, including judicial review—the power of courts to review and strike down government actions that are incompatible with the Constitution. So, just as the Court can frustrate the efforts of Congress to establish law by overturning its legislation, Congress can block the Court's attempts to create policy by overriding its decisions or taking other retaliating steps.

Finally, justices must take account of the potential reaction of the general population to any standard they seek to establish. It is one thing for the Court to dispose of the particular controversy between parties, but quite another to establish a general rule that members of society will respect and follow. If the *Craig* decision, for example, was to succeed in setting the standard for future sex discrimination cases, the substantive rule embodied in the decision would have to be one that the people would accept and use. These concerns go directly to the importance of the Court's legitimacy in the eyes of the population. As we later argue, legitimacy and its effect on the Court's efficacy is in large part a function of the willingness of the justices to take account of this third set of social and political institutions— those governing the relationship between the Court and society.

The lesson from *Craig* is clear: goal-oriented justices face complex strategic decisions in their efforts to affect the law. In attempting to create rules that reflect their own preferences, they must take account of three different strategic relationships: the relationship among the justices, of the Court to the other branches of government, and of the Court to the public. Their success in creating particular laws depends on their ability to anticipate the reactions of those other actors to their decisions; that is, the effectiveness of a particular justice depends on how skillful she is at developing reliable expectations of the actions of others. It is in this task of expectation formation that social and political institutions play a crucial role.

This assumption is what guides us. To examine it more fully, we devote this chapter and the next to a discussion of how various institutions affect Supreme Court decision making. But, first, we offer a general account of how rules help actors to establish expectations.

INSTITUTIONS AND THE FORMATION OF EXPECTATIONS

The central argument of this chapter and the next is that justices must take account of these three sets of rules if they are to accomplish their goal of creating legal standards for the society.[1] The reason, as *Craig* counsels, is simple: because Supreme Court opinions are the product of the interdependent choices of nine justices, the ability of any one justice to establish laws she most prefers is in part a function of her ability to adapt to the choices of the others. Her success or failure hinges on her ability to make dependable predictions about the future behavior of the others. Rules help by providing information about how people are expected to act in particular situations. For example, certain expectations are established by the rules of the road: we cannot drive safely unless we know what to expect from others at lights and stop signs. Court rules perform the same kind of function.

For institutions—be they traffic laws or the Rule of Four—to play this role, however, two conditions must hold. First, only those rules that are widely known and generally accepted by members of the community will be effective. When knowledge of the rules is socially shared, people have a common basis for anticipating the choices of other actors. This is not to say that rules determine exactly what people are going to do—a driver may not stop at a red light—but rules establish the constraints on the range of acceptable behavior.

Second, before an individual can confidently rely on institutional rules as a basis for expectation formation, she must have good reason to believe that other actors will comply with them. Institutions ensure compliance by a combination of information provided about the choices of other actors and the threat of sanctions imposed by other actors in the event of noncompliance.

We can demonstrate how information can affect compliance with a simple analytical example, the case of pure coordination depicted in Table 4-1. Each player has an interest in making a decision that will produce a coordinated outcome, either (A,A) or (B,B). In the case of pure coordina-

TABLE 4-1
Pure-Coordination Problem

Player I	Player II	
	A	B
A	3,3	0,0
B	0,0	3,3

Note: Both players prefer 3 to 0. If both select A or both select B, they obtain 3; otherwise they obtain 0.

tion, the players are indifferent between these two outcomes, but they both prefer either to failing to coordinate, either (A,B) or (B,A). The problem is that the efficacy of their ultimate choice is contingent on each knowing the choice of the other. For example, player I prefers to choose A if player II chooses A, but he prefers to choose B if player II selects B. Without additional information about the other player's reputation or the social context of the interaction, player I does not know how to make the most effective choice because he does not know what player II is going to do. If, however, there is a rule that governs such interactions, the choice is much easier. If the rule dictates that actors should select A, that information will aid player I's task. If he knows that player II is familiar with the rule, he can reasonably assume that player II will follow it. Player I therefore has the information he needs to make his own choice successful: the information aids his task of expectation formation *and* provides him with a reason also to comply with the rule. As long as he is confident that player II will comply, player I has no incentive not to comply. In this sense, the information alone is enough to ensure compliance because the information gives the actors an incentive to comply with the rules. This is the logic of self-enforcing institutions and the primary mechanism of compliance for informal institutions.

But, in situations where the interaction is more complicated than the case of pure coordination, information alone may not ensure compliance. In this type of situation, sanctions become important. Two types of sanctions, formal and informal, are relevant to our analysis. Formal sanctions are attached to a state's legal rules: if an actor does not comply with the law, he may be punished by public officials. In the case of Supreme Court justices, impeachment is an extremely severe form of sanction for noncompliance with the law.

Informal sanctions are attached to the various conventions and norms that evolve over time to structure social relations. If an actor does not comply with these social norms, it is likely that the other actors will apply informal sanctions, which can range from ostracism to a refusal to interact cooperatively with the offending party. Such norms and the accompanying sanctions are the primary sources of institutional constraint on Supreme Court justices. If a justice occasionally violates a norm, the other justices can invoke simple forms of informal sanctioning as a way of reinforcing the validity of the norm. For example, when a chief justice violates the opinion assignment norm by selecting a writer from among the members of the minority, justices in the majority may temporarily challenge his authority. But, if a justice (or a group of justices) consistently fails to conform to prevalent legal norms, the informal sanction might be outright rejection of her decisions, resulting in her loss of legitimacy and, ultimately, her efficacy. In either case the primary effect of sanctions is to increase the costs and diminish the benefits of noncompliance with institutional rules.[2]

With the importance of rules and norms in mind, we now turn to a more detailed discussion of how various institutions affect Supreme Court decision making. For purposes of analysis, we divide the material into two chapters, reflecting the fact that different rules are grounded in different relationships. In what follows, we consider two internal rules that structure the deliberation among the justices—the Rule of Four and the norm governing opinion assignment. Chapter Five takes up several external rules that govern the relationship between the Court and the other branches of government (the separation of powers system) and those that establish the relationship between the Court and the general public (precedent and issue creation).[a]

---

a. It is worth noting that, despite the division Chapters Four and Five create, both internal and external rules affect the decision making of individual justices and, therefore, the internal dynamics of their deliberations. For example, as we discuss in the next chapter, the norm of *stare decisis* is grounded primarily in the relationship between the Court and the public, but it also has a profound effect on the internal dynamics of the Court because of the way it structures choice.

THE INTERNAL INSTITUTIONS OF THE COURT

Since 1790 the U.S. Supreme Court has promulgated formal rules—ranging from the responsibilities of its clerk to the maximum length of briefs—to govern its activities. These rules, which the justices most recently amended in 1995, are written down and available to all to read; one can even access them via the Internet.[3]

But they are not the only rules the Court maintains. Over time, the justices have established other institutions to govern relations among the members. Some, including the convention that the chief justice speaks for the majority in "important" cases, have been around since the days of John Marshall. Others, such as the use of seriatim opinions, have not survived. (Before Marshall became chief justice, each justice wrote his own opinion. Marshall persuaded his colleagues to write "opinions of the Court" instead.) Still other norms—the Rule of Four, for example—are of relatively recent vintage.

Variation also exists in the degree to which the Court enforces and follows these institutions. A few—for example, the norm requiring a majority for precedent—are not very different from a formal rule in that the justices virtually always follow them. At the other end of the spectrum are certain conventions that the Court often, but does not always, follow, such as authorship of important opinions by the chief.[4]

As different as these and other internal rules may be, they are all, ultimately, institutions. They provide information to the justices, and this information helps them formulate expectations about the preferences and likely actions of their colleagues, which in turn enables them to make rational decisions. This part of the decision-making process is one of the many lessons of *Craig*.

To demonstrate these effects, we consider two informal institutions of the Court: the Rule of Four and the norm governing the assignment of majority opinions. We focus on these two because they govern different parts of the decision-making process. The Rule of Four comes into play at the review stage, and opinion assignments, at the merits phase. They also differ in the extent to which they help justices arrive at reliable expectations about what their colleagues will do.

The Rule of Four

Of the many institutions governing the justices' work, the Rule of Four is perhaps the best known and for good reason. Although its origins remain a mystery, at least since 1924 justices have made the rule's existence a matter of public record. In that year, Justices Willis Van Devanter and George Sutherland staged a colloquy before a congressional committee:

> Justice Van Devanter: In our conference a vote is taken on the question whether the petition shall be granted or refused, in the same way that we vote on other cases. If there be occasion for discussion, the discussion is had as in other matters. Not only that, but whenever the vote is relatively close the conference makes it a practice to grant the petition.
> Justice Sutherland: Even though a majority be against it?
> Justice Van Devanter: Yes. For instance, if there were five votes against granting the petition and four in favor of granting it, it would be granted, because we proceed upon the theory that when as many as four members of the court, and even three in some instances, are impressed with the propriety of our taking the case the petition should be granted. This is the uniform way in which petitions for writs of certiorari are considered.[5]

Nearly fifty years later, Chief Justice Burger proposed that the Court issue the following statement in response to media reports that the justices had supplanted the Rule of Four with a Rule of Three:

> To clarify any possible confusion relating to granting writs of certiorari, the procedure pending a full complement of nine Justices is to hold for reconsideration any petition that receives three votes. No petitions are granted on less than four votes.[6]

The Rule of Four, therefore, has two important characteristics of all institutions: the justices share knowledge of it, and they have informed external communities of its existence and maintenance.

Moreover, like all institutions, the Rule of Four provides information to assist the justices in making choices. Most obvious is that a justice knows that she *generally* must attract at least three other votes to hear a case. If she does not, she will need to bargain with her colleagues, perhaps by circulating a dissent from a certiorari denial, to attain the requisite number.

As the emphasis on the word "generally" indicates, exceptions occur. Consider, for example, the course of events in *New York v. Uplinger,* in which a lower court struck down a state law that prohibited loitering "in a public place for the purpose of engaging, or soliciting another person to engage, in deviate sexual intercourse or other sexual behavior of a deviate nature." [7] Four justices had voted to hear the case, but Brennan voted to deny cert, no doubt fearing that his colleagues would reverse the lower court's decision. During the conference on the merits, Brennan led a charge to have the Court dismiss certiorari as improvidently granted (a "DIG"). He took this step, we suspect, because he thought it would produce the best possible outcome, given his distaste for the law. A DIG, while establishing no Supreme Court precedent, would at least allow the lower court ruling to stand. As it turned out, Brennan was able to secure a majority of five for the DIG by circulating an unsigned written (per curiam) opinion. But the opinion elicited a harshly worded dissent from Rehnquist, who had voted to grant certiorari and against Brennan's DIG:

> Today the Court dismisses the writ of certiorari in this case as improvidently granted. . . . In so doing the Court leaves untouched a decision invalidating *in toto* a statute designed to protect individual citizens and residential neighborhoods from lewd conduct that affronts peoples' sensibilities in the most intimate of matters and that made people apprehensive about walking neighborhood streets. Four members voted to grant certiorari in this case, yet the majority advances no convincing reason for sidestepping the "Rule of Four" and dismissing the case now.[8]

With these words, Rehnquist was doing more than informing Brennan that he well understood his motives for the DIG. He was making a public proclamation that Brennan's opinion conflicted with the Rule of Four (because four justices wanted to decide the case) and diminished the rule's importance. Justice Stevens also expressed concern. In a private memorandum to Brennan, dated March 1, 1984, he wrote, "If you can get five votes on your per curiam, I will happily make a sixth; alternatively I can make a fifth if one of the original votes to grant will join you. I am most reluctant, however, to join this kind of disposition over the dissent of four Members of the Court, who voted to grant the case, even though, as you know, I think this was a particularly unwise grant." [b]

---

b. The view that Rehnquist and Stevens seem to be supporting is that a justice who voted to deny cert should not, on her own, DIG the case. This view may be something of a norm itself, as a private memo sent to Justice John Harlan from Douglas in 1969 suggests:

> I enclose a recirculation in no. 32, which adopts your suggestion that the writ be dismissed as improvidently granted.
>
> Since I voted to deny the cert, it would not be open for me on my own to dismiss as improvidently granted, but since you voted to grant, I certainly could join you and your suggestion. Hence, I have put it on that ground, rather than affirmance.

Memorandum from Justice Douglas to Justice Harlan, 12/9/69, re: no. 32, *National Labor Relations Board v. Rutter-Rex Co.,* 396 U.S. 258 (1969).

What concerned Rehnquist and Stevens was that in any case in which only four justices supported certiorari, a subset of deniers could turn around and try a DIG, as Brennan had done. If this behavior occurred on a regular basis, justices would be unable to develop reliable expectations about the course of cases that attain a minimum winning certiorari vote, and, in the long term, it would undermine the rule as a norm structuring the internal dynamics of the Court.

Rehnquist eventually withdrew his dissenting opinion in *Uplinger,* but he may have won the larger battle. During the rest of the Burger Court years, the Court voted to DIG only one case, and it was by a conference vote of 6-3.[9] But we would not want to conclude that DIGs (above the objections of four justices) will never occur again.[c] Indeed, this deviation and others from the Rule of Four would not be unexpected from a Court full of policy-oriented justices. Rather, what the *Uplinger* story suggests is that systematic departures from the Rule of Four remain rare because they may generate informal sanctions such as a Rehnquist-type dissent, which would make public otherwise private information about the certiorari vote. Accordingly, the rule assures the justices that, in the main, cases obtaining four or more votes will receive consideration on their merits.

Uplinger suggests another way the Rule of Four figures into the justices' strategic calculations: it helps them anticipate what their colleagues will do at the plenary stage. Brennan's knowledge of the justices' votes on certiorari, coupled with his beliefs about their preferences, must have propelled him to try the DIG. He felt certain that the majority would reject his preferred position and that a DIG was the best he could do. More generally, as we pointed out in Chapter Three, the Rule of Four invites forward thinking. Policy-oriented justices know that if they are to attain their goals they must take those cases that they believe will lead to their preferred outcomes and reject those that will not. But if they fail at the review phase, as Brennan did in *Uplinger,* then they can use their knowledge of certiorari votes to bargain at the later stages. Seen in this way, the Rule of Four assists justices in making their strategic calculations throughout the decision-making process.

But—and this is crucial—just because justices know of the existence of the Rule of Four and realize that it induces prospective thinking does not

---

c. In fact, during the first ten terms of the Rehnquist Court, the justices used the DIG on nineteen cases. But only one, *City of Springfield v. Kibbe,* 480 U.S. 257 (1987), elicited dissenting votes from four members of the Court.

mean that they will be able to gauge *with certainty* their colleagues' future actions. The rule only helps them to formulate guesses that they must supplement with other information, such as knowledge of their colleagues' prior policy preferences. There are two reasons. In *Uplinger* we saw evidence of the first—the existence of multiple strategies for making choices at the cert stage. The second is the ability of justices to cast ambiguous cert votes.

We begin with the strategy problem, namely, that forward thinking does not always lead justices to adopt one particular strategy over others. As we discussed in Chapters Two and Three, the reversal strategy—voting to *grant* certiorari and then voting to *reverse* on the merits—may be the most common, and the DIG, the least. But in between are others, including the aggressive grant approach, in which justices take cases to *affirm* a lower court outcome that they favor. The existence of multiple strategies makes it difficult for justices to formulate expectations about their colleagues' likely actions unless they take into account other factors.

To see this, recall the reaction to White's dissent from the Court's denial of certiorari in *Bowers v. Hardwick*.[10] Apparently believing that White was pursuing an *aggressive grant* strategy, Brennan and Marshall expressed their support for White's dissent. But, when Rehnquist (Brennan's ideological opposite) also joined the dissent, Brennan changed his vote, presumably because Rehnquist's "join" made him aware that White was actually pursuing a reversal strategy. By the same token, justices will be unable to formulate reliable expectations about their colleagues' future actions if they base those expectations solely on the assumption that they will follow a *reversal strategy*. Figure 4-1, which shows the progression of the vote in *Secretary of Interior v. California*, makes this abundantly clear. Note that if a justice believed that all of her colleagues were voting to grant because they wanted to reverse or voting to deny cases because they wanted to affirm, she would have predicted an outcome of affirmance by a 5-4 vote. But, because Chief Justice Burger deviated from this pattern, she would have miscalculated the eventual outcome unless she took into account other information about his preferences—as Brennan did about Rehnquist's in *Bowers*.

Equally confounding to justices attempting to formulate expectations about their colleagues' likely behavior at the merits stage is the ambiguous certiorari vote. Typically, such a vote takes the form of a "Join 3" or a "pass." Because justices cast these votes for many different reasons—as one justice put it, "All nine of us use the term [Join 3]. But I think we each have our

Figure 4-1   Certiorari, Expected, and Final Votes in *Secretary of Interior v. California*

Justice	Certiorari Vote		Expected Merits Vote		Actual Merits Vote
Burger (cj)	⟶ deny	⟶	affirm	⟶	reverse
Brennan	⟶ deny	⟶	affirm	⟶	affirm
White	⟶ grant	⟶	reverse	⟶	reverse
Marshall	⟶ deny	⟶	affirm	⟶	affirm
Blackmun	⟶ deny	⟶	affirm	⟶	affirm
Powell	⟶ grant	⟶	reverse	⟶	reverse
Rehnquist	⟶ grant	⟶	reverse	⟶	reverse
Stevens	⟶ deny	⟶	affirm	⟶	affirm
O'Connor	⟶ grant	⟶	reverse	⟶	reverse
Court	⟶ certiorari granted (4-5 vote)	⟶	affirm (5-4 vote)	⟶	reverse (5-4 vote)

Data Source: Docket sheets of Justice William J. Brennan Jr., Library of Congress, and Lewis F. Powell Jr., Washington and Lee University School of Law. Brennan's and Powell's certiorari vote tallies were identical.

Note: Secretary of Interior v. California, 464 U.S. 312 (1984), involved the Department of the Interior's sale of oil and gas leases on the Outer Continental Shelf off the coast of California. Resolving the dispute required the Court to interpret a section of the Coastal Zone Management Act.

The *expected merits vote* is the vote we would anticipate if justices vote to take cases they want to reverse and deny cases they want to affirm.

own meaning" [11]—they may be even less useful in formulating expectations about outcomes at the merits stage than an outright grant or deny.[d] To see why, examine the votes in *United States v. Yermain* and *Secretary of State v. Munson* in Figure 4-2. In *Yermain* eight justices cast votes to grant, which would—if justices were following a reversal strategy—create the expectation that the Court would reverse by a vote of 8-1. As we can see, this is not precisely what happened, nor, given the presence of the affirmative grant strategy, should we always expect it to happen. But, at the very least, the outcome, a vote to reverse, was foreseeable. In *Munson* three justices voted to grant, three to deny, two to Join 3, and one to pass. Under such circumstances it would be difficult to make predictions: the pass vote provides no information, and the Join 3s, although indicating some will-

---

d. Justices may have different interpretations of a "Join 3," but, at the very least, a Join 3 vote tells the others that the justice agrees to supply a vote in favor of cert.

Figure 4-2   Certiorari, Expected, and Final Votes in Cases Containing Clear and Ambiguous Certiorari Votes

Clear Case: United States v. Yermain

Justice	Certiorari Vote	Expected Merits Vote	Actual Merits Vote
Burger (cj)	⟶ grant[a]	⟶ reverse	⟶ reverse
Brennan	⟶ grant	⟶ reverse	⟶ affirm
White	⟶ grant	⟶ reverse	⟶ reverse
Marshall	⟶ grant	⟶ reverse	⟶ reverse
Blackmun	⟶ grant	⟶ reverse	⟶ reverse
Powell	⟶ deny	⟶ affirm	⟶ reverse
Rehnquist	⟶ grant	⟶ reverse	⟶ affirm
Stevens	⟶ grant	⟶ reverse	⟶ affirm
O'Connor	⟶ grant	⟶ reverse	⟶ affirm
Court	⟶ certiorari granted (8-1 vote)	⟶ reverse (8-1 vote)	⟶ reverse (5-4 vote)

Ambiguous Case: Secretary of State v. Munson

Justice	Certiorari Vote	Expected Merits Vote	Actual Merits Vote
Burger (cj)	⟶ Join 3	⟶ reverse?	⟶ reverse
Brennan	⟶ deny	⟶ affirm	⟶ affirm
White	⟶ deny	⟶ affirm	⟶ affirm
Marshall	⟶ grant	⟶ reverse	⟶ affirm
Blackmun	⟶ Join 3	⟶ reverse?	⟶ affirm
Powell	⟶ grant	⟶ reverse	⟶ reverse
Rehnquist	⟶ grant	⟶ reverse	⟶ reverse
Stevens	⟶ pass	⟶ ?	⟶ affirm
O'Connor	⟶ deny	⟶ reverse	⟶ reverse
Court	⟶ certiorari granted (5-3 vote)[b]	⟶ reverse?[b]	⟶ affirm (5-4 vote)

Data Source: Docket sheets of Justice William J. Brennan Jr., Library of Congress, and Lewis F. Powell Jr., Washington and Lee University School of Law. With one exception, Brennan's and Powell's certiorari vote tallies were identical: Powell had O'Connor "passing" in *Munson*. We used Brennan's records here because, in parentheses next to O'Connor's name, Powell wrote that he thought he recorded her vote incorrectly.

Note: United States v. Yermain, 468 U.S. 63 (1984), involved a federal law prohibiting anyone from making a false or fraudulent statement within the jurisdiction of a federal agency. To establish a violation of the law, the U.S. government must prove beyond a reasonable doubt that the statement was made with knowledge of its falsity. In this case, the Court addressed the question of whether the government also must prove that the false statement was made with actual knowledge of federal agency jurisdiction. In *Secretary of State v. Munson*, 467 U.S. 947 (1984), the Court assessed the constitutionality of a Maryland statute that prohibited a charitable organization, in connection with any fund-raising activity, from paying expenses of more than 25 percent of the amount raised during the activity, but authorized a waiver of this limitation if it worked to prevent the organization from raising contributions.

The expected merits vote is the vote we would anticipate if justices vote to take cases they want to reverse and deny cases they want to affirm.

[a]Burger's vote was to grant, vacate, and remand.
[b]Outcomes occurring if we count Join 3s as votes to grant certiorari.

ingness to hear a case, are almost as difficult to interpret because the motivation behind them differs from justice to justice. As it turned out in *Munson,* one of the Join 3 justices ultimately voted to reverse and the other to affirm. Note too that a prediction (however tentative) of reversal would not hold.

In short, ambiguous votes and multiple strategies complicate the task justices face in using the information they obtain from the certiorari vote to formulate expectations. The Rule of Four—a norm of no small consequence—certainly assists them in making these calculations, but they must supplement that information with other evidence concerning their colleagues' preferences. Only by doing so are they likely to feel confident in the beliefs they formulate.

The Assignment of Majority Opinions

In May 1972 William Douglas, who was the senior associate justice at the time, prepared the following memo:

Dear Chief Justice:
Your note to me dated April 24 about the assignment of No. 71-492—*Lloyd Corporation v. Tanner* [involving the constitutionality of a ban on the distribution of handbills inside a privately owned shopping center]—came when I was out of town and when I returned you were away. Hence this late answer.

You apparently misunderstand. *Lloyd* is already assigned to Thurgood [Marshall] and he's at work on an opinion. Whether he will command a majority, no one knows.

Under the Constitution & Acts of Congress, there are no provisions for assignment of opinions. Historically, the Chief Justice has made the assignment if he is in the majority. Historically, the senior in the majority assigns the opinion if the Chief Justice is in the minority.

You led the Conference battle against affirmance and this is your privilege. But it is also the privilege of the majority, absent the Chief Justice, to make the assignment. Hence, *Lloyd* was assigned and is assigned.

The tragedy of compromising on this simple procedure is illustrated by last Term's *Swann* [*v. Charlotte-Mecklenburg County Board of Education*]. You who were a minority of two kept the opinion for yourself and faithfully wrote the minority position which the majority could not accept. Potter [Stewart] wrote the majority view and the majority agreed to it. It was not circulated because we thought you should see it. After much effort your minority opinion was transformed, the majority prevailed, and the result was unanimous.

But *Swann* illustrated the wasted time and effort and frayed relations which result when the traditional assignment procedure is not followed.

If the Conference wants to authorize you to assign all opinions, that will be a new procedure. Though opposed to it, I will acquiesce. But unless we make a frank reversal in our policy, any group in the majority should and must make the assignment.

This is a two-edged sword. Byron [White] might well head up five members of the Court, you, Bill Brennan, Potter Stewart, and I being in the minority; and we might feel very strongly about it. But in that event it is for Byron to make the assignment. It is not for us in the minority to try and outwit Byron by saying "I reserve my vote" and then recast it to control the assignment. That only leads to a frayed and bitter Court full of needless strains and quarrels.

Lloyd stays assigned to Thurgood.[12]

Douglas's words provide us with two insights about majority opinion assignments: the justices believe they are important, and an institution governs how they are made. We consider both.

THE IMPORTANCE OF THE CHOICE OF OPINION WRITER. Without a doubt, justices view the opinion assignment—the choice of the opinion writer—as critical. Douglas said as much in the *Lloyd* memo. He also wrote a memo concerning an earlier case, *United States v. United States District Court,* which asked whether the president has the authority to authorize electronic surveillance in matters of national security without obtaining prior judicial approval. Douglas noted:

Traditionally an opinion would therefore be in the province of the senior Justice to assign. That was not done in this case and the matter is of no consequence to me as a matter of pride and privilege—but I think it makes a tremendous difference in the result.[13]

To put it another way, the author of the initial opinion draft can significantly affect the policy the Court produces because the opinion writer's first draft establishes the initial position over which justices bargain. Depending on the writer's preferences, the first draft can be crafted broadly or narrowly, can ignore or apply past precedents, and can fashion various kinds of policy.[14] Moreover, the opinion writer is in a position to accept or reject bargaining offers from her colleagues. In making this decision, all writers face similar constraints—for example, the need for a majority for precedent—but their willingness to make alterations will be condi-

tioned on other factors, especially the distance between the policy preferences of the opinion writer and the justice requesting changes.[15] In short,
the "privilege" of drafting a majority opinion gives a justice a great deal of
control of a case.[16]

Opinion writers matter in another way—in the extent to which they,
and not just the content of the opinion, help make policy palatable to
external actors, including the other political institutions and the public.[17]
Anecdotal evidence abounds: Chief Justice Harlan Fiske Stone assigned
Korematsu v. United States, in which the Court permitted the government
to relocate Japanese Americans to camps during World War II, to the civil
libertarian, Hugo Black; and Earl Warren selected former attorney general
Tom Clark to write the Court's opinion in *Mapp v. Ohio,* which created the
exclusionary rule.[18] There is also systematic evidence, albeit of an indirect
nature. In a study of the assignment patterns of Chief Justices Warren,
Burger, and Rehnquist, Forrest Maltzman and Paul J. Wahlbeck found that
chiefs attempt to encourage specialization by assigning opinions to justices
who have substantive expertise in the particular issue area under consideration.[19] This practice may reflect the chief's interest in facilitating the effi-
cient operation of the Court, as justices with expertise may be more likely
to produce opinions in a timely fashion. But it may also indicate the chief's
desire to have his Court produce "quality" opinions that will have a greater
chance of being accepted and respected by the external community.

THE INSTITUTION GOVERNING MAJORITY OPINION ASSIGNMENTS. From the
Douglas memorandum and scholarly analyses, then, we learn that it matters who writes the opinion. The memo also lends weight to another
insight, which has particular relevance to the central concern of this chapter: the opinion assignment procedure has all of the makings of an institution. For one thing, contemporary justices share common knowledge of it.
Douglas makes this point when he notes the historical roots of the rule in
his *Lloyd* memorandum. For another, it is generally followed.[e] And, when
it is not, reactions are swift. Both Brennan and Stewart took issue with

---

e. There are some exceptions that early Courts created and contemporary justices
accept. For example, following a practice that dates back at least to 1881, the Court
permits newcomers to select their first case for opinion. See David Danelski, "The
Influence of the Chief Justice in the Decisional Process of the Supreme Court," in
American Court Systems, ed. Sheldon Goldman and Austin Sarat (New York: Longman,
1975), 499. In cases in which no clear conference consensus emerges, the chief justice
may ask justices with differing viewpoints to write memoranda.

some of Burger's opinion assignments, and Douglas's attacks are legendary. Not only did he protest about *Lloyd,* but he also complained bitterly about Burger's assignment of the 1973 abortion cases to Harry Blackmun:

> Dear Chief:
>
>   As respects your assignment . . . my notes show that there were four votes to hold parts of the Georgia [abortion] Act unconstitutional and to remand for further findings. . . . Those four were Bill Brennan, Potter Stewart, Thurgood Marshall, and me.
>
>   There were three to sustain the law as written—you, Byron White, and Harry Blackmun.
>
>   I would think, therefore, that to save future time and trouble, one of the four, rather than one of three, should write the opinion.[20]

Finally, the rule governing opinion assignments provides information to the justices—information that they can use to formulate expectations about the behavior and likely actions of other justices and, in turn, to make their own choices. For the most part, that information centers on the chief justice because chiefs have traditionally assigned somewhere between 80 percent (Burger and Rehnquist) and 95 percent (Taft and Hughes) of all opinions, and these rates convey critical messages to the justices.[21] They know, for example, that the power to assign opinions increases with seniority. Table 4-2 vividly makes this point, showing that (theoretically) the probability of assigning a majority opinion drops to near zero for Justices Scalia and Kennedy, who rank fourth and fifth in seniority, respectively.

From both theoretical and empirical vantage points, then, the institution governing opinion assignment ensures that the power rests almost exclusively with the chief justice and the senior associate. From this information, the junior justices can make the following inference: if they wish to influence the decision-making process, they must consider mechanisms other than the power to assign opinions. Perhaps that is why some scholars have observed the Court's most junior members tending to align "their political preferences with the Court's ideological center of gravity."[22] By so doing, they can offset their inability to assign opinions with the power to serve as pivots.

But this information is not all the justices can infer from the institution governing opinion assignment. As Douglas's memo in *Lloyd* suggests, it is probably no coincidence that chiefs assign most opinions. When Douglas wrote, "It is not for us in the minority to try and outwit [the opinion assigner] by saying 'I reserve my vote' and then recast it to control the

TABLE 4-2
The Probability of Assigning a Majority Opinion, 1996 Term

Justice (in order of seniority)	Vote in case					Total	Percent
	5-4	6-3	7-2	8-1	9-0		
Rehnquist (cj)	70	56	28	8	1	163	63.7
Stevens	35	21	7	1	0	64	25.0
O'Connor	15	6	1	0	0	22	8.6
Scalia	5	1	0	0	0	6	2.3
Kennedy	1	0	0	0	0	1	0.4
Total	126	84	36	9	1	256	100.0

Source: Paul H. Edelman and Jim Chen, "The Most Dangerous Justice: The Supreme Court at the Bar of Mathematics," *70 Southern California Law Review* (1996): 40.

Note: Theoretically speaking, there are 512 (2^9) possible coalitions justices could form; of these, 256 are winning coalitions of five or more justices. This table assumes that all coalitions are feasible.

Interpretation Note: This table shows, among other things, the percentage of opinions that the justices would, theoretically speaking, be able to assign. If, for example, the vote in a case were 9-0, only one coalition would be possible and because by definition it would include the chief justice (Rehnquist), he would assign the opinion. By making this sort of calculation for all the possible majority coalitions, we can see that Rehnquist would be in a position to assign 63.7 percent of all opinions.

assignment," he was telling the chief that he believed that Burger acted in a sophisticated fashion (for example, passing at conference) to ensure his ability to select the majority opinion writer.

Douglas's suspicion—that the norm governing opinion assignments induces sophisticated behavior by the chief justice—is well founded.[23] During the 1983 term, Burger cast more pass votes during conference than any other justice.[f] These data do not account for instances when the chief initially "reserved" his vote at conference and voted after all the associates

---

f. Brennan's and Powell's records differ on the number of "pass" votes cast by the justices. Brennan's tallies have Burger passing or reserving his vote six times; Blackmun, twice; White, once; and the others, never. Powell's notes reveal the following: Burger passing eleven times; Blackmun, three times; Stevens, twice; and O'Connor, Rehnquist, Powell, and Brennan, once each. Either way, it is clear that the chief cast more pass votes than his colleagues.

had expressed their views, as Powell's conference notes reveal in several landmark cases, including *Washington v. Davis, Runyon v. McCrary,* and *Coker v. Georgia.*[g] Nor do the data account for when he cast tentative conference votes, which gave him room to maneuver, as this memo—a private message to Brennan, who apparently was to lead conference on a day Burger was out sick—reveals his inclination to do:

> Here is the way I . . . line up on the argued cases. . . . As with Monday's cases, I find many of Tuesday's and Wednesday's cases difficult.
>
> No. 81-2338 *Regan v. Taxation Group with Representation of Washington*
> Tentatively I would reverse.
>
> No. 82-34 *American Paper Institute v. American Elec. Corp.*
> Tentatively, I lean to REVERSE.
>
> No. 81-1889 *Public Service Comm. of N.Y. v. Mid-Louisiana Gas Co.*
> Another close case. A slight leaning to reverse—but my review of Lewis' [Powell] notes on the discussion may turn me around.
>
> No. 81-1985 *Edward J. De Bartolo Corp. v. NLRB*
> I find it hard to accept the Board's notion that the Mall Owners were "distributing" the contractor's "product." A leaning to reverse but I'll wait.
>
> No. 67-Orig. *Idaho, Ex Rel. Evans v. Oregon*
> In general, partly influenced, I confess my confidence in the Special Master, I lean to adopt his report.
>
> No. 82-271 *Chardon v. Soto*
> A leaning to reverse, but I'll wait on review of Lewis' notes.
>
> No. 82-2147 *Ariz. v. San Carlos Tribe*
> I lean to allow the State Courts to proceed. Tentative affirm. [Brennan crossed out *affirm* and penned in *reverse?*] [24]

Nor do the data include the occasions when Burger took the assignment for himself although he was not squarely in the majority, as in *Swann,*

---

g. *Washington v. Davis,* 426 U.S. 229 (1976), challenged a qualifying test administered to applicants for positions as police officers as racially discriminatory; *Runyon v. McCrary,* 427 U.S. 160 (1976), asked whether federal law 42 U.S.C. §1981 prohibits private schools from excluding qualified children solely because they are black; and *Coker v. Georgia,* 433 U.S. 584 (1977), questioned whether the Eighth Amendment prohibits the imposition of a sentence of death for the crime of rape. In the first two cases, Burger went from a pass to the majority's position by the end of conference discussion; in the third he voted with the minority.

or when he assigned opinions to others who were not in the majority, as Stewart alleged had occurred in *Groppi v. Wisconsin:*

> Dear Chief:
>   I have some difficulties with the [opinion] assignment list circulated today. . . .
>   In No. 26, *Groppi v. Wisconsin,* my Conference notes indicate that 5 of us (White, Stewart, Brennan, Harlan, and Douglas) voted to reverse on the ground that it is a violation of due process for a state categorically to prohibit a change of venue in a misdemeanor prosecution. Hugo [Black] voted to vacate and remand. You, Thurgood [Marshall], and Harry [Blackmun] voted to affirm the judgment, Harry expressing some doubt, however. I should suppose that in light of this Conference vote Hugo [to whom the chief assigned the opinion] might have great difficulty in writing an opinion that a majority could join, and that perhaps Bill Douglas should assign the writing of the opinion to one of the 5 who voted to reverse outright.[25]

Seen in this way, the norm of opinion assignment provided important information to the justices of the Burger Court, and, given the frequency of opinion assignment by all chief justices, we suspect to the justices of other Courts as well. Because Burger went to great lengths to protect his assignment power, he introduced a kind of uncertainty into the decision-making process that would not otherwise have existed. This uncertainty had marked consequences for associate justices attempting to anticipate the reactions of the chief to their (or others') writings and for the ultimate state of the law. *Swann,* which we discussed in the previous chapter, makes this point abundantly clear, as do the landmark cases of *Roe v. Wade* and *Doe v. Bolton.*

The justices initially took up *Roe/Doe* in December 1971.[26] The conference discussion did not produce consensus over the logic to be used in resolving the case, although a plurality seemed to agree with Brennan that the "right to abortion should be given a constitutional basis." But the discussion pointed to a clear result: the pro-choice side would win by a vote of 5 (Douglas, Blackmun, Brennan, Marshall, Stewart) to 2 (Burger, White) or 4-3, depending on how Blackmun voted.[h] Despite his position in the

---

h. Because Brennan's docket sheets are difficult to interpret, we derived these votes from his notes from conference discussion, with the relevant portions as follows:

minority, Burger took charge of the opinion assignment, asking Blackmun to write it. Why he made this selection was obvious to all of his colleagues: as the most ambivalent member of the pro-choice camp (if he was, in fact, a member), Blackmun would write the narrowest possible opinion—perhaps even one that Burger could sign.

This (mis)assignment triggered a series of events. The first was the irate letter from Douglas to Burger, in which Douglas had two bones to pick: first, as the senior member of the majority, he should have assigned the opinion; second, Blackmun should not have received the assignment in any event because his docket sheet put him in the minority. Burger's response: he would not change the assignment. As he put it, "At the close of discussion of this case, I remarked to the Conference that there were, literally, not enough columns to mark up an accurate reflection of the voting. . . . I therefore marked down no votes and said this was a case that would have to stand or fall on the writing, when it was done. . . . This is still my view of how to handle . . . this sensitive case." [27]

Still uncertain of how Blackmun would dispose of the case and of what rationale he would use, some of the justices began preparing opinions. It took Douglas less than a week to circulate a memorandum opinion in *Doe* to Brennan: "Let me have your suggestions, criticisms, ideas, etc., and I will incorporate them, and then we can talk later as to strategy." [28] Brennan responded with some suggestions for revision and with the admonition that Douglas hold onto the opinion until Blackmun circulated his.

As it turned out, the wait was a long one. Not until mid-May 1972 did Blackmun send around his first draft in *Roe*—a draft that came to the "right" result in Brennan's and Douglas's minds, but did so for the wrong

------

Burger: "I can't find Texas statute unconstitutional, although it's certainly archaic and obsolete."

Douglas: "Abortion statute is unconstitutional—this is basically a medical, psychiatric problem."

Stewart: "On merits, I agree with Bill Douglas."

White: "Agree with Potter [Stewart] on all preliminaries but, on merits, [I] am on the other side."

Marshall: "Go with WOD [William O. Douglas]."

Blackmun: "On the merits, can a state properly outlaw abortions? If accept fetal life, there's strong argument that it can. But there are opposing interests—right of mother to life and mental and physical health, right of parents in case of rape, of state in case of incest. [I] don't think there's an absolute right to do what you will with [your] body. This statute is a poor statute that doesn't go as far as it should and impinges too far on her 9th Amendment rights."

(that is, narrowest possible) reasons: the restrictive Texas abortion law was void for vagueness and not because it interfered with any privacy interest. As Blackmun said in the cover memo to his draft:

> I come out on the theory that the Texas statute, despite its narrowness, is unconstitutionally vague.
>
> I think that this would be all that is necessary for disposition of the case, and that we need not get into the more complex Ninth Amendment issue. This may or may not appeal to you.[29]

Blackmun was correct: this approach did not appeal to the four solid pro-choicers, who—as Brennan noted in a memo he sent to Blackmun after receiving the *Roe* draft—wanted "a disposition of the core constitutional question." [30] Douglas also urged Blackmun to recast his draft and, at the same time, raised the opinion assignment issue again:

> In *Roe v. Wade,* my notes confirm what Bill Brennan wrote yesterday in his memo to you—that abortion statutes were invalid save as they required that an abortion be performed by a licensed physician within a limited time after conception.
>
> That was the clear view of a majority of the seven who heard argument. My notes also indicate that the Chief had the opposed view, which made it puzzling as to why he made the assignment at all except that he indicated he might affirm on vagueness. My notes indicate that Byron was not firmly settled and that you might join the majority of four.
>
> So I think we should meet what Bill Brennan calls the "core constitutional issue." [31]

And, yet, Douglas and the others were ready to sign the Blackmun draft, believing that it represented the best possible outcome.[i] Douglas went so far as to "congratulate" Blackmun on his "fine job" and expressed the hope

---

i. In a 5/31/72 memorandum to Blackmun, Brennan wrote: "[T]here are five of us (Bill Douglas, Potter [Stewart], Thurgood [Marshall], you and I) in substantial agreement with [the] opinions" [in *Roe* and *Doe*]. Their willingness to join was also a function of Burger's pushing to have the cases reargued and Blackmun's draft in *Doe v. Bolton,* which was somewhat more to their liking because it took up the privacy issue. Still, Brennan and the others had serious misgivings about its treatment of the state's interest in protecting life. For more on the *Doe* draft and the justices' reactions to it, see Lee Epstein and Joseph F. Kobylka, *The Supreme Court and Legal Change* (Chapel Hill: University of North Carolina Press, 1992), 185.

that "5 can agree to get the cases down this Term, so that we can spend our energies next Term on other matters." [32]

Burger did not share these sentiments. Despite the narrow ground on which the draft rested, he apparently thought he could do better. So he (re)initiated, with Blackmun's support, a campaign to have the cases reargued the next term, when two more Nixon appointees—Lewis Powell and William Rehnquist—would be in place.[j] This move elicited the harshest reaction yet from Douglas, who circulated the following memorandum opinion to Brennan and eventually to the rest of the Court. He apparently planned to publish this opinion and make the whole affair a matter of public record:

> The present abortion cases . . . were put down for argument last Term and were heard December 13, 1971. The Conference on the two cases was held on December 16, 1971.
>
> THE CHIEF JUSTICE represented the minority view in the Conference and forcefully urged his viewpoint on the issues. It was a seven-man Court that heard the cases and voted on them. Out of that seven there were four who took the opposed view. Hence traditionally the senior Justice in the majority would make the assignment of the opinion. The cases were, however, assigned by THE CHIEF JUSTICE, an action no Chief Justice in my time would ever have taken. For the tradition is a long-standing one that the senior Justice in the majority makes the assignment. . . .
>
> The matter of assignment is not merely a matter of protocol. The main function of the Conference is to find what the consensus is. When that is known, it is only logical that the majority decide who their spokesman should be. . . .
>
> When that procedure is followed, the majority view is promptly written out and circulated, after which dissents or concurrences may be prepared.
>
> When, however, the minority seeks to control the assignment, there is a destructive force at work in the Court. When a Chief Justice tries to bend the Court to his will by manipulating assignments, the integrity of the institution is imperiled. . . .

---

j. We say "reinitiated" because Burger's campaign to have the cases reargued actually begin in December, after conference discussion but before Blackmun circulated his draft. In his response to Douglas's letter complaining about the opinion assignment, Burger wrote that these cases "are quite probable candidates for reargument" (12/20/71).

Perhaps the purpose of THE CHIEF JUSTICE, a member of the minority in the *Abortion Cases,* in assigning the opinions was to try to keep control of the merits. If that was the aim, he was unsuccessful. Opinions in these two cases have been circulated and each commands the votes of five members of the Court. The votes are firm, the Justices having spent many, many hours since last October mulling over every detail of the cases. The cases should therefore be announced.

The plea that the cases be reargued is merely strategy by a minority somehow to suppress the majority view with the hope that exigencies of time will change the result. That might be achieved of course by death or conceivably retirement. But that kind of strategy dilutes the integrity of the Court and makes the decision here depend on the manipulative skills of a Chief Justice. . . .

I dissent with deepest regret that we are allowing the consensus of the Court to be manipulated for unworthy objectives.[33]

Douglas eventually retracted this opinion, and Burger eventually won his campaign to have the cases reargued.[k] But Burger's assumption that the new appointees would help his cause turned out to be inaccurate, as Powell planted his feet firmly in the pro-choice camp, and Blackmun eventually produced a far broader opinion in *Roe.* Even so, we should not lose sight of the main point: had it not been for this last miscalculation on Burger's part, Blackmun's first draft in *Roe,* or some approximation of it, would have represented the majority's opinion—and the law governing abortions would have been off to a very different start. All of these events occurred because of a rule that encouraged the chief justice to act in a sophisticated fashion, which in turn created enough uncertainty in the minds of the majority that it was willing to take a risk and sign an opinion that would have been far from its preferred position.

But it was not only the opinion assignment or other internal norms that led the justices to make their choices in the 1973 abortion cases. Many accounts of the *Roe v. Wade* decision also underscore the importance of external rules—rules that govern the relationship between the Court and the other branches of government and those that establish the relationship between the Court and the general public. It is to those external institutions that we now turn.

---

k. Douglas noted (without opinion) his dissent from having the cases reargued. See 408 U.S. 919 (1972).

ENDNOTES

1. For this discussion of the effects of legal institutions on the choices of Supreme Court justices, we rely on the more general analysis of social institutions in Jack Knight, *Institutions and Social Conflict* (Cambridge: Cambridge University Press, 1992). We also adopt the distinction Knight makes between institutions and organizations: institutions refer to sets of rules that structure interactions among actors, while organizations refer to collective actors who might be subject to institutional constraints. See also Douglass C. North, *Institutions, Institutional Change, and Economic Performance* (Cambridge: Cambridge University Press, 1990).

2. See, generally, James F. Spriggs II, "The Supreme Court and Federal Administrative Agencies: A Resource-Based Theory and Analysis of Judicial Impact," 40 *American Journal of Political Science* (1996): 1122–51.

3. For the Supreme Court's rules, navigate to: *http://www.law.cornell.edu/rules/supct/overview.html*.

4. See Elliot Slotnick, "The Chief Justices and Self-Assignment of Majority Opinions," 30 *Western Political Quarterly* (1978): 225; and Jeffrey A. Segal and Harold J. Spaeth, *The Supreme Court and the Attitudinal Model* (New York: Cambridge University Press, 1993), 272.

5. Hearings on S. 2060 and S. 2061 before the Senate Subcommittee on the Judiciary, 72d Cong., 2d sess. (1924), 29. Cited in memorandum of Justice Marshall to the conference, 9/21/83, re: The Rule of Four. The purpose of the colloquy was to generate congressional support for the Judiciary Act of 1925.

6. Memorandum from the chief justice to the conference, 11/4/71.

7. *New York v. Uplinger,* 467 U.S. 246 (1984).

8. Dissenting opinion of Justice Rehnquist in *New York v. Uplinger,* circulated 3/8/84; retracted 3/15/84.

9. *United States v. Quinn,* 475 U.S. 791 (1986).

10. *Bowers v. Hardwick,* 478 U.S. 186 (1986). Only White voted to grant cert. Rehnquist wanted to reverse summarily; the rest voted to deny.

11. Quoted in H. W. Perry, *Deciding to Decide* (Cambridge: Harvard University Press, 1991), 168.

12. *Lloyd Corporation v. Tanner,* 407 U.S. 551 (1972). Letter from Justice Douglas to the chief justice, 5/1/72. Douglas wrote "cancel" at the top, so it is unclear if he sent it to Burger.

13. *United States v. United States District Court,* 407 U.S. 297 (1972). Memorandum from Justice Douglas to Justice Powell, 3/8/72, re: 70-153, *United States v. United States District Court.*

14. See, generally, David Danelski, "The Influence of the Chief Justice in the Decisional Process of the Supreme Court," in *American Court Systems,* ed. Sheldon Goldman and Austin Sarat (New York: Longman, 1975); and Forrest Maltzman and Paul J. Wahlbeck, "May It Please the Chief? Opinion Assignments in the Rehnquist Court," 40 *American Journal of Political Science* (1996): 421–443.

15. See Lee Epstein, Carol Mershon, Jeffrey A. Segal, and Harold J. Spaeth, "Research on the Formation of Opinion Coalitions on the U.S. Supreme Court" (proposal to the National Science Foundation; funded as SBR-9320284).

16. Jim Chen, "The Mystery and Mastery of the Judicial Power," 59 *Missouri Law Review* (1994): 281.

17. See Danelski, "The Influence of the Chief Justice"; Walter F. Murphy, *Elements of Judicial Strategy* (Chicago: Chicago University Press, 1964).

18. *Korematsu v. United States,* 323 U.S. 214 (1944); *Mapp v. Ohio,* 367 U.S. 643 (1961). These examples come from David M. O'Brien, *Storm Center,* 4th ed. (New York: Norton, 1996), 303–304.

19. Maltzman and Wahlbeck, "May It Please the Chief?"

20. *Roe v. Wade,* 410 U.S. 113 (1973); and *Doe v. Bolton,* 410 U.S. 179 (1973). Letter from Justice Douglas to the chief justice, 12/18/71, re: 70-40, *Doe v. Bolton.*

21. See Danelski, "The Influence of the Chief Justice"; and Segal and Spaeth, *The Supreme Court and the Attitudinal Model.*

22. We adopt this discussion from Paul H. Edelman and Jim Chen, "The Most Dangerous Justice: The Supreme Court at the Bar of Mathematics," 70 *Southern California Law Review* (1996): 38–43. The quote is on page 42.

23. Although we are interested in exploring only the implications of Douglas's suspicion, we note that there is a well-developed body of literature that examines majority opinion assignments made by the chief justice. For an excellent review of this literature, as well as a creative attempt to elucidate the main factors, see Maltzman and Wahlbeck, "May It Please the Chief?"

24. Letter from Chief Justice Burger to Justice Brennan, 3/24/83.

25. *Groppi v. Wisconsin,* 400 U.S. 505 (1971). Letter from Justice Stewart to the chief justice, 12/29/73. Stewart ended up writing for the majority.

26. Some of the material in this discussion of *Roe* comes from Lee Epstein and Joseph F. Kobylka, *The Supreme Court and Legal Change* (Chapel Hill: University of North Carolina Press, 1992), 183–192.

27. Memorandum of the chief justice to Justice Douglas, 12/20/71, re: *Roe* [sic] *v. Bolton,* 70–40.

28. Letter from Justice Douglas to Justice Brennan, 12/22/71.

29. Memorandum of Justice Blackmun to the conference, 5/18/72, re: *Roe v. Wade,* 70-18.

30. Memorandum of Justice Brennan to Justice Blackmun, 5/18/72, re: *Roe v. Wade,* 70-18.

31. Letter from Justice Douglas to Justice Blackmun, 5/19/72.

32. Memorandum of Justice Douglas to Justice Blackmun, 5/31/72, re: Abortion Cases. This memo was, in part, a response to Burger's (and Blackmun's) suggestion that the cases be reargued.

33. Memorandum opinion of Justice Douglas in no. 70-18, *Roe v. Wade,* and no. 70-40, *Doe v. Bolton.* First draft circulated only to Justice Brennan on 6/2/72; circulated to the rest of the Court on 6/13/72, as a dissent from the decision to put the cases over for reargument.

CHAPTER FIVE

The Institutional Context II

In Chapter Four we investigated how goal-oriented justices take into account rules that structure their relations with their colleagues. But the institutional context is more complex than that. In addition to internal rules, justices need to consider two sets of institutions that establish their relationship with relevant external actors. First, because they serve in one of three branches of government, their decisions are subject to the checks and balances inherent in the separation of powers system instantiated in the Constitution. To create efficacious law—that is, policy that the other branches will respect and with which they will comply—justices must take into account the preferences and expected actions of these other government actors. Second, because the justices operate within the greater social and political context of the society as a whole, they need to be attentive to the informal norms that reflect dominant societal beliefs about the rule of law in general and the role of the Supreme Court in particular. To the extent that these rules affect the way the American people respond to the decisions of the Court, they also affect the justices' ability to influence the substantive content of the law.

The overall contention of this chapter, then, is straightforward: if the members of the Court wish to create efficacious policy, they not only must be attentive to institutions that govern their relations with their colleagues but also take account of the rules that structure their interactions with external actors. In other words, these external institutions, like internal rules, serve as constraints on the justices' acting on their personal policy preferences. In this chapter we flesh out this claim by exploring the major institutions that govern the Court's relationship with other government actors (the separation of powers system) and with the American people (norms of legitimacy).

SEPARATION OF POWERS

During the conference discussion of *Monell v. Department of Social Services* (1978), in which the justices considered whether to affirm a lower court decision holding that city officials and municipalities are immune from damage suits filed under the Civil Rights Act of 1871, a 1961 case, *Monroe v. Pape,* received a great deal of attention.[1] Because *Monroe* held that Congress did not intend to bring cities under the act's coverage, some of the justices wondered whether they could reverse the lower court's decision in *Monell* without disturbing *Monroe.* When it was Justice Blackmun's turn to speak, he first expressed his general disagreement with the *Monroe* precedent, saying that the Court "was mistaken as to the legislative history." But he went on, "If we leave *Monroe* 100 percent intact we must affirm. Congress has accepted *Monroe.*"[2] Blackmun's simple statement, we believe, is indicative of a larger phenomenon. When it comes to making decisions, the justices must be attentive to the preferences of the other institutions and the actions they expect them to take if they want to generate enduring policy.

This claim, as we explained in Chapter One, flows from the logic of an institution underlying the U.S. Constitution, the separation of powers system. That system, along with informal rules that have evolved over time, such as the power of judicial review, endows each branch of government with significant powers and authority over its sphere. At the same time, it provides explicit checks on the exercise of those powers; each branch can impose limits on the primary functions of the others. For example, the judiciary may interpret the law and even strike down laws as being in violation of the Constitution, but Congress can pass new legislation, which the president may sign or veto. (See Figure 1-1, page 14.)

Seen in this way, the rule of checks and balances provides justices and all other government actors with important information: policy in the United States emanates not from the separate actions of the branches of government but from the *interaction* among them. It follows that for any set of actors—whether justices, legislators, or executives—to make authoritative policy, they must take account of this institutional constraint by formulating expectations about the preferences of the other relevant actors and what they expect them to do when making their own choices.

This general claim, however, requires some clarification. While we believe that the separation of powers system operates across a range of substantive issues, we also believe that it imposes a more significant constraint on cases involving statutory questions than on constitutional questions.[3] It is easy to understand why this claim holds in statutory cases. Suppose, as Figure 5-1 shows, that Blackmun was correct in his *Monell* conference remarks that Congress's ideal policy was *Monroe* and the relevant congressional committees, those with the power to introduce legislation to overturn *Monell,* were slightly to the left of Congress. In denoting the ideal points (the actors' preferred position on the policy) of J, M, and C in Figure 5-1 and those that follow, we assume that the actors prefer an outcome that is nearer to that point than one that is farther away. Further suppose that the Court genuinely preferred to overrule *Monroe.* If the Court did not take into account Congress's preference and placed the policy precisely where it wanted it, it would give the committees incentive to introduce legislation to override its decision. The reason is that the committees prefer any point on the line between C(M) and M to J.[a] Congress would be agreeable to the override proposal because it too preferred M to J, and the legislature would be well within its power to take this step because it can overturn the interpretations the Court gives to its laws. Indeed, between 1967 and 1990, Congress disturbed some 120 Court decisions.[b]

---

a. In Figure 5-1 and in the figures to come, C(M) represents the committees' indifference point "where the Court can set policy which the committees like no more and no less than the opposite policy that could be chosen" by Congress. See William N. Eskridge Jr., "Overriding Supreme Court Statutory Interpretation Decisions," 101 *Yale Law Journal* (1991): 378.

b. Ibid., 344. The number of overrides raises an interesting question: If we are correct and the Court takes into account government preferences and likely actions when it reaches decisions, why does the Court occasionally produce policy that Congress/president later overturn? One explanation is that the Court fails to take account of the external constraint imposed by the separation of powers systems. But, as our analysis later indicates, this does not seem to be the case; at the very least, in their private conferences justices attempt to form beliefs about the preferences of other actors. Another explanation is that the Court believes its decisions can provide the

Figure 5-1   Hypothetical Distribution of Preferences over the
Question of Liability Under the Civil Rights Act of 1871

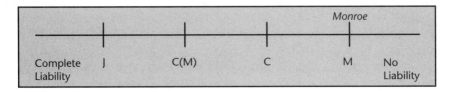

Note: The policy, *Question of Liability,* is whether city officials and municipalities are immune from damage suits filed under the Civil Rights Act of 1871.

J = ideal point of majority of Court; *C(M)* = indifference point of congressional committees; *C* = ideal point of relevant congressional committees; *M* = ideal point of median legislator in Congress.

Definitional Note: An *ideal point* is the actor's preferred position on the policy. We assume that actors prefer an outcome that is nearer to that point than one that is farther away. The *median legislator* is the legislator that divides Congress into two equal halves on the particular policy dimension. *Indifference* occurs when actors like one policy outcome as well as another; that is, both outcomes are at least as good as each other. Above we show the indifference point of the congressional committees, C(M), which (in this depiction) is the policy outcome that they view as desirable as the ideal outcome desired by the median member of Congress. For more details, see James D. Morrow, *Game Theory for Political Scientists* (Princeton, N.J.: Princeton University Press, 1994).

Cases involving constitutional interpretation present a different situation. Although the separation of powers system endows Congress and the president with weapons they can deploy against the Court, they do not deploy them very often. The infrequency of congressional responses to constitutional decisions, coupled with the difficulty involved in overturning them, means the justices may be less attentive to the preferences and likely actions of other government actors in constitutional disputes than in statutory cases. However, there are three reasons why we would not expect the Court to ignore completely the external constraint imposed by the separation of powers system in constitutional cases.

First, the other two branches of government have the power to alter constitutional policy established by the Court. Congress can propose con-

legislature with information, which can persuade members of Congress to reevaluate their positions. Finally, it is possible that the Court does not know with certainty what the other government actors will do. In these situations, the justices can only form estimates, which, like all estimates, may be wrong.

stitutional amendments, and it has even passed legislation to override constitutional decisions. The Religious Freedom Restoration Act of 1993
(RFRA) provides a case in point. RFRA, which directed courts to use a
particular standard of law to adjudicate First Amendment free exercise of
religion claims, was enacted to undercut the Court's 1990 decision in
Employment Division v. Smith.[4]

It is worth noting that Congress does not often propose constitutional
amendments or even legislation to override the Court. Moreover, when
the legislature attempts to direct the justices on how to adjudicate constitutional cases, the Court may not follow. Indeed, in *City of Boerne v. Flores*
(1997) not only did the majority overturn RFRA, but also it rebuked the
"political" branches:

> Our national experience teaches that the Constitution is preserved best
> when each part of the government respects both the Constitution and the
> proper actions and determinations of the other branches. When the Court
> has interpreted the Constitution, it has acted within the province of the
> Judicial Branch, which embraces the duty to say what the law is. *Marbury
> v. Madison*. When the political branches of the Government act against the
> background of a judicial interpretation of the Constitution already issued,
> it must be understood that in later cases and controversies the Court will
> treat its precedents with the respect due them under settled principles,
> including *stare decisis,* and contrary expectations must be disappointed.
> RFRA was designed to control cases and controversies, such as the one
> before us; but as the provisions of the federal statute here invoked are
> beyond congressional authority, it is this Court's precedent, not RFRA,
> which must control.[5]

Shortly after the decision in *City of Boerne* was announced, Congress
held hearings to discover how it might be circumvented.[6] Therefore, the
game over RFRA may not be over, with the possibility always existing that
the Court will eventually buckle under. The more general point, however,
is this: because Congress has in the past overridden the Court, the justices
have reason to believe that the legislature will do so in the future, and this
may be enough to cause them to, at the very least, pay some attention to
its preferences.

Second, the U.S. Constitution provides the elected branches with other
weapons that may not be related to specific policies, that they can use to
"punish" justices for their decisions. Congress, for example, can hold judicial salaries constant, impeach justices, and pass legislation to remove the

Figure 5-2   Approximate Distribution of Preferences over the Rights
of Witnesses in Subversive Activities Cases, 1957–1959

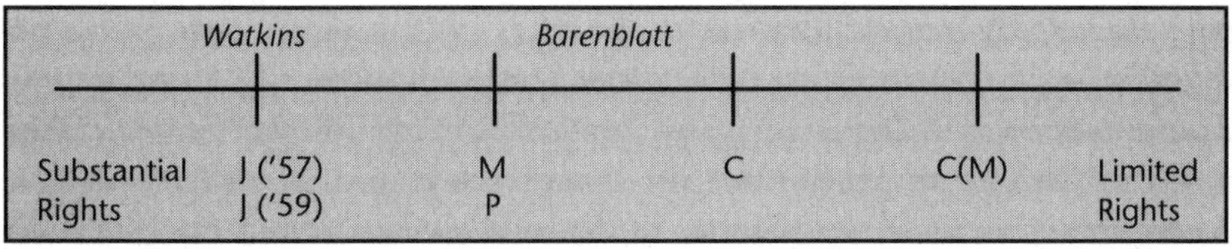

Watkins		*Barenblatt*		
Substantial	J ('57)	M	C	C(M)	Limited
Rights	J ('59)	P			Rights

Note: The policy, *Rights of Witnesses*, pertains to the rights of witnesses to refuse to answer questions put to them by congressional committees investigating subversive activities in the United States.

J ('57) = ideal point of majority of Court in 1957; J ('59) = ideal point of majority of Court in 1959; M = ideal point of median legislator in Congress; C = ideal point of relevant congressional committees; P = ideal point of the president; C(M) = indifference point of congressional committees.

Definitional Note: An *ideal point* is the actor's preferred position on the policy. We assume that actors prefer an outcome that is nearer to that point than one that is farther away. The *median legislator* is the legislator that divides Congress into two equal halves on the particular policy dimension. *Indifference* occurs when actors like one policy outcome as well as another; that is, both outcomes are at least as good as each other. Above we show the indifference point of the congressional committees, C(M), which (in this depiction) is the policy outcome that they view as desirable as the ideal outcome desired by the median member of Congress (and, here, the president). For more details, see James D. Morrow, *Game Theory for Political Scientists* (Princeton, N.J.: Princeton University Press, 1994).

Court's ability to hear certain kinds of cases. Although the government rarely deploys these weapons, their existence may serve to constrain policy-oriented justices from acting on their preferences. The *Watkins/Barenblatt* pair, described in Chapter Two, provides a nice illustration.[7] In these cases the Court considered similar constitutional questions pertaining to the rights of witnesses to refuse to answer questions put to them by congressional committees investigating subversive activities in the United States. In *Watkins* the Court ruled for the witness, but in *Barenblatt* it ruled against him. A possible explanation for the shift is depicted in Figure 5-2, which provides an approximation of the ideal points of the major players. At the time the cases were decided, the Court was to the left of (more liberal than) Congress, the president, and the relevant congressional committees. Given this configuration, the Court's decision in *Watkins,* which put the policy at its ideal point, provided the committees with incentive to introduce legislation to override its decision. The reason is that the committees preferred any point on the line between C(M) and M/P to J. Congress and the president would have favored legislation to override because they too preferred M/P to J. In fact, responding to *Watkins* and other liberal decisions, members of Congress proposed numerous Court-curbing laws, including some that would have removed the Court's jurisdiction to hear cases involving subversive activities. Therefore, in *Barenblatt,* the Court had every reason to misrepresent its true policy preferences to protect its legitimacy and reach a result to the right of the congressional median (M), which is precisely the course of action it took.

Finally, government actors can refuse, implicitly or explicitly, to implement particular constitutional decisions, thereby decreasing the Court's ability to create efficacious policy. *Immigration and Naturalization Service v. Chadha* provides a case in point.[8] Theoretically speaking, *Chadha* nullified, on constitutional grounds, the one-house legislative veto, that is, the ability of either house of Congress to reject policy produced by executive agencies. In practice, however, Congress has passed more than two hundred new laws containing legislative vetoes since *Chadha,* and agencies continue to pay heed to congressional rejections of their policy. The problem here is that the Court fashioned a rule that was "unacceptable" to the other branches of government and, as a result, the rule has been "eroded by open defiance and subtle evasion." [9] There are several explanations as to why the Court established such an ineffective rule, but the relevant point is simple enough: once the Court reached its decision it had to depend on Congress to implement it. Because Congress failed to do so, the Court was unable to set long-term policy.[c]

Hence, although we believe that the constraint imposed by the separation of powers system operates to a greater extent in statutory cases than in constitutional cases—a sensible claim because Congress can more easily overturn the Court's construction of its statutes than it can constitutional provisions—we do not believe that it is wholly inoperative in constitu-

---

c. *Chadha* raises the question of why the Court occasionally produces inefficacious policy. In this case, we know it was not because the justices failed to take into account the preferences of other actors. In his dissenting opinion, Justice White anticipated the congressional reaction, as did Chief Justice Burger, the author of the majority opinion. During the conference discussion, Powell recorded Burger as saying veto issue is "highly sensitive politically. Wish we could avoid the issue." After the conference vote, a worried Burger circulated six drafts of his opinion, knowing that Congress was going to look at it with a jaundiced eye.

tional cases. The *Watkins/Barenblatt* example and others we shall offer make that plain; they illustrate our belief about the importance of the separation of powers system—and its importance in a range of disputes.

In the material that follows, we attempt to provide greater support for the claim by addressing three questions to which it gives rise. (1) Where do justices obtain information about the preferences and likely actions of other government actors? (2) Are justices attentive to those preferences and likely actions? (3) If justices are attentive, do their beliefs affect the choices they make?

Information About the Preferences and Likely Actions of Other Government Actors

Before considering whether justices take into account the preferences of other actors and whether their "accounting" affects their choices, we must deal with a threshold question: Where do justices obtain the information necessary to formulate such beliefs? This question must come first because, if justices cannot obtain the necessary information, they cannot act in the manner we suggest or cannot do so effectively. This is not to say that justices must know with certainty where Congress or the president stand on particular issues, but that they need to be able to make some calculation about the nature of the political context in which they are operating.

Two sources supply information to the justices. The first is the media. We have no reason to suspect that justices, like other Americans, do not obtain information about current events from newspapers, magazines, television, and radio. Because many justices held political positions before their appointment to the Court (see Table 2-3, page 37), it would be difficult to believe that they relinquish their interest in politics once on the bench any more than they shed their political preferences. Moreover, during our examination of the files of Justices Marshall, Brennan, and Powell, we came across many clippings of newspaper stories and editorials about specific cases—those the Court had decided and those awaiting action. Occasionally, justices even circulate copies of newspaper stories, with commentary, to their colleagues, as the following memorandum, dated October 1, 1985, from Justice Powell illustrates:

> The enclosed article from the October 7 issue of *U.S. News & World Report* entitled "As Liability-Insurance Squeeze Hits Everyone" may be of interest.

It is not easy to disagree with the insurers that the cause of this intolerable situation lies primarily with "lawyers, juries, and the courts." The article is relevant to the cert petition we considered today involving the new statute enacted by California with respect to the liability of physicians.

In another instance, Powell forwarded to Stevens, and only to him, an article relevant to *NCAA v. Board of Regents* (1984). The case asked whether the National Collegiate Athletic Association's plan for televising its member schools' football games violated the Sherman Anti-Trust Act—Stevens was assigned to write the majority opinion but had yet to circulate it. This memo accompanied the article:

Dear John:
    One of my clerks brought the enclosed article to my attention.
    It suggests the kind of market that will exist in free competition, and provides details as to the basketball experience.[10]

These examples suggest that justices pay attention to how the press reports on issues on their docket and on their activities; and we do not imagine that the clippings found in their files are the only articles they read.

    A second source of information—briefs of the parties and of amici curiae—enables justices to make potentially precise calculations because these briefs are geared toward the specific issues at hand. To see this, consider the arguments contained in an amicus curiae submission filed by several states in *United States v. Leon*. These "friends" wanted the justices to eradicate the exclusionary rule as not constitutionally mandated. In support of their position, they "informed" the Court that:

Several justices have expressly stated that the exclusionary remedy is not of constitutional dimension, and this view is concurred in by the current President [Reagan] and a number of members of Congress.[11]

This sort of preference delineation is not at all unusual, as Table 5-1 shows. The data, from briefs filed in a random sample of 1990 term cases, suggest that justices can readily obtain information on the preferences of the institutions of the federal government and of the states. We should not take these figures to mean that justices regard all of this information as credible, but they certainly show that the majority of briefs filed in constitutional and nonconstitutional cases attempt to define the preferences of other political actors. In fact, at least one brief provided this kind of information in all but two of the fourteen cases in our sample.

TABLE 5-1
Delineation of Preferences in Attorneys' Briefs

Delineated Preferences of Other Government Actors?	Briefs Filed in Constitutional Cases		Briefs Filed in Nonconstitutional Cases		Total	
	n	%	n	%	n	%
Yes	18	75.0	21	80.8	39	78.0
No	6	25.0	5	19.2	11	22.0
Total	24		26		50	

Data Sources: U.S. Supreme Court Records and Briefs, BNA's Law Reprints; Harold J. Spaeth, United States Supreme Court Judicial Database (updated annually) (Ann Arbor, Mich.: Inter-University Consortium for Political and Social Research, 1997), published as study no. 9422.

Note: This is a random sample of cases decided during the 1990 term. It includes four constitutional cases and ten nonconstitutional cases. We used Spaeth's U.S. Supreme Court Judicial Database to classify the basis of the decision as constitutional or not. We thank Harold J. Spaeth for running these data for us.

Coding Rules: For each case, we read the briefs filed by the parties and by amici curiae, if any. If the brief mentioned the preferences of the federal government or of a state, we coded it as delineating a preference. To obtain the data, navigate to: http://www.artsci.wustl.edu/~polisci/epstein/choices/.

Attention to the Preferences and Likely Actions of Other Government Actors

Assuming that justices can obtain information about the preferences and likely actions of other actors, the next question is: Do they attempt to take account of their beliefs about those preferences/actions when making choices? Blackmun's comment during the *Monell* conference provides some evidence that they do. But is this sort of accounting typical? The fact that written submissions often include information about other political units, as shown in Table 5-1, suggests that attorneys believe that *Monell* is not unusual. Given the constraints on how long a brief can be, why would lawyers include this information if they thought it would be trivial to the justices?

It is also true that majority opinions often comment on the preferences of various government actors, as *Heckler v. Edwards* exemplifies. In this case the Court was asked to determine whether a federal appellate court could dismiss, for lack of jurisdiction, the government's appeal from a district court decision in which it declared a section of the Social Security Act unconstitutional, but in which the government challenged only the district court's remedy. The justices noted that "neither Congress nor the agency had modified the statute or implementing regulation at the time this case was argued." [12]

Constitutional criminal cases provide another kind of example. In these sorts of disputes, justices occasionally record the number of states that do or do not follow a particular practice. Illustrative is *Gregg v. Georgia,* in which the Court considered whether a state capital punishment law, passed in response to its 1972 decision in *Furman v. Georgia* (striking down existing death penalty laws), violated the Constitution.[13] In ruling that the revised statute was, in fact, constitutional, the justices took note of the preferences of the states: "in response to *Furman* . . . [t]he legislatures of at least 35 States have enacted new statutes that provide for the death penalty." [14]

One might argue that these *public* statements are mere window dressing, designed to lead government actors into believing that justices are taking their preferences seriously, that they are preemptive strikes by the Court to guard against override attempts. If this were so, we would not expect to find justices taking government preferences into account in their *private* deliberations, for it is difficult to imagine that a group of intelligent individuals would attempt to formulate beliefs about external actors among themselves and use those beliefs to persuade their colleagues to take particular actions, as Blackmun did in *Monell,* if they did not think they were important.

To assess the extent to which justices are attentive to the preferences/likely actions of other government actors, we examined Brennan's conference memoranda—the typed versions of the statements he made at conference and that he occasionally read verbatim—and the notes that he and Powell took during the justices' private discussions of cases orally argued during the 1983 term. We coded comments, such as the one Blackmun made in *Monell,* as attempts to engage in belief formation.[d]

---

d. We coded only those occasions when justices made comments about the preferences of government actors (for example, the president), branches (for example, Congress), or units (for example, the states). We excluded statements noting a lack of information about such preferences, such as when Powell recorded Stevens as saying in *Brown v. Hotel & Restaurant Employees,* 468 U.S. 491 (1984): "Odd [that] NLRB filed no brief." For the data, visit our web site: *http://www.artsci.wustl.edu/~polisci/epstein/choices/.*

TABLE 5-2

Attention to the Preferences and Likely Actions of Government Actors During Conference Discussion

Attentive to Preferences/Likely Actions of Other Government Actors?	Constitutional Cases		Nonconstitutional Cases		Total	
	n	%	n	%	n	%
Yes	32	46.4	60	69.8	92	59.4
No	37	53.6	26	30.2	63	40.6
Total	69		86		155	

Data Sources: Conference notes and conference memoranda of Justice William J. Brennan Jr., Library of Congress; conference notes of Justice Lewis F. Powell Jr., Washington and Lee University School of Law; Harold J. Spaeth, *United States Supreme Court Judicial Database* (updated annually) (Ann Arbor, Mich.: Inter-University Consortium for Political and Social Research, 1997), published as study no. 9422.

Note: The data are from Brennan's conference memoranda and Powell's and Brennan's notes of discussions of cases orally argued during the 1983 term that were listed in Brennan's register, with the exception of original cases. The unit of analysis was citation: if two or more cases were combined under one U.S. cite, we included only the lead case. We used Spaeth's U.S. Supreme Court Judicial Database to classify the basis of decisions as constitutional or not. We thank Harold J. Spaeth for running these data for us.

Coding Rules: We begin with Justice Brennan's conference memo, a typed version of his conference statement, which—according to Powell's conference notes—Brennan more than occasionally read verbatim. If this memo took into account the preferences or likely actions of other government actors, we coded the case as "attentive." If this memo did not take into account such factors, we examined Brennan's and Powell's notes of the comments of other justices. To obtain the data, navigate to: *http://www.artsci.wustl.edu/~polisci/epstein/choices/*.

We also noted whether the case at hand involved largely constitutional or nonconstitutional matters. Table 5-2 displays the results.

Several findings are worthy of note. First, in more than half the cases at least one justice explicitly stated her beliefs about the preferences/likely actions of other government actors, and some of the remarks were even more explicit than Blackmun's in *Monell.* Consider Brennan's comments in *Norfolk Redevelopment and Housing Authority v. Chesapeake & Potomac Telephone Company,* in which the Court was asked to determine whether a utility company is a "displaced person" within the meaning of the Uniform Relocation Act of 1970.[15] After noting his view of Congress's intent in the legislation at hand, Brennan added:

> Congress is in the process of enacting legislation which would prospec-
> tively overrule the Fourth Circuit's holding, while also allowing utilities to
> obtain relocation assistance in certain limited circumstances. It is interest-
> ing to note that even if applicable, none of these circumstances would
> cover the present case.

In other words, Brennan attempted to formulate beliefs about congressional preferences and likely actions by looking at the legislature's intent
and its current behavior. Interesting too is that Congress was not the only
actor to whom Brennan was attentive. In *Immigration and Naturalization
Service v. Phinpathya,* involving the meaning of the term "continuous physical presence" within the Immigration and Nationality Act, Brennan noted
his belief that Congress's purpose was not to punish aliens who left the
country to avoid "undue hardship." [16] Brennan also claimed that he drew
"support for this position from the Attorney General's acquiescence in
Wadman [*v. INS*] in 1964, combined with his [position] in this case." [17]

A second finding appears to bode less well for our argument: in only 46
percent of constitutional cases (but in 70 percent of nonconstitutional
cases) do justices attempt to account for the preferences and likely actions
of other actors. It would, at first blush, seem to give ammunition to those
who argue that the external constraint of the separation of powers system
does not apply to constitutional disputes. But another look at the data suggests a different interpretation. Of the thirty-seven constitutional cases in
which justices made no belief-formulation attempt, eighteen involved
issues of criminal rights and procedures.[18] In such cases, the justices need
not exert too much energy trying to discern the government's preferences
because they are typically against the accused.

If we eliminate these criminal cases from consideration, the percentage
of conference attempts increases to about sixty. While this figure is still
below that in nonconstitutional disputes (not an unexpected finding on our
account), it lends support to the notion that justices more than occasionally attend to the preferences/likely actions of other government actors.

Effect of Justices' Beliefs About the Preferences and Likely Actions of Other Government Actors

Our primary argument in this section is that the institution of the
American separation of powers system serves as a constraint on justices acting on their personal preferences. If that assertion is correct, we should find
evidence of the constraint operating on many of the choices justices make

and, ultimately, affecting the law they create. We have already supplied some support for this claim. Earlier we provided data to show that the Court considers the preferences of the president and Congress when making its decisions over which cases to hear and decide. We also described the results of a study suggesting that chief justices seek to assign opinions to colleagues who will be in the best position to make the majority view palatable to external actors.[19]

Perhaps even more important is a range of data showing that justices' beliefs about government actors affect their decisions on the merits of cases—decisions that, in turn, have the potential of becoming policy for all of society. We first consider analyses of two cases of historical importance, *Marbury v. Madison* and *Ex parte McCardle*.[20]

In Chapter Two, we invoked *Marbury* to illustrate the point that justices act strategically with regard to other political actors when pursuing their goals. Chief Justice Marshall took the action that he did—denying Marbury his job while establishing judicial review—because it was the best he could do given:

- his own preferences (Marshall wanted to establish judicial review and give Marbury his appointment);
- Jefferson's preferences (he favored judicial review, but disfavored giving Marbury his appointment);
- Marshall's and Jefferson's beliefs about the political context in which they operated (their belief that Congress would have supported Jefferson if Jefferson had tried to have Marshall impeached).

To support the claim that Marshall crafted the best solution he could, we offer Figure 5-3, which we derived from a game-theoretic analysis of the *Marbury* case.[21] The top half of the figure shows what might have happened had Jefferson not favored judicial review *and* Marshall and Jefferson believed that Congress supported the president. Note that, under these circumstances, no matter what Marshall did, Jefferson would have attempted to impeach him and judicial review would not have been established. The bottom half of the figure presents the possible course of events had Marshall believed that Jefferson favored judicial review and that Congress favored Marshall. If that were the case, Marshall might have behaved in a sincere fashion—giving Marbury his commission and establishing judicial review. But, because it is quite possible that Jefferson would have refused to deliver the commission, such a move could have generated a clash between the president and the Court.

Figure 5-3   Alternative Paths in *Marbury v. Madison*

1. If Jefferson does not favor the establishment of judicial review and Marshall and Jefferson believe that the political environment strongly favors Jefferson, then:

> Marshall refuses to give Marbury his position and fails to establish judicial review ⟶
> Jefferson attempts to have Marshall impeached

2. If Jefferson favors the establishment of judicial review and Marshall and Jefferson believe that the political environment strongly favors Marshall, then:

> Marshall gives Marbury his position and establishes judicial review ⟶
> Jefferson refuses to deliver Marbury's commission

Note: This figure depicts only those events directly related to *Marbury* and omits some paths of play. For more details, including the derivation of the results, see Jack Knight and Lee Epstein, "On the Struggle for Judicial Supremacy," 30 *Law and Society Review* (1996): 87–120.

Seen in this way, the effect of the external constraint imposed by the separation of powers system is dramatic. Under a different set of beliefs and preferences, judicial review—the Court's most powerful tool—may not have been established, or a major showdown between Jefferson and Marshall could have resulted, with either the Court or the president emerging in a seriously weakened form.

The effect of the separation of powers system on the development of law was no less felt in the post–Civil War case of *Ex parte McCardle*.[22] After the war Congress, in the control of the Radical Republicans, imposed restrictions on the South. Known as the Reconstruction laws, they in effect placed the region under military rule. Journalist William McCardle opposed these measures and wrote editorials urging resistance to them. As a result, he was arrested for publishing allegedly "incendiary and libelous articles" and held for a trial before a military tribunal, established under Reconstruction.

Because he was a civilian, not a member of any militia, McCardle alleged that he was being illegally held. He petitioned for a writ of habeas corpus, which is an order issued to determine if a person held in custody is being unlawfully detained or imprisoned. His petition was based on an 1867 act giving federal judges the power to grant habeas corpus to any person restrained in violation of the U.S. Constitution. After this effort failed, McCardle appealed to the U.S. Supreme Court.

When the Court heard arguments in early March 1868, it was clear to most observers that "no Justice was still making up his mind": the Court's sympathies lay with McCardle.[23] But before the justices could issue their decision, Congress, on March 27, enacted a law that repealed the 1867 Habeas Corpus Act and removed the Supreme Court's authority to hear appeals emanating from it; it even threatened to remove the Court's jurisdiction to hear all Reconstruction cases. These moves were meant to punish the Court or, at the very least, to send it a strong message. Two years before *McCardle,* in 1866, the Court had invalidated President Lincoln's use of military tribunals in certain areas, and Congress did not want to see the Court take similar action in this dispute.[24] The legislature's feelings were so strong on this issue that, after President Andrew Johnson vetoed the 1868 repealer act, Congress overrode the veto.

The Court responded by redocketing the case for oral arguments in March 1869. During the arguments and in its briefs, the government made its position clear: "When the jurisdiction of a court to determine a case or a class of cases depends upon a statute and that statute is repealed, the jurisdiction ceases absolutely." In short, the government contended that the Court no longer had authority to hear the case and should dismiss it. Despite the fact that the justices wanted to rule in favor of McCardle and make clear to Congress that it could not subject civilians to military trials when civilian courts were in operation, it did not take this step. Rather, after considering the preferences and likely actions of Congress, the justices acted in a sophisticated fashion: they acceded to the government's wishes and declined to hear the case.

This move helped the justices avoid a major collision with the legislature at a time when the Court's prestige was particularly low, thereby ensuring its ability to make future policy.[e] It also established a precedent of no small consequence. *McCardle* suggests that Congress has the authority

---

e. The Court's image was still suffering from its decision in *Scott v. Sandford,* 19 How. 393 (1857), in which the Court struck down the Missouri Compromise, even though Congress had already repealed it. The Court ruled that Congress did not have the constitutional power to regulate slavery in the territories. In addition, the justices said that blacks could not be considered in a legal sense to be citizens of the United States. Some scholars suggest that *Scott* not only contributed to the start of the Civil War but also that it damaged the credibility of the Supreme Court for decades to come.

to remove the Court's appellate jurisdiction as it deems necessary. This policy provides the legislature with potential leverage over the Court in a range of disputes and is yet another reason why the justices must be attentive to the interests of the other branches of government.[f]

To us, *Marbury* and *McCardle* are good examples of our point in this section. But it could be argued that this is all they are—unusual examples—and that in the main the justices do not view the institution of the separation of powers system as a constraint on their policy preferences. We have two responses. The first is that even if *Marbury*, *McCardle*, and other landmark cases are the exceptions, they cannot be ignored.[25] After all, it was the strategic interactions in these cases—whether between Marshall and Jefferson or the Court and the Radical Republican Congress—that generated some of the most important rulings in American history. We have only to consider how different the law might be had Jefferson not favored judicial review or had the post–Civil War Court failed to take into account the preferences of Congress.

Second, as it turns out, these cases are not anomalous, as William Eskridge's study of the development of civil rights policy from 1962 to 1990 makes clear.[26] Overall, Eskridge shows that it is difficult to understand how the Court reached many of its decisions without taking into account the preferences of the majority of justices *and* those of the president, Congress, and the relevant congressional committees. In other words, he provides strong evidence of the claim we make: the separation of powers system serves as an external constraint on justices acting on their own

---

f. Since *McCardle,* Congress has considered, but not enacted, legislation to limit the Court's appellate jurisdiction. Many of these proposals have involved controversial issues such as abortion, prayer in school, and busing, leading to the conclusion that modern Congresses are no different from the one that passed the 1868 repealer act: the legislature would like to use the Exceptions Clause (Article III, section 2) as a way to restrain the Court, but has yet to do so successfully.

Moreover, in spite of *McCardle,* justices continue to debate whether Congress may use the Exceptions Clause in this way. In *National Mutual Insurance Co. v. Tidewater Transfer,* 337 U.S. 582 (1949), Justice Frankfurter wrote, "Congress need not give this Court any appellate power; it may withdraw appellate jurisdiction once conferred and it may do so even while a case is sub judice [before a judge]." Thirteen years later, in *Glidden Co. v. Zdanok,* 379 U.S. 530 (1962), Justice Douglas remarked, "There is a serious question whether the *McCardle* case could command a majority view today."

Figure 5-4   Distribution of Preferences over Civil Rights Policy, 1972–1981

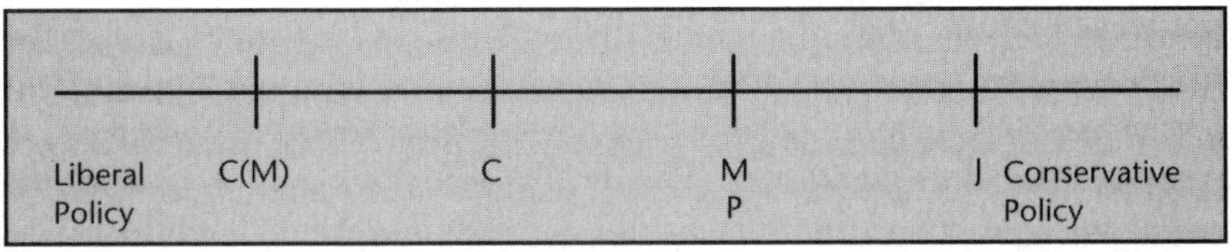

Source: William N. Eskridge Jr., "Reneging on History? Playing the Court/Congress/President Civil Rights Game," 79 California Law Review (1991): 650.

Note: By Preferences over Civil Rights Policy Eskridge means preferences concerning civil rights legislation passed by Congress. Examples include the Civil Rights Act of 1964 (attempting to eliminate many forms of discrimination in major areas of American life); the Age Discrimination Act Amendments of 1978 (prohibiting "arbitrary age discrimination in employment"); and the Pregnancy Discrimination Act of 1978 (forbidding employment discrimination of grounds of pregnancy).

$C(M)$ = indifference point of congressional committees; C = ideal point of relevant congressional committees; M = ideal point of median legislator in Congress; P = ideal point of the president; J = ideal point of majority of Court.

Definitional Note: An ideal point is the actor's preferred position on the policy. We assume that actors prefer an outcome that is nearer to that point than one that is farther away. The median legislator is the legislator that divides Congress into two equal halves on the particular policy dimension. Indifference occurs when actors like one policy outcome as well as another; that is, both outcomes are at least as good as each other. Above we show the indifference point of the congressional committees, $C(M)$, which (in this depiction) is the policy outcome that they view as desirable as the ideal outcome desired by the median member of Congress (and, here, the president). For more details, see James D. Morrow, Game Theory for Political Scientists (Princeton, N.J.: Princeton University Press, 1994).

policy preferences. And he shows just how this constraint operates to affect policy in the United States.[g]

Figure 5-4, which depicts the preferences of the Court, Congress, congressional committees, and the president over civil rights policy between 1972 and 1981, illustrates the power of Eskridge's argument. Note that, under this preference distribution, the Court is to the right of Congress, the congressional committees, and the president. If the separation of pow-

---

g. Almost every study, both before and after Eskridge's, that examined the separation of powers system comes to the conclusion we report: it acts as a constraint on justices acting on their policy preferences. See, for example, C. Herman Pritchett, *Congress versus the Supreme Court* (Minneapolis: University of Minnesota Press, 1961); Walter F.

ers system operates in the way that we (and Eskridge) suggest, we should see the Court consistently behaving in a sophisticated fashion—in this example, reaching decisions that are more liberal than its sincere preferences. The reason is simple: should the Court place policy on its ideal point, it would give the congressional committees, who prefer any policy to the left of the Court's sincere preference, every incentive to attempt an override. The committees would understand that the median member of the legislature and the president are also to the left of the Court and would therefore be amenable to moving policy in a more liberal direction.

Although this prediction does not hold in every case, it explains some of the most important and seemingly anomalous Burger Court decisions, with *United Steelworkers v. Weber* providing a good example.[27] The Court, which had previously voiced disapproval of affirmative action programs in constitutional litigation, held that Title VII of the Civil Rights Act permitted a voluntary plan—a policy outcome Eskridge explains:

> Justice Stewart, who voted with the *Weber* majority, had voted the year before against the constitutionality of voluntary state affirmative action. Another majority justice explained his vote in *Weber* as a response to societal developments that had overtaken the original congressional expecta-

---

Murphy, *Congress and the Supreme Court* (Chicago: University of Chicago Press, 1962); Pablo T. Spiller and Rafael Gely, "Congressional Control of Judicial Independence: The Determinants of U.S. Supreme Court Labor-Relations Decisions, 1949–1988," 23 *RAND Journal of Economics* (1992): 463–492; Gerald N. Rosenberg, "Judicial Independence and the Reality of Political Power," 54 *Review of Politics* (1992): 369–398; William N. Eskridge Jr. and John Ferejohn. "The Article I, Section 7 Game," 80 *Georgetown Law Journal* (1992): 523; Linda R. Cohen and Matthew L. Spitzer, "Solving the *Chevron* Puzzle," 57 *Law and Contemporary Problems* (1994): 65–110.

An important exception is Jeffrey Segal's study, "Separation-of-Powers Games in the Positive Theory of Congress and Courts," 91 *American Political Science Review* (1997): 28–44, which provides empirical evidence to show that "the institutional protections granted the Court mean that with respect to Congress and the presidency" the justices almost never need to vote other than sincerely.

Whether Segal's conclusion will hold as scholars continue to produce research on this important topic, we cannot say at this point. See, for example, Andrew D. Martin, "Designing Statistical Tests of Formal Theories: The Separation of Powers and the Supreme Court" (paper presented at the 1997 annual meeting of the Law of Society Association, St. Louis, Mo.). But, as noted, the preponderance of research to date surely supports our assertion that *Marbury* and *McCardle* are not anomalous.

tions. Both of these justices may have been sensitive to the pressures for
affirmative action created by *Griggs v. Duke Power Co.* and to [Congress's]
approval of *Griggs.* For these reasons, a Court critical of affirmative action
in constitutional cases ended up interpreting title VII to allow a broad
range of private affirmative action programs.

Eskridge goes on to write: "The conclusion from this *Weber* example suggests a broader observation: the Burger Court generally produced results in
constitutional civil rights cases (where there was little chance of its being
overridden) that were discernibly more conservative than the results it
reached in analogous cases of statutory interpretation." [28]
    Although our data provide some support for this last observation—recall
that justices are more likely to be attentive in conference discussion to the
preferences of other actors in nonconstitutional cases than in constitutional cases—we cannot ignore evidence suggesting that the external constraint of the separation of powers system is in fact operative in some constitutional cases. *Marbury v. Madison* provides one piece of evidence; cases
analyzed by other scholars provide even more. [29]

THE COURT AND THE AMERICAN PEOPLE

So far, our discussion has elucidated the importance of one institution governing relations between the Court and the external community—the
separation of powers system. What we have demonstrated is that this institution constrains judicial decision making, that justices, in their quest to
create efficacious policy, must make choices that will be acceptable to other
government actors. If they are not attentive in this fashion, they may see
results similar to what followed the *Chadha* or *Smith* cases: the other
branches fail to comply with Court policy or seek to overturn it.
    But the separation of powers is not the only institution the justices need
to consider. Because they operate within the greater social and political
context of the society as a whole, the justices also must attend to those
informal rules that reflect dominant societal beliefs about the rule of law
in general and the role of the Supreme Court in particular—the norms of
legitimacy. To the extent that these norms affect the way the American
people respond to the decisions of the Court, they affect the ability of justices to influence the substantive content of the law.
    We illustrate this argument by considering two examples of legitimacy
norms: *sua sponte,* which is the norm disfavoring the creation of issues, and

stare decisis, the norm favoring respect for precedent. We selected these two not only because they are important constraints on policy-seeking justices but also because they demonstrate the complexity of any empirical analysis designed to unearth the effects of norms on judicial decision making.

Before we turn to these examples, however, we need to clarify one point. Some might argue that these legitimacy norms are not institutions that have much to do with society as a whole; instead, they govern the relationship between the Court and members of the legal community—in other words, attorneys. We understand why some would make this claim: after all, we know of no explicit empirical evidence to suggest that most Americans take legitimacy norms seriously, that they believe it is important for the Court to refrain from creating issues or to respect previously decided cases. But there is evidence to show, first of all, that attorneys believe in the existence of these norms.[h] And, because lawyers—whether retained by interest groups, the states, the federal government, or one client—represent the public in Court, we would be hard-pressed to say that these norms do not operate between the larger community and the justices. There is also evidence demonstrating that the justices believe that these norms govern relations between them and the public, not just the legal community. A private memorandum Powell sent to Burger provides an example. In telling the chief why he planned to remain true to his position in the landmark affirmative action case, *Regents of the University of California v. Bakke,* Powell had this to say:

---

h. For one thing, they are schooled in them; many law school classes operate on the assumption that the doctrine of *stare decisis* is alive and well. In addition, research shows that, in their written briefs before the Court, attorneys cite precedent more than all other sources combined. These sources include scholarly works and state and federal constitutional provisions, statutes, and regulations. See Jack Knight and Lee Epstein, "The Norm of *Stare Decisis,*" 40 *American Journal of Political Science* (1996): 1018–35. If the major goal of attorneys in these briefs is to influence judicial decision making by persuading justices to adopt legal rules that will produce outcomes favorable to their interests, then this finding suggests that attorneys cite precedent because they believe the Court finds it persuasive. Finally, lawyers themselves acknowledge the importance of legitimacy norms. In a recent biography of former solicitor general Archibald Cox, the author reports that Cox resisted efforts by the administration to make major changes in reapportionment precedent, at least in part because he feared for the legitimacy of the Court. Ken Gormley, *Archibald Cox* (Reading, Mass.: Addison-Wesley, 1997).

I must remain with my *Bakke* analysis. I believe it is strictly in accord with
our precedents, affords a clear framework for the resolution of future cases
and will serve the country well—as indeed my *Bakke* opinion did.
Whatever anyone thinks of my rationale, the country at large—and particularly universities—have been able to live with *Bakke*.[30]

Another, even more explicit, example comes from the explanation
Justices O'Connor, Kennedy, and Souter offered for why the Court would
not overrule *Roe v. Wade*. In their joint opinion in *Planned Parenthood v.
Casey* they wrote:

A decision to overrule *Roe's* essential holding under the existing circumstances would address error, if error there was, at the cost of both profound and unnecessary damage to the Court's legitimacy, and to the
Nation's commitment to the rule of law. It is therefore imperative to
adhere to the essence of *Roe's* original decision, and we do so today.[31]

Whether O'Connor and company truly felt constrained by the legitimacy
norms or whether they merely felt compelled to say they did raises the sort
of question we take up next. What is not in doubt, however, is that they
believe the norm of *stare decisis* governs relations between them and society—and not just the legal community. They took great pains to make this
point in their writing, especially in Part III of *Casey*, as have other justices.[32]

Therefore, while it may be true that members of the legal community
think more about legitimacy norms than do other members of society, we
cannot say that these norms operate only on that community. In fact, all
the available evidence points in the other direction—that legitimacy
norms, at least in the eyes of justices, govern their relationship with the
whole of American society. Let us consider how they do so.

Sua Sponte

In 1963 the U.S. Supreme Court received seven cases for review that, in
one way or another, touched on the subject of capital punishment. In none
of these petitions did attorneys raise questions concerning the constitutionality of the death penalty; rather, all the claims hinged on procedural
matters such as challenges to the voluntariness of defendants' confessions.[33]
Prior to the conference at which the Court would decide whether to hear
these cases, Justice Arthur Goldberg circulated a memo informing his col-

leagues that he would raise this issue: "Whether and under what circumstances, the imposition of the death penalty is proscribed by the Eighth and
Fourteenth Amendments to the U.S. Constitution." He recognized that
none of the attorneys had briefed this issue; nonetheless, he felt that the
Court should consider the question because he was convinced that "evolv-
ing standards of decency . . . now condemn as barbaric and inhumane the
deliberate institutionalized taking of human life by the state." Most of
Goldberg's colleagues were startled by his memo, complaining that it went
well beyond their authority, that to implement his plan, the Court would
have to proceed *sua sponte* ("on its own, without prompting or suggestion"). In the end, the justices not only rejected the memo's suggestion but
also refused to hear the cases.

This story suggests that a particular variant of the *sua sponte* doctrine,
namely the practice of disfavoring the creation of issues not raised in the
record before the Court, is a norm.[i] We can speculate on why the majority of the Court was so taken aback by Goldberg's memo and why it took
the action it did: because the memo deviated from a norm the justices had
come to accept, they "sanctioned" Goldberg by rejecting his invitation to
reconsider the constitutionality of capital punishment.[34]

Framed this way, the norm disfavoring the creation of issues is as vital to
the functioning of the Court as the institutions we have discussed here and
in Chapter Four. If the norm of *sua sponte* did not exist, the justices would
be free to raise any issue they wished in any case, even if the attorneys had
not briefed the issue. The implications of such behavior are enormous.
Justices would act a good deal more like members of Congress, who are
free to engage in "issue creation," and less like jurists, who must wait for
issues to come to them. We could imagine rational, policy-seeking justices
attempting, as a matter of course, to append new issues to cases that had

---

i. Other variants of the *sua sponte* doctrine obligate a court to act, rather than prohibit it from acting, on its own. Most pertain to trial courts, such as the duty to conduct *sua sponte* inquiries into defendants' competence to stand trial. A few implicate
appellate courts; for example, if an appellate court believes it does not have jurisdiction
to hear a particular dispute, it is obliged to say so even if no party has raised the issue.
Here, we focus only on the variant preventing a court from acting without prompting, the norm disfavoring the creation of issues. For more details, see Lee Epstein,
Jeffrey A. Segal, and Timothy Johnson, "The Claim of Issue Creation on the U.S.
Supreme Court," 90 *American Political Science Review* (1996): 845.

been accepted, briefed, and argued as a way to manipulate case outcomes, just as members of Congress add riders to legislative proposals.[35]

Additional implications of a Court operating free from a norm disfavoring issue creation are easy to develop.[j] But the general point is simple: without this norm the Court would no longer resemble a legal body in the way that scholars, attorneys, and jurists—not to mention Article III of the U.S. Constitution—contemplate such fora. More to the point, regular deviations from this norm would undermine the Court's legitimacy. The public believes that the Court's legitimate judicial function involves resolving the issues before it, not the creation of new issues.[36] As one scholar put it, "When the parties choose issues, there is little opportunity for judges to pursue their own agendas and, as a consequence, the proceedings are not only fairer, but are perceived to be fairer." But, if the Court departs from this practice, it

> raises questions as to the impartiality of [its] actions, and such speculation tarnishes the Court's legitimacy. Litigant control of the issues is important to satisfy not only the parties, but society as well. . . . When the Court [discovers] issues that the litigants have not presented, the Court erodes its credibility and trespasses on the soul of the adversarial system.[37]

---

j. We know from the congressional literature that legislators seek to make good policy and to gain reelection, but they face considerable uncertainty about the substantive and political ramifications of various courses of action. Interest groups reduce the risk for legislators. By lobbying and mustering grassroots pressure, interest groups provide valuable information on the views of organized and attentive constituents. See John Mark Hansen, *Gaining Access: Congress and the Farm Lobby, 1919–1981* (Chicago: University of Chicago Press, 1991). They also provide insight into the possible policy consequences of their actions. See Keith Krehbiel, *Information and Legislative Organization* (Ann Arbor: University of Michigan Press, 1991). If the justices were unconstrained by a norm disfavoring issue creation, they would face uncertainty—not about their constituents, but about the actions their colleagues might take and about the political, economic, and social ramifications of their decisions. However, the information that attorneys and interest groups provide to the Court might not be as valuable as the information provided to Congress. If the justices could transform a case in which attorneys raised First Amendment claims into a case involving search and seizure or privacy or capital punishment, the attorneys, interest groups, and other "lobbyists" would have difficulty identifying even the proximate grounds on which the Court would decide the case. Indeed, the justices—recognizing that attorneys were not in a position to provide them with useful information—might simply disregard written submissions.

The question, then, is whether the Goldberg story is an anomaly; that is, do justices regularly deviate from the norm disfavoring the creation of issues? Available evidence suggests that they do not.[38] A comparison of the briefs filed in a sample of cases decided during the Court's 1988 term with the *U.S. Reports* summaries (the syllabi) of those cases shows that the Court virtually never created a major issue that was not part of the existing record; in fact, all but one of the ninety-one syllabi points were covered in the briefs of the parties.[39] This pattern suggests that the Court does not regularly adjudicate *major* issues that were not a part of the written record.[k]

At the same time, however, we do not wish to suggest that violations of the norm never occur. We have already recounted the story of Justice Goldberg's memo; the study of the 1988 term unearthed another, which occurred in *Patterson v. McLean Credit Union*. The Court granted certiorari in *Patterson* to consider whether a federal law, 42 U.S.C. § 1981, provides a remedy for racial harassment. Yet, after oral arguments, the justices requested attorneys to brief a question no party (or amicus curiae) had raised: "Whether or not the interpretation of 42 U.S.C. § 1981 adopted by this Court in *Runyon v. McCrary* should be reconsidered."[40] To some legal scholars, this kind of request is a clear violation of the *sua sponte* norm: when courts ask for rearguments on matters that the parties did not brief, they engage in issue creation.[41]

Although we are sympathetic to this claim, two factors dampen our enthusiasm. First, if the Court did not respect the norm disfavoring issue creation, it would have reconsidered *Runyon* without asking for rearguments. In other words, if the Court could discover issues, it could also reexamine past cases *sua sponte*. Seen in this way, the *Patterson* order may lend further support for the existence of the norm of *sua sponte,* rather than sup-

---

k. We stress "major" because Court opinions, which can run more than one hundred pages, might well contain issues that are not summarized in the syllabi. So this research strategy cannot tell us whether the Court brings up secondary issues on its own.

The collectors of the data acknowledged this limitation. See Epstein, Segal, and Johnson, "The Claim of Issue Creation," 848. They nevertheless felt, as do we, that the data support the existence of the norm. But Kevin T. McGuire and Barbara Palmer took them to task for (1) ignoring specific cases, such as *Marbury v. Madison,* in which they claim that the justices clearly created issues, and (2) ignoring statements by Court members that the majority was in fact engaging in issue creation. See McGuire and Palmer, "Issues, Agendas, and Decision Making on the Supreme Court," 90 *American Political Science Review* (1996): 853–865. As to the first criticism, we have both a specific and general response. The specific one is that because McGuire and Palmer rely

ply ammunition to refute it. Second, like the Goldberg memo, the request for reargument in *Patterson* elicited negative responses. Four justices dissented, asserting that "neither the parties nor the Solicitor General [as an amicus curiae] have argued that *Runyon* should be reconsidered."[42] In addition, journalists took aim at the Court's majority; legal scholars denounced the order as an example of brute activism; and, at the end of the day, the Court did not overrule *Runyon*.[43] We do not claim that the overwhelmingly negative reaction to the reargument order led to the decision to retain *Runyon,* but, because of the fuss following the Court's request in *Patterson,* analysts have speculated that "it may be a long time before the Court requests rehearing *sua sponte.*"[44]

Stare Decisis

From our discussion of *sua sponte,* we learn that it is no great mystery why Goldberg's memo so disturbed his colleagues or why the *Patterson* order so alarmed the community. In both instances, justices were perceived as attempting to violate a legitimacy norm that serves as a constraint on the Court. Another legitimacy norm—*stare decisis* or the norm favoring respect for precedent—we believe, operates in much the same way as the norm of *sua sponte:* it serves as a constraint on justices acting on their personal preferences. In what follows, we provide some documentation for our belief, but first we address a basic question: Why would justices follow precedent in those situations in which they would prefer to create a different rule?[45]

To begin to develop a response, let us (re)consider the task that justices face: they seek to establish a rule as close as possible to their most preferred policy position but, to accomplish this, they must take account of the

---

on secondary sources, rather than on the Court's records, they get *Marbury* wrong. Marbury's attorney did, in fact, raise the issue of judicial review when he argued that Section 13 of the Judiciary Act of 1789, under which his client had brought suit, was constitutional (see *Marbury* at 148). More generally, neither the authors of the study they criticize nor we argue that the norm of *sua sponte* holds in every case. Rather, they (and we) say that "while occasional deviations from the norm are not unexpected, regular and systematic deviations should be rare." Epstein, Segal, and Johnson, "The Claim of Issue Creation," 849. Surely, the data support that expectation.

The second criticism is amply addressed by Epstein, Segal, and Johnson. The appendix to their study shows that, more often than not, charges of issue creation (1) come from justices who are writing separately from the majority and (2) are mistaken, that, in fact, one or more of the attorneys raised the issue or mischaracterized the majority's position perhaps in an effort to bolster their own.

strategic nature of their choice. On the one hand, as we have already discussed, they must be attentive to the strategic dimensions of the decision-making process within the Court itself; for example, only those rules to which at least five members of the Court subscribe will be established. Therefore, they may have to modify their most preferred policy choice in order to accommodate the preferences of the other members of the Court. On the other hand, they must be attentive to the strategic dimensions of judicial decision making outside of the Court: if justices want to establish a legal rule of behavior that will govern the future activity of the members of the society in which their Court exists, they will be constrained to choose from among the set of rules that the members of that society will recognize and accept.[46] If the Court seeks to establish rules that the people will not respect and with which they will not comply, it risks undermining its fundamental efficacy.

For at least two reasons, it is on this external strategic dimension that a norm favoring respect for precedent can significantly affect decision making by constraining judicial choice. First, there are prudential reasons to suggest that justices might follow precedent rather than their own policy preferences. *Stare decisis* is one way courts respect the established expectations of a community. To the extent that members of a community base their future expectations on the belief that others will follow existing laws, the Court has an interest in minimizing the disruptive effects of overturning existing rules of behavior. If the Court makes a radical change, the community may not be able to adapt, resulting in a decision that does not produce an efficacious rule.

There are also normative reasons why justices may follow precedent rather than their own preferences. If a community has a fundamental belief that the "rule of law" requires the Court to be constrained by precedent, the justices may follow the belief even if they do not personally accept it. The constraint follows from the justices' understanding that the community's belief affects its willingness to accept and comply with the Court's decisions. If the members of the community believe that the legitimate judicial function involves the following of precedent, then they will reject as normatively illegitimate the decisions that regularly and systematically violate precedent. To the extent that justices are concerned with establishing rules that the community will accept, they will keep in mind the fact that the community must regard these rules as legitimate. In this way, a norm of *stare decisis* can constrain the actions of even those Court members who do not share the view that justices should be constrained by past decisions.

If a norm of respecting precedent exists on the Court, in what ways would it manifest itself? The problem in answering this question is that the norm of respecting precedent is general and individual cases are specific. And, as we noted in our discussion of *sua sponte,* individual violations of the norm will not result in society's rejection of the Court; only regular and systematic deviations from the norm could undermine the Court's legitimacy. Accordingly, evidence of individual instances of deviation do not demonstrate that the norm has no effect. As long as justices generally comply with the norm, they will be free to deviate from precedent in those cases in which their personal preferences so differ from the precedent that they feel compelled to change the existing law.

Seen this way, the best way to document the existence of the norm of *stare decisis* would be a detailed, systematic analysis of the evolution of the law in various substantive areas. We take a somewhat more modest approach here, providing evidence of two types of behavior that are consistent with the existence of such a norm and inconsistent with the claim that precedent does not matter for Supreme Court decision making: the use justices make of precedent during their private conferences and the use they make of it in their opinions.

USE OF PRECEDENT DURING CONFERENCES. One source of evidence in support of the existence of a norm favoring respect for precedent is the extent to which justices invoke it in their conference discussions. The fact that justices use precedent as a source of persuasion in their *private* communications suggests that they believe it can have an effect on their colleagues' choices. It is one thing for the justices to ground their public proclamations in the rhetoric of precedent, but quite another for them to use it in their private deliberations. In addition, the use of precedent in conference discussions lends support to the claim that a norm favoring precedent also exists in society. Justices who wish to see their rulings followed by the community will give priority to those rules that are consistent with a norm favoring respect for precedent if they believe that such a norm exists. Therefore, one reason why justices might be persuaded to adjust their position on the holding in a case in the direction of precedent is that such an adjustment may ensure society's acceptance of the ruling.

Table 2-1 (page 30) shows that about 25 percent of justices' conference comments center on past cases. Table 5-3 displays the results of a somewhat different analysis, which focuses on the invocation of precedent in discussions of the landmark case of *Edelman v. Jordan* and its progeny.[1] These fresh data allow us to investigate more directly how justices deal with precedent from one related case to the next.

Table 5-3 shows that in every case but two at least one justice mentioned a previously decided case. As our earlier analysis revealed, a particular precedent was often central to the justices' comments. In *Atascadero State Hospital v. Scanlon,* for example, O'Connor simply said, *"Pennhurst* decided this case and I'd reverse"; and in *Green v. Mansour,* Blackmun noted that he would "reverse on *Atascadero."* In both instances, the justices relied on *Edelman* progeny similar to the disputes they were discussing.

At other times, the justices struggled with competing precedents, and the conflict is evident in their remarks and in their votes. *Edelman* provides another interesting illustration. During the conference discussion, Stewart said, "Same jurisdiction issue here as in *Hagans* but can't solve it the same way. Can't possibly find *Parden* type waiver here. My problem comes down to *Ex parte Young."* [m] But White and Blackmun seemed to disagree. White argued, "Conditions of scheme are such that [the] state had to agree to dis-

---

1. By "progeny" we mean subsequent cases that followed from the *Edelman* precedent. We derive this list from Jeffrey A. Segal and Harold J. Spaeth, "The Influence of Stare Decisis on the Votes of U.S. Supreme Court Justices," 40 *American Journal of Political Science* (1996): 991, which also provides a detailed operational definition of progeny. See pages 979–980.

We selected *Edelman,* in part, because of the availability of data. In an essay responding to Segal and Spaeth's assertion that justices rarely "subjugate their preferences to the norms of *stare decisis"* (page 987), we used the case to demonstrate that *stare decisis* is a norm that structures judicial decisions. See Knight and Epstein, "The Norm of Stare Decisis," which relied exclusively on Brennan's conference notes. (Here, we also incorporate Powell's.) Our rationale for using *Edelman* was that of all the landmark cases included in Segal and Spaeth's sample, it generated the greatest number of progeny and its progeny span the longest length of time.

The important points here are that *Edelman* and its successors allow us to explore how justices go about using precedent in their private deliberations and how they do so from one related and successive case to the next over a relatively long period of time.

m. *Hagans v. Lavine,* 415 U.S. 528 (1974), challenging a New York regulation permitting the state to recoup prior unscheduled payments for rent from subsequent grants under the AFDC program. *Parden v. Terminal Railway Co.,* 209 U.S. 123 (1964),

burse as Feds required—a *Parden* type waiver." Blackmun noted that he did not "think that there's an 11th Amendment problem. It's not the Missouri case where state had something forced on it. This comes down on *Parden* side." [n] Powell simply could not make up his mind: at first he passed and then tentatively voted to affirm. But, in a December 17, 1973, memo, he told the chief justice he had "reexamined" his position and wanted his vote recorded in favor of reversal:

> The case is still a close one for me because we may leave the respondents remediless. Yet we have not extended *Ex parte Young* to cover the compelling of a state to pay money from general tax funds to private citizens. Before I go that far, I will have to be satisfied that there was a waiver by the state. I have reread *Parden* and [the Missouri case] and concluded that there is no waiver here.

Clearly, these kinds of statements—not to mention the data presented in Tables 2-1 and 5-3—provide documentation of the use of precedent in the private deliberations of the Court. We recognize that these findings are not definitive evidence of a precedential effect on decision making, but they are evidence of behavior consistent with the existence of a norm favoring respect for precedent. In addition, it is behavior that makes little sense if the justices think that precedent has no impact on their ultimate decisions.

USE OF PRECEDENT IN PUBLISHED OPINIONS. Although a norm favoring precedent could manifest itself in many ways in the opinion-formation process, we focus on the products of that process: the final, published versions of the opinion, especially two aspects of opinions—the claims writers make and the way they treat precedent.

As all students of the Court know, justices invoke numerous justifications for their opinions, from the intent of the Framers to the plain mean-

---

asking whether a state that owns and operates a railroad in interstate commerce may successfully plead sovereign immunity in a federal court suit brought against the railroad by its employee under the Federal Employers' Liability Act. *Ex parte Young,* 209 U.S. 123 (1908), asking whether a suit by a stockholder against a corporation to enjoin the directors and officers from complying with the provisions of a state statute alleged to be unconstitutional, was properly before the Court.

n. The Missouri case was *Employees v. Public Health and Welfare Dep't,* 411 U.S. 279 (1973), asking whether employees of state health facilities could bring suit for overtime pay due them under the Fair Labor Standards Act or whether such a suit was barred by the Eleventh Amendment.

TABLE 5-3
Justices' Appeals to Precedent During Conference Discussion

Case	Burger	Douglas	Brennan	Stewart	White	Marshall	Blackmun	Powell	Rehnquist	Stevens	O'Connor	Scalia
Edelman v. Jordan, 415 U.S. 651 (1974)[a]	Yes	No	No	Yes	Yes	No	Yes	Yes	Yes	NC	NC	NC
Fitzpatrick v. Bitzer, 427 U.S. 445 (1976)[b]	No	NC	No	Yes	No	No	No	No	Yes	Yes	NC	NC
Milliken v. Bradley (II), 433 U.S. 267 (1977)[c]	Yes	NC	No	Yes	No	No	No	Yes	Yes	Yes	NC	NC
Hutto v. Finney, 437 U.S. 678 (1978)[d]	No	NC	No	No	No	No	No	No	No	No	NC	NC
Florida Dep't v. Treasure Salvors, 458 U.S. 670 (1982)[e]	Yes	NC	No	NC	No	No	No	No	Yes	No	No	NC
Guardians Ass'n v. New York City Civil Service Comm., 463 U.S. 582 (1983)[f]	Yes	NC	Yes	NC	Yes	No	Yes	Yes	Yes	Yes	Yes	NC

Case												
Pennhurst State Hospital v. Halderman, 465 U.S. 89 (1984)[g]	No	NC	No	NC	Yes	No	Yes	No	Yes	Yes	Yes	NC
Oneida County v. Oneida Nation, 470 U.S. 226 (1985)[h]	Yes	NC	Yes	NC	Yes	Yes	Yes	Yes	Yes	No	Yes	NC
Atascadero State Hospital v. Scanlon, 473 U.S. 234 (1985)[i]	No	NC	Yes	NC	No	No	No	No	No	No	Yes	NC
Green v. Mansour, 474 U.S. 64 (1985)[j]	Yes	NC	Yes	NC	Yes	No	Yes	No	Yes	Yes	No	NC
Papasan v. Allain, 478 U.S. 265 (1986)[k]	No	NC	No	NC	No	No	No	No	No	No	No	NC
Welch v. Texas Highways Dep't, 483 U.S. 468 (1987)[l]	NC	NC	No	NC	Yes	No	Yes	No	No	Yes	Yes	Yes

Source: Adapted from Jack Knight and Lee Epstein, "The Norm of Stare Decisis," 40 American Journal of Political Science (1996): 1027, which relied exclusively on Brennan's conference notes. Here we use both Brennan's and Powell's.

Note: Yes = cited precedent in conference remarks or agreed with another justice who cited precedent; No = failed to cite precedent in conference remarks or agreed with another justice who did not cite precedent; NC = not on Court.

(Table continues)

TABLE 5-3 (Continued)

Data Note: There was one other progeny of *Edelman v. Jordan: PATH v. Feeney*, 495 U.S. 299 (1990). Because Justice Brennan's papers are not available for this term, we exclude it from the table.

Coding Rules: We examined Brennan's and Powell's conference notes for each of the *Edelman* progeny. We coded "yes" or "no" based on the definitions listed above.

[a] Involving whether the Eleventh Amendment ("The Judicial power of the United States shall not be construed to extend to any suit in law or equity, commenced or prosecuted against one of the United States by citizens of another State, or by Citizens or Subjects of any Foreign State") protects state officials from being sued for allegedly administering a federal-state program in a manner inconsistent with federal laws and the Fourteenth Amendment.

[b] Asking whether Congress, in determining what legislation is appropriate for enforcing the Fourteenth Amendment, can provide for suits against states that conflict with the Eleventh Amendment in other contexts.

[c] Taking up two questions concerning the remedial powers of federal district courts in school desegregation cases: (1) whether a court can, as part of a desegregation decree, order certain educational programs for children who have been subjected to past acts of de jure segregation and (2) whether, consistent with the Eleventh Amendment, a court can require state officials found responsible for constitutional violations to bear some of the costs of those programs.

[d] Challenging a district court order involving remedies for Arkansas prisons, including an award of attorneys' fees to be paid out by the Department of Corrections, which the state claimed violated the Eleventh Amendment.

[e] Involving a federal court attempt to take custody of property held by two state officials and bring it within the jurisdiction of the court; the specific question was does the Eleventh Amendment immunize the property from the federal court's process.

[f] Asking, as a threshold question, whether the private plaintiffs in the case needed to prove discriminatory intent to establish a violation of Title VI of the Civil Rights Act of 1964 and administrative implementing regulations promulgated under the act.

[g] Asking whether the Eleventh Amendment prohibits a federal court from ordering state officials to conform their conduct to state law.

[h] Asking whether several tribes can bring a suit for damages for the occupation and use of tribal land allegedly conveyed unlawfully in 1795.

[i] Asking the Court to determine whether states and state agencies are subject to suit in federal court by litigants seeking monetary relief under the Rehabilitation Act of 1973 or whether such suits are proscribed by the Eleventh Amendment.

[j] Asking whether the Eleventh Amendment prohibits the granting of relief for a claim that the director of the Michigan Department of Social Services miscalculated benefits under the federal Aid to Families with Dependent Children (AFDC) program.

[k] Considering whether the claims of Mississippi school officials and children that they were denied the economic benefits of public school lands granted by the United States to the state more than one hundred years ago are barred by the Eleventh Amendment.

[l] Asking whether the Eleventh Amendment bars a state employee from suing the state in federal court under the Jones Act, which provides that any seaman injured in the course of his employment may sue for damages in federal district court.

ing of the words of statutes. Even those who are skeptical about the importance of precedent acknowledge that "appeal to precedent is the primary justification justices provide for the decisions they reach." [47] Several pieces of evidence support this claim. First, very few Supreme Court opinions— majority, dissenting, or concurring—do not cite previously decided cases. A perusal of any volume of the *U.S. Reports* supports this claim, as does our analysis of the number of citations contained in the opinions in *Edelman* and its progeny. As Table 5-4 shows, in all but three of the twenty-eight opinions, citations to precedent exceeded those to all other sources combined. What is more, the average opinion cited 2.01 previously cited cases per *U.S. Reports* page; that figure was .93 for all other authorities.

Second, we note Glenn Phelps and John Gates's study, which found that 80 percent of the constitutional arguments used by Justices Brennan and Rehnquist were based on precedent.[48] Our analysis of the justifications used in majority and dissenting opinions in *Edelman* and its progeny comes to the same general conclusion. Although justices occasionally invoke other legal resources, *stare decisis* predominates. Indeed, in only a handful of the opinions listed in Table 5-4 did an appeal to precedent fail to form the core of the argument.

The data reported here are limited to a few cases, but we doubt that any scholar of the judicial process would take issue with the conclusion that precedent is a prominent feature of most opinions. What they may suggest, however, is that our data actually support a counterargument: the invocation of the precedent justification by both dissenting and majority opinions renders it meaningless. But this position begs the question of why justices use it. Why would justices feel compelled to invoke precedent, not just occasionally but regularly, especially when many other justifications exist? The answer is clear. The justices' behavior is consistent with a belief that a norm favoring precedent is a fundamental part of the general conception of the function of the Supreme Court in society at large. To the extent that compliance with this norm is necessary to maintain the Supreme Court's legitimacy, such a belief will constrain the justices from deviating from precedent in a regular and systematic way.

We now turn to the way the Court treats precedent in its opinions. If the justices consistently overturned principles established in past cases, we could not label *stare decisis* a "norm"—in the sense that norms establish expectations about future behavior. But the justices do not behave this way. No matter how one counts the number of alterations of precedent, the numbers border on the trivial: the Congressional Research Service reports

TABLE 5-4

Justices' Citations to Authorities in Their Opinions

Case	Citations to Precedent (Average per page)	Citations to Other Authorities (Average per page)
Edelman v. Jordan, 415 U.S. 651 (1974)[a]		
Majority opinion	1.42	0.58
Dissenting opinion #1	2.20	0.60
Dissenting opinion #2	1.00	2.00
Dissenting opinion #3	1.56	0.78
Fitzpatrick v. Bitzer, 427 U.S. 445 (1976)[b]		
Majority opinion	1.00	1.00
Milliken v. Bradley [II], 433 U.S. 267 (1977)[c]		
Majority opinion	1.57	0.22
Hutto v. Finney, 437 U.S. 678 (1978)[d]		
Majority opinion	1.43	0.67
Dissenting opinion	1.22	0.56
Florida Dep't v. Treasure Salvors, 458 U.S. 670 (1982)[e]		
Judgment	.68	0.11
Guardians Ass'n v. New York City Civil Service Comm., 463 U.S. 582 (1983)[f]		
Judgment	1.39	0.78
Dissenting opinion #1	3.21	2.26
Dissenting opinion #2	2.20	.70
Pennhurst State Hospital v. Halderman, 465 U.S. 89 (1984)[g]		
Majority opinion	2.15	0.27
Dissenting opinion #1	4.00	2.00
Dissenting opinion #2	2.49	0.46
Oneida County v. Oneida Nation, 470 U.S. 226 (1985)[h]		
Majority opinion	2.20	0.64

(Table continues)

TABLE 5-4 *(Continued)*

Atascadero State Hospital v. Scanlon, 473 U.S. 234 (1985)[i]		
Majority opinion	2.42	0.75
Dissenting opinion #1	0.70	0.63
Dissenting opinion #2	7.00	3.00
Dissenting opinion #3	4.00	1.00
Green v. Mansour, 474 U.S. 64 (1985)[j]		
Majority opinion	1.90	0.70
Dissenting opinion #1	1.00	0.67
Dissenting opinion #2	1.33	1.00
Dissenting opinion #3	3.00	1.00
Papasan v. Allain, 478 U.S. 265 (1986)[k]		
Majority opinion	1.29	0.63
Welch v. Texas Highways Dep't, 483 U.S. 468 (1987)[l]		
Judgment	1.67	0.79
Dissenting opinion	1.08	0.52
PATH v. Feeney, 495 U.S. 299 (1990)[m]		
Majority opinion	1.10	1.60

Source: Jack Knight and Lee Epstein, "The Norm of *Stare Decisis,*" 40 *American Journal of Political Science* (1996): 1027.

Note: We included only opinions dissenting in full.

Coding Rules: Precedent: we counted the number of citations to precedent. We did not double count or include lower court citations to the case at hand. Authorities: we counted the number of citations to all other authorities, including constitutional provisions, statutes, regulations, scholarly works, and so forth. We did not double count.

$$\text{The average number per page} = \frac{\text{number of citations}}{\text{number of pages of opinion in } U.S. \text{ Reports}}$$

[a] Involving whether the Eleventh Amendment ("The Judicial power of the United States shall not be construed to extend to any suit in law or equity, commenced or prosecuted against one of the United States by citizens of another State, or by Citizens or Subjects of any Foreign State") protects state officials from being sued for allegedly administering a federal-state program in a manner inconsistent with federal laws and the Fourteenth Amendment.

[b] Asking whether Congress, in determining what legislation is appropriate for enforcing the Fourteenth Amendment, can provide for suits against states that conflict with the Eleventh Amendment in other contexts.

^c Taking up two questions concerning the remedial powers of federal district courts in school desegregation cases: (1) whether a court can, as part of a desegregation decree, order certain educational programs for children who have been subjected to past acts of de jure segregation and (2) whether, consistent with the Eleventh Amendment, a court can require state officials found responsible for constitutional violations to bear some of the costs of those programs.

^d Challenging a district court order involving remedies for Arkansas prisons, including an award of attorneys' fees to be paid out by the Department of Corrections, which the state claimed violated the Eleventh Amendment.

^e Involving a federal court attempt to take custody of property held by two state officials and bring it within the jurisdiction of the court; the specific question was does the Eleventh Amendment immunize the property from the federal court's process.

^f Asking, as a threshold question, whether the private plaintiffs in the case needed to prove discriminatory intent to establish a violation of Title VI of the Civil Rights Act of 1964 and administrative implementing regulations promulgated under the act.

^g Asking whether the Eleventh Amendment prohibits a federal court from ordering state officials to conform their conduct to state law.

^h Asking whether several tribes can bring a suit for damages for the occupation and use of tribal land allegedly conveyed unlawfully in 1795.

ⁱ Asking the Court to determine whether states and state agencies are subject to suit in federal court by litigants seeking monetary relief under the Rehabilitation Act of 1973 or whether such suits are proscribed by the Eleventh Amendment.

^j Asking whether the Eleventh Amendment prohibits the granting of relief for a claim that the director of the Michigan Department of Social Services miscalculated benefits under the federal Aid to Families with Dependent Children (AFDC) program.

^k Considering whether the claims of Mississippi school officials and children that they were denied the economic benefits of public school lands granted by the United States to the state more than one hundred years ago are barred by the Eleventh Amendment.

^l Asking whether the Eleventh Amendment bars a state employee from suing the state in federal court under the Jones Act, which provides that any seaman injured in the course of his employment may sue for damages in federal district court.

^m Asking whether the Eleventh Amendment bars a suit in federal court against an entity created by two states to operate certain transportation facilities.

Figure 5-5   Cases Overruled as Percentage of Cases Available for Overruling

Percent

Decade

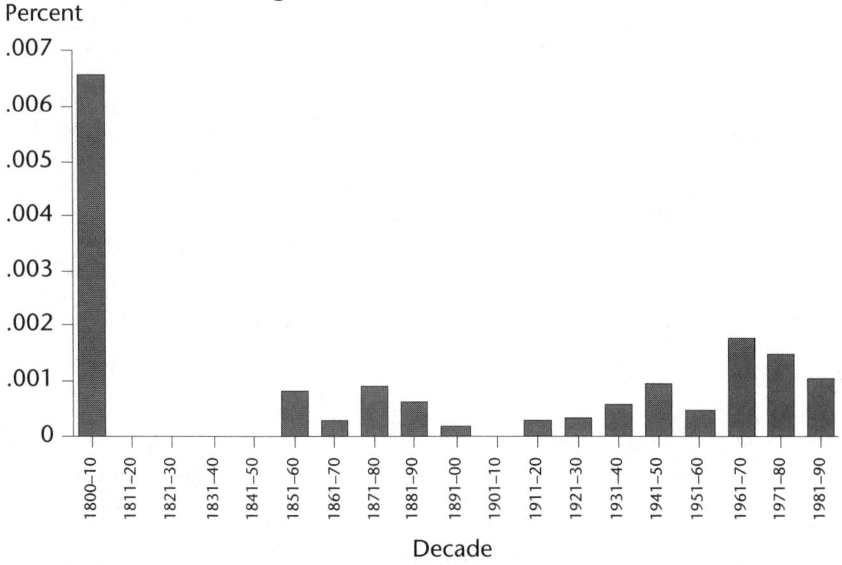

Source: Jack Knight and Lee Epstein, "The Norm of *Stare Decisis,*" 40 *American Journal of Political Science* (1996): 1031. The data are available at: *http://www.artsci.wustl.edu/~polisci/ epstein/choices/*.

Note: Percent = $\dfrac{\text{number of cases overruled per decade}}{\text{cases available for overruling}}$

Where: cases available for overruling = cumulative number of opinions of the Court per decade.

that the Court has overturned prior decisions in only 196 of the cases decided through 1990; and Saul Brenner and Harold Spaeth, using a different rule, claim that the Vinson through Rehnquist Courts overruled about 2.5 cases per term.[49]

Figure 5-5 provides yet another perspective on the data: it displays cases overruled as a percentage of all cases available for overruling, that is, all cases decided by the Court with a full opinion. The story that it tells could not be clearer: even with the greater propensity to alter precedents starting with the 1960s, the percentages remain minute.

We recognize that the explicit abandonment of precedent is the most extreme method of disposing of prior decisions the justices no longer find

useful; certainly, they maintain rulings on the books that they have effectively gutted. But, the main point, as Lawrence Baum highlights, is this:

> The Court adheres to precedents far more often than it overturns them,
> either explicitly or implicitly. . . . Certainly most justices accept the princi-
> ple that "any departure from the doctrine of *stare decisis* demands special
> justification." Like the law in general, the rule of adhering to precedent
> hardly controls the Court's decisions, but it does structure and influence
> them.[50]

We believe that the relevant data support Baum's sentiment, and that
they are consistent with the claim that a norm of *stare decisis* exists in the
Supreme Court. Even so, one might challenge our interpretation of the
evidence for a norm of *stare decisis* (and a norm of *sua sponte*) by suggesting that all we have shown is that judges act strategically as if there were
such a norm. This point seems related to a fairly common view that,
although precedent does not have any real effect on the justices, there are
reasons why legal actors maintain the myth of the normative rule of law.

These challenges undermine their own arguments and provide the best
basis for rejecting them. First, if good reasons exist to maintain the "myth"
of the rule of law, such as those offered here about the importance of maintaining the legitimacy of the Court in the society at large, and if the justices act with knowledge of them, those reasons have a causal effect on the
decisions of the Court. Second, there is only one plausible reason for a justice to invoke precedent strategically: that it will be effective in persuading
others to accept his preferred position. Invoking precedent will be effective only if the others believe in its importance. This follows from the fact
that the strategic use of norms depends on the acceptance of the norm by
some segment of a community.[51] Put simply, unless some members of society accept a norm favoring respect for precedent, there will be no way of
affecting behavior strategically by invoking such a norm. The same holds
for the norm disfavoring the creation of new issues.

ENDNOTES

1. *Monell v. Department of Social Services,* 436 U.S. 658 (1978); *Monroe v. Pape,* 365
U.S. 167 (1961).

2. Quoted from Powell's transcripts of conference discussion. Brennan's notes
are similar. He records Blackmun saying, *"Monroe suggests we must affirm. If we*

want to pull back from it, have a problem that Congress hasn't. Have to affirm because I think I'm bound by it."

3. For a somewhat different point of view, which suggests that the constraint is equally operative in constitutional cases, see Harry Stumpf, "Congressional Responses to Supreme Court Rulings: The Interaction of Law and Politics," 14 *Journal of Public Law* (1965): 377–395; and James Meernik and Joseph Ignagni, "Judicial Review and Coordinate Construction of the Constitution," 41 *American Journal of Political Science* (1997): 447–467.

4. *Employment Division v. Smith,* 494 U.S. 872 (1990).

5. *City of Boerne v. Flores,* — U.S. — (1997).

6. Linda Greenhouse, "Laws Urged to Restore Religion Act," *New York Times,* National Edition, July 15, 1997, A11.

7. *Watkins v. United States,* 354 U.S. 158 (1957); *Barenblatt v. United States,* 360 U.S. 109 (1959).

8. *Immigration and Naturalization Service v. Chadha,* 462 U.S. 919 (1983).

9. See Louis Fisher, "The Legislative Veto: Invalidated, It Survives," 56 *Law and Contemporary Problems* (1993): 288.

10. *NCAA v. Board of Regents,* 468 U.S. 85 (1984). The article, "Drop in Ratings of Televised Basketball Worries Broadcasters, College Officials," by N. Scott Vance, appeared in *The Chronicle of Higher Education,* April 4, 1984, 25. Justice Powell included it in his memo to Justice Stevens, 4/6/84, re: 83-271, *NCAA v. Board of Regents.*

11. *United States v. Leon,* 468 U.S. 897 (1984). Brief of amicus curiae filed by Kansas, Missouri, South Dakota, Wisconsin, and the Gulf & Great Plains Legal Foundation in *United States v. Leon,* 82-1771.

12. *Heckler v. Edwards,* 465 U.S. 870 at 874 (1984).

13. *Gregg v. Georgia,* 428 U.S. 153 (1976); *Furman v. Georgia,* 408 U.S. 238 (1972).

14. *Gregg v. Georgia,* 428 U.S. 153 at 179 (1976).

15. *Norfolk Redevelopment and Housing Authority v. Chesapeake & Potomac Telephone Company,* 464 U.S. 30 (1983).

16. *Immigration and Naturalization Service v. Phinpathya,* 464 U.S. 183 (1984).

17. *Wadman v. Immigration and Naturalization Service,* 329 F. 2d 812 (1964), in which a lower federal appellate court wrote that a strict construction of the relevant section of the immigration act is "inappropriate."

18. We used Spaeth's definition to classify cases as criminal or noncriminal disputes. See Harold J. Spaeth, *United States Supreme Court Judicial Database* (Ann Arbor, Mich.: Inter-University Consortium for Political and Social Research, published as study no. 9422, 1997, updated annually), 64–65.

19. Forrest Maltzman and Paul J. Wahlbeck, "May It Please the Chief? Opinion Assignments in the Rehnquist Court," 40 *American Journal of Political Science* (1996): 421–443.

20. *Marbury v. Madison,* 1 Cr. 137 (1803); *Ex parte McCardle,* 7 Wall. 506 (1869).

21. Jack Knight and Lee Epstein, "On the Struggle for Judicial Supremacy," 30 *Law and Society Review* (1996): 87–120. This essay contains a detailed history of the case, a game-theoretic analysis of the main events in the Marshall-Jefferson inter-action, and a detailed explanation of the findings reported in this paragraph and Figure 5-3, including why Jefferson might have sought to impeach Marshall, even if the chief justice had not established judicial review or had given Marbury his commission.

22. We adopt this discussion from Lee Epstein and Thomas G. Walker, "The Role of the Supreme Court in American Society: Playing the Reconstruction Game," in *Contemplating Courts,* ed. Lee Epstein (Washington, D.C.: CQ Press, 1995).

23. Charles Fairman, *History of the Supreme Court of the United States,* vol. VII: *Reconstruction and Reunion* (New York: Macmillan, 1971), 456.

24. This action came in *Ex parte Milligan,* 4 Wall. 2 (1866). For more details, see Epstein and Walker, "The Role of the Supreme Court in American Society."

25. See, for example, Rafael Gely and Pablo T. Spiller's analysis of *Grove City College v. Bell,* 465 U.S. 555 (1984), in "A Rational Choice Theory of Supreme Court Statutory Decisions with Application to the *State Farm* and *Grove City* Cases," 6 *Journal of Law, Economics and Organizations* (1990): 263–300; Gely and Spiller's study of the "switch in time that saved nine" in "The Political Economy of Supreme Court Constitutional Decisions: The Case of Roosevelt's Court-Packing Plan," 12 *International Review of Law and Economics* (1992): 45–67; and Linda R. Cohen and Matthew L. Spitzer's examination of *Chevron v. Natural Resources Defense Council,* 467 U.S. 837 (1984), in "Solving the *Chevron* Puzzle," 57 *Law and Contemporary Problems* (1994): 65–110.

26. William N. Eskridge Jr., "Reneging on History? Playing the Court/Congress/President Civil Rights Game," 79 *California Law Review* (1991): 613–684.

27. *United Steelworkers v. Weber,* 443 U.S. 193 (1979).

28. According to Eskridge, "Stewart, the necessary fifth vote in *Weber* (the Court split 5-2), was part of the five-justice majority invalidating the affirmative action plan in *Regents of the University of California v. Bakke,* 438 U.S. 265 (1978). Justices Stevens and Powell, who did not participate in *Weber,* were also part of the *Bakke* majority." The other majority justice was Blackmun, concurring in *Weber,* 443 U.S. 193 at 209–216 (1979). See Eskridge, "Reneging on History?" 651–652.

29. See, for example, C. Herman Pritchett, *Congress versus the Supreme Court* (Minneapolis: University of Minnesota Press, 1961); Walter F. Murphy, *Congress and the Supreme Court* (Chicago: University of Chicago Press, 1962); Murphy, *Elements of Judicial Strategy* (Chicago: University of Chicago Press, 1964); and Christina Wolbrecht, "Separation of Powers, Constitutional Interpretation, and the Free Exercise of Religion: A Formal Model," Washington University Political Science Working Paper (on file with the authors).

30. Memorandum from Justice Powell to Chief Justice Burger, 6/13/80, re: 78-

1007, *Fullilove v. Klutznick.* In *Regents of the University of California v. Bakke,* 438 U.S. 265 (1978), a judgment for the Court, Powell wrote that, absent a history of racial discrimination demanding a strong remedy, affirmative action programs that set quotas for particular racial or ethnic groups violate the Equal Protection Clause, but minority status may play a role in the admissions process.

31. *Roe v. Wade,* 410 U.S. 113 (1973); *Planned Parenthood v. Casey,* 505 U.S. 833 at 869 (1992) (emphasis added).

32. For additional quotes, see Saul Brenner and Harold J. Spaeth, *Stare Indecisis* (Cambridge: Cambridge University Press, 1995), 5. The authors, however, question whether the justices are "concerned with legitimacy in the eyes of Court commentators or in the eyes of the general public."

33. We take the discussion of *sua sponte* from Lee Epstein, Jeffrey A. Segal, and Timothy Johnson, "The Claim of Issue Creation on the U.S. Supreme Court," 90 *American Political Science Review* (1996): 845–852.

34. There are other possible explanations, such as the Court's unwillingness to involve itself in a controversial issue in the wake of *Brown v. Board of Education,* 347 U.S. 483 (1954). See Ian Gray and Moira Stanley, *A Punishment in Search of a Crime* (New York: Avon Books, 1989), 330.

35. See, for example, Randall Calvert and Richard F. Fenno Jr., "Strategy and Sophisticated Voting in the Senate," 56 *Journal of Politics* (1994): 349–376.

36. See, for example, Karl N. Llewellyn, *The Common Law Tradition* (Boston: Little, Brown, 1960). See also Christopher J. Peters, "Adjudication as Representation," 97 *Columbia Law Review* (1997): 337–338.

37. Rosemary Krimbel, "Rehearing Sua Sponte in the U.S. Supreme Court: A Procedure for Judicial Policymaking," 65 *Chicago-Kent Law Review* (1989): 943.

38. See Epstein, Segal, and Johnson, "The Claim of Issue Creation on the U.S. Supreme Court."

39. The one exception was the following point, listed in the syllabus to *City of Richmond v. J. A. Croson Co.,* 488 U.S. 469 (1989):

> The "evidence" relied upon by JUSTICE MARSHALL's dissent, the city's history of school desegregation and numerous congressional reports, does little to define the scope of any injury to minority contractors in the city or the necessary remedy, and could justify a preference of any size or duration.

Because this issue implicates a dissenting opinion filed in the case, it is understandable why it was not covered in any of the briefs of the parties.

40. *Runyon v. McCrary,* 427 U.S. 160 (1976); *Patterson v. McLean Credit Union,* 491 U.S. 164 (1989); *rehearing ordered,* 485 U.S. 617 (1988); *certiorari granted,* 484 U.S. 814 (1987). The quote is from the 1988 rehearing order, at 617.

41. See, for example, Wayne Cook, "The Rehearing Evil," 14 *Iowa Law Review* (1928): 36–62; Ronan Degnan and David W. Louisell, "Rehearing in American

Appellate Courts," 34 *Canadian Bar Review* (1956): 898–938; and Krimbel, "Rehearing Sua Sponte in the U.S. Supreme Court."

42. *Patterson v. McLean Credit Union,* 485 U.S. at 617 (1988).

43. See, for example, Tamar Jacoby and Ann Daniel, "Why Open a Closed Case? Upheaval on the Court," *Newsweek,* May 9, 1988, 69; and Krimbel, "Rehearing Sua Sponte in the U.S. Supreme Court."

44. Krimbel, "Rehearing Sua Sponte in the U.S. Supreme Court," 933.

45. We adopt the discussion that follows from Jack Knight and Lee Epstein, "The Norm of *Stare Decisis,*" 40 *American Journal of Political Science* (1996): 1018–35.

46. Jack Knight, "Interpretation as Social Interaction" (typescript, Washington University, St. Louis, Mo., 1994).

47. Jeffrey A. Segal and Harold J. Spaeth, "The Influence of *Stare Decisis* on the Votes of U.S. Supreme Court Justices," 40 *American Journal of Political Science* (1996): 972.

48. Glenn A. Phelps and John B. Gates, "The Myth of Jurisprudence," 31 *Santa Clara Law Review* (1991): 567–596.

49. Congressional Research Service, *The Constitution of the United States of America: Analysis and Interpretation,* 2117–27; and *1990 Supplement,* 265–266 (Washington, D.C: Government Printing Office, 1987, 1991). Brenner and Spaeth, *Stare Indecisis.*

50. Lawrence Baum, *The Supreme Court,* 5th ed. (Washington, D.C.: CQ Press, 1995), 149.

51. Jon Elster, "The Strategic Use of Argument," in *Barriers to Conflict Resolution,* ed. Kenneth Arrow et al. (New York: Norton, 1995).

CHAPTER SIX

Implications of the Strategic Account

In the Preface, we noted the argument that Walter F. Murphy made in *Elements of Judicial Strategy*. In this closing chapter, we are tempted simply to say that Murphy and those who have followed in his footsteps were right, that justices behave in precisely the way they suggested. After all, if *Choices* has demonstrated anything, it is that strategic rationality is a plausible approach to study the range of judicial choices.

But to end so abruptly would be to give short shrift to the implications of our account. In what follows, we explore two. The first centers on the emergence of law in American society; the second, on the study of courts.

IMPLICATIONS FOR THE EMERGENCE OF LAW

Fundamental to our account is that law is best conceptualized as the set of formal rules that structure all aspects of our lives. This notion is not without controversy, but it captures the way we Americans treat laws—as rules of behavior in our everyday lives—and the way we back them up—with the formal enforcement power of the state. Seen in this way, the substantive content of these rules gives life to the policy commitments our society hopes to achieve.

What role do courts play in establishing these rules? Over the years, this question has generated many responses, and the traditional answer is that the judicial branch interprets the laws that the legislative and executive branches make. Social scientists long ago rejected this account and replaced it with a more realistic conception that incorporated the fact that when judges engage in legal interpretation, they often change the existing set of rules so extensively it would be misleading to say that they are not making new law. The acknowledgment of this fact—that judges, along with legislators and executives, make law—not only challenged some of our basic beliefs about the rule of law, but also carried with it important implications about judicial autonomy and discretion. Our analysis of strategic behavior on the Supreme Court clarifies and develops some of these implications.

First, the judicial branch shares with the other branches of government a defining characteristic: it is a primary forum for the resolution of social and political conflict. Even when we take account of the distinctive institutional nature of the judicial process, law is profoundly political. To the extent that judges make law, it is the way their decisions are transformed into the rules that govern social life. We suggest a particular conception of this process: law, as generated by the Supreme Court, evolves in an incremental way. Each decision of each term of the Court modifies and builds on the existing body of legal rules and procedures. Over time, justices converge on specific common features of their decisions and, in so doing, establish new rules, new law.[1] Although this process is slow and incremental, it is nonetheless political because the decisions of justices are strategic and aimed at affecting the substantive content of these rules. Therefore, to a significant degree, law is the cumulative product of numerous short-term strategic decisions made by the justices over the various terms of the Court. *Craig v. Boren* makes this point with force; and, since our discussion of that case in Chapter One, we have tried to identify the basic mechanisms by which short-term strategic decisions produced new legal rules in many other cases and how those judicial choices may have long-term policy effects.

Second, if we are interested in explaining democratic politics in general and the development of specific policies in particular, we ignore the judicial branch of government at our peril. In the specialized division of labor that characterizes contemporary political science, the courts and the choices of judges have received scant attention from scholars other than those whose interests are related either to judicial behavior or to certain areas of political theory. Our analysis highlights the important strategic implications of the separation of powers system in the U.S. constitutional framework.

We have emphasized only one aspect of that system, of the dynamic strategic interaction that produces American policy and law—the effects of the other branches of government on judicial decisions. But, if we conceive of democratic law making as an ongoing game among the actors in all three branches of government, as we do, it is clear that all students of politics must give greater attention to the role courts play in this process. We believe, and hope we have demonstrated, that the strategic approach to analyzing judicial decisions provides a promising and fruitful way of understanding this interrelationship.

Third, because the "new" conception of judicial behavior acknowledges the political nature of courts, many observers have concluded that judges are unconstrained political advocates who threaten the normative legitimacy of the rule of law by making whatever choices they want. We can see why scholars have reached such a conclusion. But the inference from the political motivation of judges to a fundamental threat to legitimacy *may*, on our account, be mistaken. Our analysis explains the different ways judicial decision making is constrained by the actions of others and by social and political institutions. This analysis suggests that the legitimacy of the system of law may be sustained even if judges act in political ways. The relevant question therefore becomes: Can the legitimacy of the system be grounded primarily in the institutional constraints on judicial decision making rather than in the actions of the judges themselves? We believe that a strategic conception of courts can help us identify the factors necessary to answer this question.

IMPLICATIONS FOR THE FUTURE STUDY OF COURTS AND LAW

The preceding sentence leads us back to a more general point we made at the beginning of *Choices:* this book marks a beginning, not the end, of an inquiry into judicial decision making. Nothing we have written since changes that. We have offered an account of judicial decisions, assessed the plausibility of that account, and explored some of its predictions against evidence mined largely from the papers of several justices. But, if we have done our job, much work remains because we hope that we have made a compelling case for applying strategic analysis to future studies of the Supreme Court, regardless of whether those studies are grounded in the literature of judicial politics or jurisprudence.

To put it more concretely, we believe that our account has implications both for what we study and how we study it. Beginning with the focus of our inquiries, a lesson—if not *the* lesson—of this volume is that explorations of the Supreme Court should not begin and end with examinations of the vote, as they have for so many years.[a] Rather, we must explore the range of choices that contribute to the development of law.

The implications of this statement are twofold. The first is obvious: we encourage researchers to pick up where we have left off and invoke the strategic account to understand the choices justices make: to accommodate the concerns of other justices in majority opinions, to bargain, to circulate a dissent from the denial of certiorari, to engage in persuasion, and, yes, to vote in a particular way and to change that vote, to name just a few. The second implication is less obvious, as it centers on the emphasis of our studies rather than on particular topics. What it suggests is that research building on *Choices* should attempt to explain discrete choices, but that we would be disappointed if that is all our work generated—studies designed to explain the decision to accommodate or bargain or to persuade or to vote in a particular way and so on. We hope that future scholarship does not lose sight of the ultimate goal: to understand how these choices come together to explain the substantive content of law.

Certainly, there will be debates about how we go about developing predictions from this theory—and we have a few thoughts along these lines. We realize that many may be surprised that a book on strategic analysis of the Supreme Court contains no game-theoretic, or formal, models. But that reaction would reflect a misunderstanding of the nature of our enterprise. Our goal has been to develop a picture of judicial choice, a conception of the mechanisms of strategic behavior that characterize decision making on the Court. As such our task has been to analyze the basic logic of strategic action, identify the ways it manifests itself in the choices of justices, and provide a framework for understanding its implications for research on the Court. If we have provided a basis for incorporating strategic choice into various approaches to studying the Supreme Court, we have accomplished our goal.

More generally, we would argue, strategic analysis is not synonymous with formalization; various forms of strategic behavior can be fruitfully

---

a. This is not to say that scholars of the Court have ignored the choices we have considered; indeed, our citations indicate otherwise. However, many of those works have been done in isolation and without a unified theoretical underpinning.

analyzed without a formal model. Seminal works such as Thomas C. Schelling's *The Strategy of Conflict* and Douglass C. North's *Institutions, Institutional Change, and Economic Performance* are two examples.[2] Many historical accounts of the Court, therefore, can benefit from incorporating the logic of strategic action and, by so doing, can significantly enhance our understanding of judicial decision making. But the fact that strategic analysis is not synonymous with formal models does not diminish the importance of formal analysis for many central issues related to the Court. For example, if scholars want to explain a particular line of decisions or a substantive body of law as the *equilibrium* outcome of the interdependent choices of the justices and other actors, they must demonstrate why the choices are in equilibrium, and a formal model is an essential part of such a demonstration. The benefits of formal analysis should not be underestimated. The basic point here is that the degree of formalization of the analysis depends on the nature of the explanation that is desired. While formalization is often crucial to explanations of judicial behavior, we cannot emphasize enough the basic idea that strategic behavior is a broader and more extensive phenomenon than what can be captured by formal equilibrium analysis.

Seen in this way, our account provides a set of tools to unite scholars who analyze legal doctrine and those who focus on judicial behavior. While these analysts agree on the fundamental importance of law, for decades upon decades they have talked past each other, exhibiting fundamental disagreements over how best to study judicial decisions. To be sure, strategic rationality cannot resolve all of these debates, but it can provide a mechanism for understanding what is important to both groups—how law evolves from judicial action.

ENDNOTES

1. This is a theme we both have developed in previous research. See Lee Epstein and Joseph F. Kobylka, *The Supreme Court and Legal Change: Abortion and the Death Penalty* (Chapel Hill: University of North Carolina Press, 1992); and Jack Knight, *Institutions and Social Conflict* (Cambridge: Cambridge University Press, 1992).

2. Thomas C. Schelling, *The Strategy of Conflict* (Cambridge: Harvard University Press, 1960); and Douglass C. North, *Institutions, Institutional Change, and Economic Performance* (Cambridge: Cambridge University Press, 1990).

APPENDIX A
The Processing of Supreme Court Cases

Occurs Throughout Term

Court Receives Requests for Review (5,000–7,000)
- appeals (e.g., suits under the Civil Rights and Voting Rights Acts)
- certification (requests by lower courts for answers to legal questions)
- petitions for writ of certiorari (most common request for review)
- requests for original review

Occurs Throughout Term

Cases Are Docketed
- original docket (cases coming under its original jurisdiction)
- appellate docket (all other cases)

Occurs Throughout Term

Justices Review Docketed Cases
- Chief justice, in consultation with the associate justices and their staffs, prepares discuss lists (approximately one quarter of docketed cases)
- Chief justice circulates discuss lists prior to conferences

Fridays

Conferences
- selection of cases for review, for denial of review
- Rule of Four: four or more justices must agree to review most cases

Begins Mondays After Conference

Announcement of Action on Cases

Clerk Sets Date for Oral Argument
- usually not less than three months after the Court has granted review

Attorneys File Briefs
- appellant must file within forty-five days from when Court granted review
- appellee must file within thirty days of receipt of appellant's brief

Seven Two-Week Sessions, From October Through April on Mondays, Tuesdays, Wednesdays

Oral Arguments
- Court typically hears four cases per day, with each case receiving one hour of Court's time

Wednesday Afternoons, Fridays

Conferences
- discussion of cases
- tentative votes

Drafting and Circulation of Opinions ◄— **Assignment of Majority Opinions**

Reporting of Opinions
- U.S. Reports (U.S.) (official reporter systems)
- Lawyers' Edition (L.Ed.)
- Supreme Court Reporter (S.Ct.)
- U.S. Law Week (U.S.L.W.)
- electronic reporter systems (WESTLAW, LEXIS)
- Legal Information Institute (via the Internet: http://www.law.cornell.edu/supct/)

Issuing and Annoucing of Opinions

Source: Lee Epstein, Jeffrey A. Segal, Harold J. Spaeth, and Thomas G. Walker, *The Supreme Court Compendium: Data, Decisions, and Developments,* 2d ed. (Washington, D.C.: Congressional Quarterly, 1996), Figure 1-1.

The Court's Rule 10, governing considerations for review on writ of certiorari, states:

Review on a writ of certiorari is not a matter of right, but of judicial discretion. A petition for a writ of certiorari will be granted only for compelling reasons. The following, although neither controlling nor fully measuring the Court's discretion, indicate the character of the reasons the Court considers:

(a) a United States court of appeals has entered a decision in conflict with the decision of another United States court of appeals on the same important matter; has decided an important federal question in a way that conflicts with a decision by a state court of last resort; or has so far departed from the accepted and usual course of judicial proceedings, or sanctioned such a departure by a lower court, as to call for an exercise of this Court's supervisory power;

(b) a state court of last resort has decided an important federal question in a way that conflicts with the decision of another state court of last resort or of a United States court of appeals;

(c) a state court or a United States court of appeals has decided an important question of federal law that has not been, but should be, settled by this Court, or has decided an important federal question in a way that conflicts with relevant decisions of this Court.

A petition for a writ of certiorari is rarely granted when the asserted error consists of erroneous factual findings or the misapplication of a properly stated rule of law.

Index

Note: Index locators with n. refer to lettered footnotes, numbered endnotes, or source notes. Locators with fig. and t. refer to figures and tables.